CONSTITUTIONAL PROBLEMS OF THE EUROPEAN UNION

CONSTITUTIONAL PROBLEMS OF THE EUROPEAN UNION

TREVOR C HARTLEY

Professor of Law
London School of Economics

·HART·
PUBLISHING

OXFORD and PORTLAND, OREGON

Hart Publishing
Oxford and Portland, Oregon

Published in North America (US and Canada) by
Hart Publishing c/o
International Specialized Book Services
5804 NE Hassalo Street
Portland, Oregon
97213-3644
USA

Distributed in the Netherlands, Belgium and Luxembourg by
Intersentia, Churchillaan 108
B2900 Schoten
Antwerpen
Belgium

Hart Publishing Ltd is a specialist legal publisher based in Oxford, England.
To order further copies of this book or to request a list of other
publications please write to:

Hart Publishing Ltd, Salter's Boatyard, Oxford OX1 4LB
Telephone: +44 (0)1865 245533 or Fax: +44 (0)1865 794882
e-mail: mail@hartpub.co.uk
www.hartpub.co.uk

British Library Cataloguing in Publication Data
Data Available
ISBN 1 901362–46–9 (cloth)

Typeset in Bembo 10pt
by Hope Services (Abingdon) Ltd.
Printed and bound Great Britain by
Biddles Ltd,
www.biddles.co.uk

Foreword

In twenty years, there could be a European Federation, a United States of Europe, of which Britain would be a part. This is far from certain, but it is not fanciful. It could happen. If it does, Brussels will be the capital of Europe; Strasbourg and Luxembourg will also be important centres. There will be a President of Europe and a European Government; the European Parliament will make laws and the European Court will give rulings. The European Police Force will see they are carried out and the European Army will undertake operations, probably in Eastern Europe and the Arab world.

Britain will be a province of Europe, as it was in Roman times long ago. There will still be a Parliament at Westminster, dealing with local matters, but its sessions will be much reduced. Able, ambitious people will look to the European Parliament for a career; Westminster will attract only second-raters. The British courts will still function, but important matters will be beyond their jurisdiction. They will have the last word on British law, but only if their rulings do not conflict with European policies. London will be a provincial city.

Even if things do not happen in quite this way, there is little doubt that the Union will constitute a major force: there are no signs that it is about to collapse or wither away. It will have a substantial effect on the lives of its citizens and on the lives of people in neighbouring countries. Its laws and institutions will decide the major issues facing Europe. Whatever one feels about it, therefore, it is vital to understand its nature and characteristics, to know what sort of entity it is.

The purpose of this book is to contribute towards such an understanding by scrutinizing the Union from the constitutional and legal angle: we will ask whether the European Court, the supreme authority on Community law, behaves as a court ought to behave; we will examine the vague and elastic nature of Community law and see whether this causes problems for those who have to deal with it; we will consider whether the division of power between the Union and the Member States is based on any sort of principle, and, if so, whether that principle is consistently applied; we will examine the enforcement of Community law and the problems caused by the different levels of compliance in different Member States; and, finally, we will look at the foundations of the Union's legal system and consider whether the Member States have ceded their sovereignty.

Some Community specialists believe that these are questions that ought not to be discussed: they feel that by drawing attention to them one could sow the seeds of suspicion and distrust towards the Union in the minds of ordinary citizens. But they are the most fundamental—the most vital—questions to be asked if we are to understand the true nature of the Union. They are questions we *must* ask—and try to answer.

It is hoped that this book will be of interest not only to experts in Community law, but to all lawyers—indeed, to non-lawyers as well—who want to understand the Community. To make this possible, an introductory chapter has been added to provide the necessary background.

TREVOR HARTLEY

London School of Economics
1 September 1998

Contents

Contents

Detailed Table of Contents

Acknowledgments

Many of the ideas in this book were first put forward in talks and articles. The critique of the European Court that now constitutes Chapters 2 and 3 was first tried out in lectures given in 1994 in Galway, Ireland, and Bergen, Norway. I then wrote an article, originally sketched out on the long flight from the Western USA to London, which was published under the title "The European Court, Judicial Objectivity and the Constitution of the European Union" in (1996) 112 LQR 95. Although Chapters 2 and 3 have been almost completely rewritten, I have re-used a few paragraphs and I am grateful to Francis Reynolds, editor of the Law Quarterly Review, for permission to do so.

Chapter 4 is based on an article originally published in the Cambridge Law Journal, "Five Forms of Uncertainty in European Community Law" [1996] CLJ 265. It has been extensively modified and largely rewritten; nevertheless, a few paragraphs of the original remain. I would like to thank Michael Prichard, editor of the Cambridge Law Journal, for permission to incorporate them into this book.

The genesis of Chapters 7–9 (on sovereignty) was a talk given in Trier at a conference organized by the Trier Academy of European Law (ERA) and published under the title "The Community Legal Order: A British View" in Volume 21 of the Academy's series: Jean-Denis Mouton and Torsten Stein (eds.), *Towards a New Constitution for the European Union?* (1997), 57. At a little over five pages, this article contains only the barest outline of what now constitutes Chapters 7–9. It has been completely rewritten.

The assistance that is most valuable to me is that of my wife, Sandra, who reads all my work and helps me to improve it.

TREVOR HARTLEY

Abbreviations

AJIL	Americal Journal of International Law
Am.Jo.Comp.L	American Journal of Comparative Law
BVerfGE	Bundesverfassungsgericht
BYIL	British Yearbook of International Law
CDE	Cahiers de Droit Européen
CLJ	Cambridge Law Journal
CMLR	Common Market Law Reports
CMLRev.	Common Market Law Review
COREPER	Committee of Permanent Representatives
EAEC	European Atomic Energy Community
EC	European Community
ECB	European Central Bank
EC Bull.	Bulletin of the European Communities
ECJ	European Court of Justice
ECR	European Court Reports
ECSC	European Coal and Steel Community
EEA	European Economic Area
EEC	European Economic Community
EFTA	European Free Trade Association
ELJ	European Law Journal
ELRev.	European Law Review
EP	European Parliament
EU	European Union
Euratom	European Atomic Energy Community
ICLQ	International and Comparative Law Quarterly
JO	Journal officiel (French version of OJ)
JCMS	Journal of Common Market Studies
LIEI	Legal Issues of European Integration
LQR	Law Quarterly Review
MLR	Modern Law Review
OJ	Official Journal (of the European Communities)
PL	Public Law
RDI	Rivista di Diritto Internazionale

Rec.	Recueil de la jurisprudence de la Cour de Justice des Communautés européennes (French version of ECR)
RIW	Recht der Internationalen Wirtschaft
RMC	Revue du Marché Commun
RTDE	Revue Trimestrielle de Droit Européen
SEA	Single European Act
TEU	Treaty on European Union (Maastricht Agreement)
YEL	Yearbook of European Law

Note on Numbering of Treaty Articles

The Articles in the EC Treaty and the Treaty on European Union were renumbered by the Treaty of Amsterdam, which was signed in 1997 but is not yet in force. In view of this, the new numbers are inserted in curly brackets (braces) after the old ones. Thus, for example, a reference to "Article 100a {94} EC" is a reference to the provision originally numbered Article 100a and renumbered Article 94. Articles introduced, or substantially modified, by the Treaty of Amsterdam are referred to by their new numbers only. Curly brackets indicate that they are not yet in force.

Table of Cases (European Courts: Alphabetical)

Table of Cases (European Courts: Numerical Order)

Table of Cases (British Courts)

1

Background

The French Government proposes that the entire Franco-German output of coal and steel should be placed under the control of a common High Authority, in an organization open to the participation of the other European countries.

Robert Schuman (1950)

Determined to lay the foundations for an ever closer union among the peoples of Europe . . . [the Member States] . . . [h]ave agreed as follows . . .

Preamble to the EC Treaty (1957)

ORIGINS

The European enterprise began on 18 April 1951 when the six original Member States—three large countries[1] and three small[2]—met in Paris to sign the Treaty establishing the European Coal and Steel Community (ECSC).[3] The Treaty was the result of a French initiative, the "Schuman Plan", the announcement[4] of which by the French Foreign Minister, Robert Schuman, marked a change in French policy towards Germany from one of attempted subordination to one of friendship.[5] Right from the start, the Community was based on a Franco-German partnership: the Schuman Plan expressly envisaged a pooling by France and Germany of their coal and steel

---

[1] Germany, France and Italy.
[2] Belgium, the Netherlands and Luxembourg.
[3] It entered into force on 25 July 1952. For the background, see William Diebold, *The Schuman Plan* (1959).
[4] On 9 May 1950.
[5] For the full text, see Documents on International Affairs, 1949–1950, pp. 315–317.

resources; other countries were invited to join, but only Germany was mentioned by name.[6]

It is also clear that, at least in Schuman's eyes,[7] the fundamental purpose of the Plan was political. The Schuman Declaration emphasized that it constituted the first step towards a European federation, the establishment of which was "indispensable for the preservation of peace"; it also said that the pooling of production that would occur under the ECSC would show that "any war between France and Germany would become, not merely unthinkable, but physically impossible". These words, forgotten by some, do much to explain the thinking of present-day French and German leaders on European integration.

There were various reasons why coal and steel were chosen for the new project. Then known as "heavy industry", this sector of the economy was regarded as the foundation on which other sectors, including armaments, rested; a major employer, it was in economic difficulties; its geographical distribution meant that a common approach made particular sense;[8] and the idea of an international solution had political advantages both with regard to the Saar, a territory of importance for these industries which was then in contention between France and Germany,[9] and to the policy of rebuilding the German economy, a policy supported by the United States and Britain but until then opposed by France.[10] Boldly conceived, the Schuman Plan thus operated on three levels: it solved political and economic problems in the short term; provided a sound basis for France's relations with Germany in the middle term; and laid

[6] See the extract quoted above at the head of this Chapter.

[7] It seems that the Plan was conceived hurriedly and in some secrecy; it was agreed by the Cabinet after only brief discussion: Diebold, n. 3 above, p. 8.

[8] Geographically fairly compact but divided between four states, the industry was concentrated in southern Belgium, Luxembourg, northern France, Lorraine, the Saar and the Ruhr. Schuman was himself from Lorraine and had grown up at a time when that territory was ruled by Germany.

[9] It was reunited with Germany in 1957.

[10] The International Agreement on the Ruhr (1949) provided (at French insistence) for Allied supervision of the coal and steel industry of the Ruhr through an international institution, the International Authority for the Ruhr, on which the United States, Britain, France and Germany had three votes each and the Benelux countries one each; however, this did not function effectively, because the Germans were naturally against it, and the British and Americans doubted the wisdom of trying to keep Germany indefinitely in a position of subordination. The ECSC provided an acceptable substitute; indeed, prominent German politicians had called for such an alternative as early as 1948: Diebold, n. 3 above, pp. 35–37.

the foundations for a new Europe in the long term. Although the ECSC was limited to a comparatively small sector of the economy, its creation was of lasting significance because the European Union of today is based on the blueprint of 1951, a blueprint which made an original contribution to the solution of international problems through the establishment of international organizations.

Generally speaking, international organizations have an institutional structure designed to provide a framework for intergovernmental co-operation. One might thus expect some sort of council, where the member states are represented, together with a secretariat to prepare the ground for meetings of the council and to carry out its decisions. The normal rule is that member states are not bound by decisions of the organization unless they consent; consequently, decisions of the council must be unanimous if they are to be binding, though there may be provision for majority voting if dissidents are free to declare that they do not accept the outcome. (As we shall see in Chapter 7, some international organizations have moved beyond this; nevertheless, it remains the traditional pattern.)

As soon as one looks at the structure of the Community, however, it is apparent that its founders rejected this concept: from its very inception, the Community was intended to be something more than a traditional international organization. It is equally clear, on the other hand, that the federal model was also rejected. The basic principle of a federation is that there is a democratic legislature, elected by the people of the federation, which enacts its laws. There is an executive which is either chosen by the legislature or, as in the case of America, elected by the people. An essential feature of a federation is that the federal institutions exercise power independently of the States, a feature that is acceptable because they obtain their legitimacy directly from the people.

The distinguishing characteristic of the Community is that it is founded on neither of these models. The framers of the ECSC Treaty found a third way, one in which the Community was governed by an institution, the High Authority, which was independent of the Member States but which did not derive its power from democratic elections. This was acceptable because the Treaty itself laid down the programme it was to pursue and the objectives it was to attain. The Member States agreed to these when they signed the Treaty. Having done so, they were not at liberty to block the implementation of that programme and the attainment of those objectives, even though particular aspects might be contrary to their interests. True enough, there was a Council of Ministers, in which the Member States were represented, and which looked like the deliberative body of a typical international organization; but this was intended to deal with unforeseen problems and major crises: the day-to-day running of the Community was in the hands of the High Authority, the members of which, though chosen by the national governments, were independent of them during their terms of office.

Since the High Authority was independent of the national governments and was not subject to direct democratic control, it was necessary to have some alternative mechanism to prevent it from abusing its authority. A Court of Justice was therefore established with the power to annul any act of the High Authority that was contrary to the Treaty and generally to ensure that the law was observed. Provision was also made for an Assembly, the members of which were to be designated by the national parliaments from among their members. It was largely without power, and in no way resembled the legislature of a federation, but it could force the resignation of the members of the High Authority if a motion of censure was passed by a two-thirds majority.[11] However, if it exercised this power—which it never did—it had no say in the appointment of their successors; moreover, the existing members would remain in office until the Member States had made new appointments.[12]

A COMMUNITY OF INTERESTS

A joint enterprise, whether political or economic, flourishes only if it is based on a community of interests. What is the community of interests that makes the European Community possible? Since it was originally a French idea, we will start with France.

France

For France, the greatest prize has always been political: the ending of what the Schuman Declaration called the century-old conflict

---

[11] Art. 24 ECSC.
[12] Art. 10, last paragraph, ECSC.

between France and Germany. Three times in the previous hundred years, France had fought Germany. Defeated by Prussia in 1870, France was able—with British assistance—to hold the German advance in 1914, and ultimately, when the United States entered the war, to gain victory—though at a terrible cost in lives. She then pursued a policy towards Germany whose harshness was regarded by some as partly responsible for the rise of Hitler, an event which in turn led to the attack of 1940, when France surrendered and was occupied. Although Germany was eventually defeated, this was achieved by the Soviet Union, the United States and Britain: (Free) France played only a minor role.

After World War II, it was clear to those Frenchmen far-sighted enough to see such things that in the long term France could not contain Germany by military means alone. That had been tried and had failed. Divided and defeated, with her industry in ruins, Germany might not have seemed a threat in 1950; nevertheless, her potential—economic, military and political—was inevitably greater than that of France. Today, this potential has been realized: stronger economically and financially than France and with a significantly greater population, Germany is the leading nation of Western Europe. Only in the military sphere, where the possession of nuclear weapons still gives her the advantage, can France claim pre-eminence.

In this situation, France could have allied herself with Britain and America against Germany. This was the policy that had been pursued during the two World Wars. In 1950, however, America and Britain saw the Soviet Union as the main enemy and needed Germany's support to meet the Communist threat; they were not, therefore, disposed to join with France in an anti-German alliance. In these circumstances, Schuman's idea of not merely forming an alliance with Germany, but of seeking to merge France and Germany in a European Federation whose institutions France hoped to control, though hazardous, was masterly. If successful, it would permanently eliminate the German threat and eventually allow Europe to act independently of both the United States and the Soviet Union.

Though France's confidence in this strategy has fluctuated over the years—de Gaulle believed in partnership with Germany,[13] but was hostile to European supranationalism—it has nevertheless brought

---

[13] This was cemented by the Franco-German Treaty of Co-operation, signed in 1963 by de Gaulle and Adenauer.

rewards. Without the German relationship, France's influence in the Community would be diminished; without the Community, France would carry less weight in the world. Moreover, France has been able to shape the Community to her own advantage: French is the working-language of the Community institutions, and the emphasis in the early days on agriculture, and the enormous subsidies, were particularly beneficial to France, the largest agricultural producer in the Community. The only anxiety in the long term is that the partnership with Germany may not survive the shift in the balance of power between the two countries.

Germany

It is easy to see why Germany accepted the Schuman Plan. In 1950, (West) Germany was not a fully sovereign state: her territory was occupied by Britain, France and the United States, and her Government was subject to restrictions, both military and political. The legacy of Nazism still determined the way other countries looked at her. Germany was not a normal country, accepted as a such by the community of nations. Regaining this position was one of her foremost objectives. When Schuman proposed the ECSC, the German coal and steel industry was subject to international control. The ECSC was also a form of international control, but in it Germany was treated as a normal country, not as an outcast. Indeed, the French made clear that politically Germany had a special status as France's partner. Joining the ECSC was thus a step on the road towards normality.

Today, circumstances have changed. Germany has regained her position in the international community and the long search for respectability is over. However, all the old suspicions would rise up again if Germany modified her pro-European stance. Moreover, Community membership serves German interests in other ways: Germany is now the dominant country in Western Europe and, together with France, leads the Community; the Community is thus an instrument that can be used to exert influence over other countries, both in the Community and outside it. Given her power and position, it is more an instrument she can use than an instrument that can be used against her. Moreover, as the dominant industrial and financial power in Europe, she derives particular benefit from the single market. Thus, though some Germans may resent the extent to which the financial burden of the Community has come to rest on their shoulders, pro-European sentiment is still the prevailing orthodoxy.

Britain

Britain is a country that has not been invaded by a foreign army for almost a thousand years. She does not fear Germany, as France does. Her traditional policy has been to maintain a balance of power among the major Continental States, so that no one country could become sufficiently strong to constitute a threat. Thus, when Napoleon was striving for hegemony, Britain supported the anti-French alliance of Germany and Russia; when first the Kaiser and then Hitler sought dominance, she supported the anti-German powers, France and Russia. Beyond this, Britain has traditionally sought to avoid Continental entanglements; instead, she has looked overseas to the English-speaking countries she founded and which were originally peopled by British emigrants. In the past, the Commonwealth formed the ideal trading area, the overseas countries supplying food and raw materials in exchange for British manufactures. In two World Wars, Commonwealth and British soldiers fought side by side in Europe, Africa and Asia.

After World War II, however, this relationship began to break down. The Commonwealth countries started developing their own manufacturing industry and introduced tariffs to protect it. The "special relationship" with the United States weakened as the disparity in power between the two countries became more marked. When the Commonwealth ceased to be a meaningful entity, Britain, which had spurned the Community when it was first established, began to rethink its policy.

As a major exporter and traditional protagonist of free trade, Britain did not want to be excluded from one of the world's foremost trading blocs. Since joining the Community, she has enthusiastically embraced its free market policies. Other aspects, however, have not been to her liking. Since she is a major food-importing country, the Common Agricultural Policy has been against her interests. Under it, Continental—mainly French—producers are doubly subsidized by Britain: the British consumer subsidizes them by paying higher prices

for food and the British taxpayer subsidizes them by paying for grants
and the buying up of unwanted produce. The Community fisheries
policy has been harmful to the British fishing industry. Moreover,
since the Community is run by Germany and France, Britain has felt
an outsider. For these reasons, she has been an unenthusiastic
Member State. Reluctant to leave, she has been cool towards further
integration. Ideally, she would like the supranational side of the
Community to be limited to free trade.

The Netherlands

It is interesting to compare British attitudes with those in the
Netherlands. In some ways, they could not be more different: the
Netherlands (together with Belgium and Luxembourg) is probably
the strongest supporter of European federalism; Britain (together
with Sweden and Denmark) is its strongest opponent. Yet, in many
ways, the two countries have much in common. Both are seafaring
nations; both had overseas empires which they once saw as the focus
for their foreign investment; both are mercantile countries living by
international trade.

However, the Netherlands is a Continental country. Her law is
based on that of France—Napoleon imposed the French Civil
Code on her when he conquered the Netherlands—and her culture is much less distinct from that of other Continental countries
than that of Britain. She lacks the strong overseas links that Britain
has. She was overrun by Germany in the Second World War, an
event made all the more traumatic by the fact that she had suc-
cessfully remained neutral in World War I and had given refuge to
the Kaiser after Germany's defeat. As a small but highly developed
country, her economy is much more integrated with that of her
neighbours than is Britain's. Economic links with Germany are
especially close.

The Dutch, therefore, see the Community not only as a new trading area to replace their lost empire, but also as a means by which
they can avoid becoming a satellite of Germany, with less influence
than a German *Land*. A Community run by France and Germany
would not have this effect; only a federal Europe run by independent
supranational institutions would produce the desired result. As a small
country, her freedom of action would be limited even if there was no

Community; a truly federal Europe would not limit that freedom much more, while it would prevent the bigger countries from throwing their weight around. From the Dutch point of view, the ideal would be a European Federation in which the Federal Republic of Germany ceased to exist and the German *Länder* were Member States in their own right.

Thus, her smaller size, her proximity to Germany (both geographical and economic), her closer ties with her Continental neighbours and the absence of links of kinship and culture with non-European countries comparable to those enjoyed by Britain—these are the reasons why her policy towards the Community has taken a different course from Britain's. It is possible that, when Britain first sought to join the Community, the Dutch hoped she would join them in fighting for a federal Europe as a way to counteract Franco-German domination. If they entertained this hope, they must have been sadly disillusioned.

Other Countries

Belgium and Luxembourg are in a similar position to the Netherlands. Sweden has something (though certainly not everything) in common with Britain. Other countries have other interests and combinations of interests. For some, Community membership is prized as an indication that they are accepted as part of the West; for others (for example, Ireland and Greece), EU grants and subsidies are important; for Finland and some of the applicants from Eastern Europe, Community membership is a means of safeguarding their independence from Russia.[14] For all Member States, membership of an organization that is demonstrably successful, and which—at least until recently—has been seen as the gateway to economic growth, cannot be other than attractive. If the Community is destined to be the major force in Europe, it is better to be inside than outside.

---

[14] Finland was ruled by Russia until 1917 and relations with Russia have dominated Finnish foreign policy ever since.

THE EEC AND EURATOM

When it became clear the ECSC was a success, the Member States applied the same formula to the remaining sectors of the economy. Instead of merging the ECSC into a wider Community, however, they created two new Communities operating alongside the ECSC—Euratom, covering atomic energy, and the European Economic Community (EEC), which covered all other areas of the economy. The EEC and Euratom Treaties were signed in Rome on 25 March 1957 and entered into force on 1 January 1958. The result was that there were three separate Communities, each with its own powers and functions.

The two new Communities had the same structure as the ECSC, the High Authority being replaced by a body known as the Commission.[15] The aim of the EEC, however, was much wider and less precisely defined than that of the ECSC, partly because its area of operation was so much broader and partly because its objectives could be attained only in the long term. As a result, its institutions had to be given wider and more general powers. Since the Member States were unwilling to confer such powers on a body they could not control, the position of the Council was enhanced at the expense of the Commission: while in the ECSC the High Authority was the main law-making organ, the EEC Treaty provided for legislation to be adopted by the Council on a proposal from the Commission. The result was to dilute the supranational character of the Community at the same time as its scope was greatly widened.

It might be thought that the shift in power from the Commission (High Authority) to the Council would have solved the problem of legitimacy, since the Council consisted of representatives of the national governments, which were themselves subject to democratic control at the national level. At first, this may have seemed to be the case. However, as ever-increasing areas of policy were taken over by

[15] At first, the High Authority continued in existence to run the ECSC, and two new bodies—both called the "Commission"—were created to run the EEC and Euratom. Subsequently, these three bodies were merged into one body, called the "Commission". This was done by a new treaty, the Merger Treaty 1965 (officially, the Convention Establishing a Single Council and a Single Commission of the European Communities). The Treaty also merged the original three Councils into one. Right from the start, there had been only one Court and one Assembly (Parliament).

the Community, it became apparent that the effect on the national governmental systems was to transfer power from the national parliaments to the national executives, since decisions that had previously been taken by the parliaments were now taken by the national governments meeting in the Council. Moreover, the *method* of decision making was also different. Debate in the national parliaments has traditionally been open and widely reported in the press; discussions in the Council, on the other hand, were conducted in strict secrecy, which meant that the public could not always be sure which side their own government had supported. This led some governments to see the handing over of policy areas to the EC as a convenient means of avoiding the blame for unpopular decisions. A government could even oppose a policy in public but secretly support it in the privacy of the Council chamber. It could then claim to have been forced to give in by pressure from the others. In these circumstances, *ex post facto* control by the national parliaments was difficult: once made, a diplomatic deal in the Council could not easily be overturned. Moreover, the rule that Community law in all circumstances prevails over national law, a rule not found in the Treaties but laid down by the European Court, ensured that legislation adopted by the Council could not be challenged at national level. This shift in the method of legislating from open debate in the national parliaments to the secret bargaining sessions of the Council is one of the causes of the popular conception that the Community is the enemy of democracy.[16]

AN EVER CLOSER UNION

Since the EEC and Euratom Treaties came into force, there have been ten major Community treaties,[17] which have either given new

---

[16] Whether the problem can be solved by the grant of greater powers to the European Parliament is considered below.

[17] The Merger Treaty 1965; the First Budgetary Treaty 1970; the First Accession Treaty 1972 (by which Denmark, Ireland and the United Kingdom joined the Community); the Second Budgetary Treaty 1975; the Second Accession Treaty 1979 (by which Greece joined the Community); the Third Accession Treaty 1985 (by which Spain and Portugal joined the Community); the Single European Act 1986; the Treaty on European Union (Maastricht Agreement) 1992; the Fourth Accession Treaty 1994 (by which Austria, Finland and Sweden joined the Community); and the Treaty of Amsterdam 1997. If the Act (annexed to Council Decision 76/787) concerning the election of the representatives of the Assembly by direct universal suffrage, OJ 1976, L278/1, is to be regarded as a Treaty, there have been 11 major Treaties since the EEC and Euratom Treaties.

powers to Community institutions or provided for the admission of new Member States. The deepening (greater powers) and widening (new members) of the Community have thus been continuous ever since it was established. No doubt they will continue in the future, in line with the Preamble to the EEC Treaty, which said that the Member States were then laying the foundations of "an ever closer union among the peoples of Europe". Unlike a normal international organization, therefore, the Community is not something that exists in more or less the same form over an extended period of time, so that once a country has come to terms with it, it can turn its attention to other things: the Community is constantly developing and the process of adjustment must also be continuous. Moreover, these developments are not the result only of Treaty amendments accepted by the Member States: some have been engineered by the European Court which, as we shall see in Chapter 2, has changed the law to hasten the process of integration.

The most important institutional developments since the establishment of the EEC and Euratom have concerned the European Court and the European Parliament.

The European Court

The change in the status of the Court has been enormous, so that today it more closely resembles the equivalent institution of a fully-fledged federation (for example, the United States Supreme Court or the German *Bundesverfassungsgericht*) than any other institution of the Community.[18] The foundations for this development were laid in the EEC Treaty, but the edifice erected on those foundations is almost entirely the work of the Court itself, which has used its existing powers of interpretation to grant itself further powers.

Although given a general power to ensure the observance of Community law,[19] the Court's main function under the scheme laid down by the ECSC Treaty was to keep the High Authority in check. The latter had the job of ensuring that the Member States obeyed the law. Thus Article 88 ECSC provided that, if the High

---

[18] See Hartley, "Federalism, Courts and Legal Systems: The Emerging Constitution of the European Community" (1986) 34 Am.Jo.Comp.L 229; Weiler, "The Community Legal System: The Dual Character of Supranationalism" (1981) 1 YEL 267.

[19] Art. 31 ECSC.

Authority considered that a Member State had failed to fulfil an obligation under the Treaty, it would take a decision to that effect (after giving the Member State a chance to defend itself). Such a decision was binding on the Member State and had to be obeyed within a time limit set by the High Authority. Failure to do so could result in sanctions.[20] The role of the Court was to hear appeals from the decision of the High Authority. The Court's other main powers were to annul acts of the High Authority in proceedings brought before it for that purpose;[21] to rule on the validity of such acts when in issue in proceedings before a national court;[22] to require the High Authority to take action where it was obliged to do so by Community law;[23] and to award damages against the Community (normally the High Authority) if it caused harm as a result of its wrongful action.[24] It also had limited powers to keep the Council and the Assembly (Parliament) in line,[25] though these have almost never been used.

Under the EEC Treaty, on the other hand, the European Court was granted more general powers.[26] In particular, Article 169 {226} of the Treaty provides that, if a Member State fails to fulfil an obligation under it, the Member State can be brought before the European Court by the Commission or another Member State: in contrast to the ECSC Treaty, the Commission cannot itself take a decision, but is restricted to a non-binding opinion.

In addition to being able to rule on the validity of Community acts in issue before national courts, the European Court was empowered by Art. 177 {234} of the EEC Treaty to rule on the *interpretation* both of Community acts and of the Treaty itself. This power, which might have seemed of only limited significance, has in fact proved

---

[20] These were to be imposed by the High Authority after obtaining the approval of the Council, the latter acting by a two-thirds majority. Sanctions have in fact never been imposed.

[21] Art. 33 ECSC.

[22] Art. 41 ECSC.

[23] Art. 35 ECSC.

[24] Art. 40 ECSC.

[25] Art. 38 ECSC allowed it to annul acts of the Assembly or Council, though this could be done only on the application of a Member State or the High Authority and only on limited grounds. Art. 41 (which allowed it to rule on the validity of High Authority acts in issue before national courts) also applied to acts of the Council.

[26] The powers granted by the ECSC Treaty remain in force, though they apply only when action is taken under that Treaty. Since this occurs only where coal and steel are involved, they are of limited importance.

immensely important, since the Court has used it as its principal instrument for developing Community law.[27]

The European Parliament

When the EEC and Euratom were first created, the European Parliament—then called the "Assembly"—was a body of little consequence. In time, this changed. It was given significant financial powers by the Budgetary Treaties of 1970 and 1975, so that it now has the last word on budgetary items for expenditure not required by the Treaties or existing legislation (so-called "non-compulsory" expenditure), and can reject the whole budget if it musters a two-thirds majority. In 1976, the Member States agreed that the members of the European Parliament (who had until then been designated by the national parliaments) would be directly elected by the peoples of the Community.[28] The first elections were held in 1979.

The Parliament's legislative powers were increased by Articles 6 and 7 of the Single European Act 1986,[29] which, when the "co-operation" procedure applies, allow it to block certain kinds of legislation unless the Council is unanimous, and by Article G(61) {8(61)}[30] of the Maastricht Agreement 1992, which introduced the joint legislative procedure which, when it applies, gives the Parliament a full veto over legislation and a significant say in amendments.[31] Article 3(1) of the Single European Act changed its official name from the "Assembly" to the "European Parliament", a title which it had itself adopted as long ago as 1962.[32] Despite these changes, however, its powers remain considerably less than those of the Council and it still cannot be regarded as a parliament in the true sense.

---

[27] This is discussed in Chapter 2.
[28] Council Decision 76/787 and annexed Act concerning the election of the representatives of the Assembly by direct universal suffrage, OJ 1976, L278/1.
[29] See now Art. 189(c) {252} EC.
[30] Inserting Art. 189(b) {251} into the EC Treaty.
[31] Neither of these procedures applies in every case.
[32] EP Resolution of 30 March 1962, JO 1962, p. 1045.

THE COMMUNITY AND THE UNION

The Maastricht Agreement (Treaty on European Union) brought about changes in nomenclature. The European Economic Community (EEC) was renamed "the European Community" (EC),[33] a term which had previously been applied (unofficially) to the whole European enterprise. The EEC Treaty then became the EC Treaty. Two new areas of activity were put on a firmer footing— the Common Foreign and Security Policy, and Co-operation in the Fields of Justice and Home Affairs (renamed in the Treaty of Amsterdam "Police and Judicial Co-operation in Criminal Matters"). Activities in these two areas are conducted on an intergovernmental basis: the Court is generally prohibited from interfering and the Commission and Parliament are largely onlookers.[34] The European enterprise is now seen as having a tripartite structure: the first "pillar" consists of the three Communities (EC, ECSC and Euratom), the second is the Common Foreign and Security Policy and the third is Co-operation in the Fields of Justice and Home Affairs (Police and Judicial Co-operation in Criminal Matters). The three "pillars" together constitute the European Union, an entity created by the Maastricht Agreement.[35]

DECISION-MAKING IN THE COUNCIL

Since the ECSC, EC and Euratom are separate entities in law, each has its own powers and procedures. Those of the EC are the most important. It will be remembered that these are exercised by the Council,[36] the body which represents the Member States. Legislation is normally adopted, on a proposal from the Commission, under the "qualified majority" voting procedure,[37] a system under which votes

---

[33] Art. G(1).
[34] For further details, see T C Hartley, *The Foundations of European Community Law* (4th ed. 1998), pp. 24–27.
[35] Art. A {1} TEU.
[36] This is now subject to the rights enjoyed by the European Parliament.
[37] See Art. 148 EC.

are weighted in favour of the big countries.[38] The total number of votes is 87; of these, 62 must be cast in favour of the measure.[39]

Although the system of qualified-majority voting was established right from the beginning in the EEC Treaty,[40] there was for many years a convention that it would not be used to outvote a Member State if that State considered its vital interests to be at stake. This convention is sometimes said to be based on the "Luxembourg Accords", though the latter do not in fact lay it down. What happened is an interesting story. The EEC Treaty envisaged that its provisions would come into force in three stages. In many instances, it provided that the Council would take decisions by unanimity during the first two stages and by a qualified majority from the beginning of the third stage, 1 January 1966. The French President, General de Gaulle, felt, however, that the Community was getting too assertive and decided that France would boycott all Community institutions. This "empty-chair" strategy began in the middle of 1965 and was aimed in part at preventing the introduction of qualified-majority voting. The French attitude created a crisis, which was resolved at a meeting in Luxembourg in January, 1966 at which the Luxembourg Accords were adopted. The first paragraph accepted that, where very important interests of a Member State were at stake, a majority vote would not be taken until an attempt had been made to reach a compromise that respected the interests of all Member States and those of the Community. What was to be done if no such solution could be found within a reasonable time? On this point, the Accords simply stated that there was a difference of view, with the French considering that no vote could ever take place and the others disagreeing. However, while the Accords expressly recorded this difference of views and made no attempt to reconcile them, the French view prevailed in practice for many years thereafter. This meant that any country could block a vote by simply declaring that its vital interests were at stake,

[38] At the one end of the scale, the four big countries—Germany, France, Italy and the United Kingdom—have ten votes each; at the other end, Denmark, Ireland and Finland have three votes each and Luxembourg has two. Relative to population, the small countries have much greater voting power than the big. Thus, for example, Denmark, Ireland, Finland and Luxembourg together have more votes than Germany, even though Germany has over five times their combined population.

[39] This is a majority of a little over 70 per cent, approximately half-way between a two-thirds and a three-quarters majority.

[40] The number of votes required has of course changed with the accession of new Member States.

a right which many regarded as a veto, though it rested on no legal foundation.[41] When Britain joined the Community, the Government publicly stated that this "political"[42] veto existed.[43]

For a number of years after Britain joined the Community, the convention continued to be respected. However, it was abused by some countries, not least by Britain, which used the veto to block agricultural price increases that were not in themselves against vital British interests. Britain's strategy was to use this as a lever to obtain a rebate on Britain's admittedly unfair budgetary contribution. Some countries saw this as blackmail, and at a meeting in 1982 the Belgian President of the Council[44] called for a vote, despite Britain's protests. Denmark and Greece, both of which wanted the price increases, joined Britain in objecting to what they (and Britain) regarded as a violation of the convention. However, the remaining Member States voted in favour and there were thus enough votes to secure a qualified majority.

It could be argued that in this instance Britain was abusing its right and the others were justified in calling for a vote. Ever since this incident, however, the "political veto" has been on the wane and voting is now common; nevertheless, a vote will still not be taken if most Member States want the matter settled by consensus. However, there is no longer a right of veto (except where this is laid down in the Treaties); there is merely a hope—possibly an expectation—that on some issues one's partners will not insist on a vote. The extent to which this happens will of course depend on the political standing of the Member State concerned.

Once qualified majority voting became common, a controversy arose over the number of votes that should be needed to adopt a measure. The problem was that each time new Member States joined the Community, the voting power of the existing Members was diluted. In particular, the number of votes needed to block a measure, the so-called "blocking minority", became larger. For example, before

[41] There are certain instances—for example, admission of new Member States—in which each Member State has a legally-recognized veto. These rights still exist.

[42] This term is used to distinguish it from the legal rights of veto mentioned in the previous footnote.

[43] See *The UK and the European Communities*, Cmnd. 4715 (1971), para. 29, and *Membership of the European Community—Report on Renegotiation*, Cmnd. 6003 (1975), para. 124.

[44] The Presidency rotates among all the Member States. At the time, it happened that it was held by Belgium.

Austria, Finland and Sweden joined, a blocking minority was 23. After they had joined, the total number of votes was greater and the number needed to pass a measure was increased proportionately. Though a blocking minority was proportionately more or less the same, it was larger in absolute terms—26. This meant that a combination of countries that together commanded 23 votes could no longer be certain of blocking any measure they wanted.

During the accession negotiations for Austria, Finland and Sweden, it was argued by Britain and Spain that the proportion of votes needed to pass a measure should be increased so that a blocking minority would remain at 23. The others did not accept this, but a compromise was reached at a meeting of the Council held in Ioannina, Greece, in 1994. Usually called the "Ioannina Compromise", this states that if Member States commanding a total of at least 23 votes indicate their intention to oppose the taking of a Council decision by a qualified majority, the Council will make every effort to find a satisfactory solution that can be adopted with fewer than 23 votes against, provided that this can be done within a reasonable period and without infringing any of the time limits laid down in Community law.[45] This compromise was intended to last only until the Treaty of Amsterdam was adopted, but it has now been extended until the next time the Community is enlarged, when it is hoped to find a better solution.[46]

THE DEMOCRATIC DEFICIT

It is generally recognized that the Community is not democratic, a fact neatly highlighted by the phrase "democratic deficit". It was

[45] For the text of the Decision, see OJ 1994, C105/1, as amended by OJ 1995, C1/1 (adjustments consequent on Norway's decision not to join the Community).

[46] See Declaration 50, adopted by the Conference at which the Treaty of Amsterdam was agreed. See also the "Protocol on the Institutions with the Prospect of Enlargement of the European Union" (a Protocol annexed to the Treaty on European Union and the EC, ECSC and Euratom Treaties) under which it was agreed that, by the entry into force of the next enlargement, the Commission will consist of only one national from each Member State (instead of two from each of the large countries, as at present), provided that the qualified-majority voting system is modified, either by re-weighting the votes or by a dual majority, "in a manner acceptable to all Member States". The idea is that, since the change in Commission membership will harm the interests of the large Member States, the system of qualified-majority voting will be modified in a way helpful to them.

originally thought that the problem would be solved once the European Parliament was directly elected by the voters of Europe, but it is now coming to be recognized that the Parliament gives the Community little more than a façade of democracy.

In the constitutional systems of the Member States, the national parliaments provide a mechanism under which the opinions, values and attitudes of the electorate can influence government policy. Admittedly, this mechanism functions imperfectly and is distorted in various ways. Nevertheless, it *does* function. In Britain, for example, there are a number of parties in Parliament, one of which usually has an overall majority and forms the government. The government then runs the country for a number of years. At the next election, the electorate holds that party responsible for what the government has done: if it approves, it will reward it by voting for it; if it does not, it will punish it by voting for some other party. Under this system, the party in power knows that it will have to answer to the electorate, and the Members of Parliament in that party will act accordingly. In most other Member States—for example, Germany, Denmark, the Netherlands or Sweden—the position is similar, except that the government is usually a coalition of two or more parties.

In the Community, on the other hand, there is no government, or, if one regards the Commission as the government, it is not a party government. No party holds power; consequently, no party is responsible for government policy. If things go well, no party can take the credit; if they go badly, no party must take the blame. The result is that when elections are held, the voters do not vote according to the governing party's record, nor indeed according to the opposition parties' promises as to what they will do if elected. In the United Kingdom, and probably in most other Member States, voters use European elections to express approval or disapproval of what their *national* government is doing: if there is a Conservative government in Britain and British voters want to express their dissatisfaction with it, they will vote Labour in the European election. This means that nothing the parties do, or do not do, in the European Parliament will affect their chances of re-election; so they are not constrained in their actions by any consideration of public opinion. For these reasons, the European Parliament fails to provide a mechanism for popular opinion to influence Community policy.[47]

---

[47] It does, however, provide a fertile field for lobbyists to conduct their operations.

It might be thought that this problem could be solved by giving the European Parliament greater powers, in particular by making the Commission responsible to it in the same way that most national governments are responsible to the national parliaments. There are, however, reasons why this will not work. Democracy presupposes that most members of the electorate think of other voters in some sense as being "one of us". This is usually expressed by a phrase such as "one nation". The terminology is not important, but what matters is that the voters as a whole should have a sense of group loyalty and belonging: they must share the same fundamental values and attitudes. Only then will the minority be willing to give in to the majority on particular points of disagreement. Since both start from the same fundamental premises, they can reason with one another, and it will always be possible that today's minority will become tomorrow's majority. The minority parties know that they could win next time and the majority party knows that it could lose next time.

If, on the other hand, the electorate is split into segments with fundamentally different values, these expectations will not apply. This occurs particularly where there are ethnic or religious differences regarded as so important by the persons concerned that they eclipse all other considerations. In such a situation, members of the opposing group are no longer "us", but "them". Sectarian parties spring up, catering exclusively for a particular group. If the whole political system becomes "tribalized" in this way, democracy will no longer work. Ethnic minority parties can never become the government because they can never win a majority of votes: except in the case of ethnic cleansing or mass immigration, they are doomed to be a permanent opposition. In such a situation, they will call for a separate state, one in which they will constitute the majority. This is why democracy has never worked properly in Northern Ireland. When the whole of Ireland was part of the United Kingdom, Irish nationalists felt alienated and demanded separation. Ulster Protestants, however, were unwilling to accept a united Ireland, even if guaranteed democratic rights, because they knew they would be in a permanent minority within it. For similar reasons, Ulster Catholics have always felt that democratic rights in the Northern Ireland political system are not a satisfactory solution for them.

The relevance of this for Europe is that the European Union is made up of a number of separate nations which have only a limited sense of being European. Citizens of other Community countries are "them", not "us". There is no feeling of being one nation. There is no European public opinion, except perhaps among the narrow elite who actually run the Community. If there was a European Government responsible to the European Parliament, voters would feel just as alienated as they do at present. Each nation would regard itself as being in a permanent minority: there would be no sense of belonging. Voters would not feel that the European President or Prime Minister spoke for them: they would not regard the European Government as *their* government.[48] This is the dilemma of European democracy.

[48] This has been pointed out by a number of writers: see, for example, Dashwood, "States in the European Union" (1998) 23 ELRev. 201 at p. 216.

2

The European Court: An Objective Interpreter of Community Law?

"When *I* use a word," Humpty-Dumpty said in a scornful voice, "it means just what I choose it to mean—neither more nor less."

Lewis Carroll, *Through the Looking-Glass* (1872), Chapter 6.

THE RULE OF LAW

The Ancient Greeks used to boast that they were ruled by laws, not men. This idea, which led eventually to the modern doctrine of the rule of law, means that those with power in a society must abide by the law, even if they disagree with it. It also means that the law must be interpreted objectively, not according to the interests, values or beliefs of the interpreter. Since governments cannot always be relied upon to do this, courts have been created to carry out the task.

The doctrine of the rule of law assumes that laws are capable of an objective existence, separate from the interests, values or beliefs of individuals or groups. Since laws are expressed in words, it assumes that words are capable of an objective meaning. This assumption is treated with derision by totalitarian politicians; but it is an assumption on which all law and legal thinking is based. Words are notoriously imprecise; their meaning is elusive and constantly changing. This cannot be ignored, least of all by lawyers; nevertheless, lawyers must believe that words are *capable* of an objective meaning.

The meaning of a word depends on the context in which it is used: in interpreting a legal text, one must consider who the author was and what he was trying to achieve; the background—political, legal or economic—must also be taken into account. Having done this, one may conclude that a particular text has no ascertainable meaning;

most legal texts, however, have some meaning, though a core of clarity may be surrounded by a periphery of imprecision.

The rule of law requires, first, that laws should be expressed in the clearest and most precise way possible; secondly, that they should be interpreted objectively; and, thirdly, that they should be obeyed and enforced. The first of these requirements, in so far as it applies to the European Union, will be examined in Chapter 4. The third requirement is discussed in Chapter 6. In this chapter we consider whether the European Court interprets Community law in a fair and objective way.

Before doing this, however, we must try to determine more precisely what standards courts should be expected to follow and what may reasonably be regarded as unacceptable behaviour. Courts are not responsible for the enactment of the law; so, if the law is vague, imprecise or even meaningless, they cannot be blamed. They nevertheless have to interpret and apply it. In such a situation they must do the best they can and give it such meaning as it may reasonably be regarded as having. Therefore, if a legal text could have a whole range of meanings and a court selects one of them as being correct, it cannot be accused of giving a ruling at variance with the text,[1] even though a series of such rulings may over a period of time change the face of the law. Where, on the other hand, the law has a clear meaning[2] and the court does not follow it, or where, though it is unclear, it is given a meaning which it could not possibly have, the court may reasonably be accused of giving a judgment contrary to the law.

The Community Treaties are the most important component of Community law and we will restrict our investigation to them. Our attention will be focused on cases in which the Court has been required to decide on the division of power between the Community and the Member States, and in particular on the extent of its own jurisdiction: these are the cases in which any departure from the text of the Treaties is likely to have the most important consequences.

[1] Whether its interpretation is good from other points of view is of course a different question.

[2] It may be objected that no text ever has a clear meaning: see, for example, Cappelletti, "The Law-Making Power of the Judge and its Limits: A Comparative Analysis" (1981) 8 Monash ULRev. 15 at pp. 16–18. Theoretically, this is true; however, in any given case only certain aspects of the text are relevant and there is no reason why these should not be clear. In other words, the text may be clear *for the purpose of the case*. Cappelletti accepts this: *ibid.*, p. 19.

To determine whether the European Court interprets the Treaties objectively, we will analyse a number of cases in which the Court has been accused of giving judgments contrary to the text of the Treaties, as well as two instances in which it has notably refused to do so. In carrying out this investigation, we will try to ascertain whether the provision in question has an objective meaning and, if it does, what this is. We will look at both the words used and the probable intention of the authors. In this chapter we will limit ourselves strictly to the question whether the European Court gives judgments contrary to the Treaties; further questions, including possible justifications for what the Court does, will be dealt with in Chapter 3.

THE COURT'S JUDGMENTS: SOME EXAMPLES

Direct Effect of Treaty Provisions

The first question to consider is the relationship between the Community Treaties and the domestic law of the Member States. Can Treaty provisions be "directly effective", that is to say, can they apply as part of the law of the land in the Member States and prevail over domestic law without the intervention of the government or legislature of the State concerned? This is an important question. Our starting point must be the principle that the effect of an international treaty in the domestic legal system of a State that is a party to it is a matter for the constitutional law of the State in question. Prior to the decision of the European Court in the *Van Gend en Loos* case,[3] this principle was universally accepted:

> [T]he effect of international law generally, and of treaties in particu-
> lar, within the legal order of a State will always depend on a rule of
> domestic law. The fundamental principle is that the application of
> treaties is governed by domestic constitutional law. It is true that
> domestic law may, under certain conditions, require or permit the
> application of treaties which are binding on the State, even if they
> have not been specifically incorporated into domestic law. But this
> application of treaties "as such" is prescribed by a rule of domestic
> constitutional law. It is not a situation reached by the application of a
> rule of international law, since such a rule, to have effect, itself

[3] Case 26/62, [1963] ECR 1.

depends upon recognition by domestic law. Indeed international law is generally uninformative in this area since it simply requires the application of treaties in all circumstances. It does not modify the fundamental principle that the application of treaties by domestic courts is governed by domestic law.[4]

In spite of this principle, the European Court has held, in a line of cases beginning with *Van Gend en Loos*,[5] that it is *Community law* that decides whether a provision of a Community Treaty is directly effective in the Member States.[6] The Treaties themselves do not deal with the question[7] and, as it is inconceivable that the authors of the Treaties would have omitted to insert an express provision if they had intended to modify the principle universally accepted at the time, one must conclude that the judgments given by the European Court in these cases are contrary to what the parties to the Treaties intended, and therefore contrary to the Treaties themselves.[8]

If the traditional principle had been applied by the European Court, the result would have been that the effect of the Treaties in

---

[4] Francis G Jacobs in Francis G Jacobs and Shelly Roberts (eds.), *The Effect of Treaties in Domestic Law* (1987), p. xxiv (Introduction).

[5] N. 3 above.

[6] In the *Van Gend en Loos* case itself the issue was slightly fudged: one might almost say that the European Court tried to disguise what it was doing; nevertheless, the principle became absolutely clear in later cases.

[7] Art. 189 {249} EC (set out below) states that Community regulations are directly applicable (directly effective, in the terminology we are using), but there is no statement that the Treaty itself is directly effective. It is sometimes argued that, since regulations are subordinate to the Treaty in the legal hierarchy, if they are directly effective, the authors of the Treaty must have intended the Treaty itself to be directly effective. This does not necessarily follow, however, since the national governments might have been prepared to allow regulations, which were intended to deal with specific issues, to be directly effective, without being prepared to accept that the wider-ranging provisions of the Treaty should have this effect. It could in fact be said with more justification that the express inclusion in the Treaty of a provision giving direct effect to regulations shows that the authors of the Treaty had given thought to the question; consequently, the omission of a similar provision regarding the Treaty itself shows that the Treaty was not intended to have direct effect.

[8] It might be thought that the existence of Art. 177 {234} EC (discussed below) indicates that the Treaty and Community legislation were intended to be directly effective as a matter of Community law: why else, it might be argued, would a procedure be established for national courts to refer to the European Court questions on the interpretation and validity of Community provisions? However, the constitutions of some of the original Member States provide that international treaties may in certain circumstances be applied directly by the national courts; in those countries, therefore, Community law could be directly effective *as a matter of national law*. Moreover, even in those countries in which this could not occur, a national court might well wish to ascertain the validity and interpretation of a Community provision even if it was not directly effective. The reasons for this are explained at p. 28, below.

the domestic law of the Member States would have varied from State to State. A given provision would have been directly effective in one but not in another; consequently, it would have been easier to enforce in one Member State than in another. Such a situation would have been undesirable; nevertheless, it is the normal situation in international law and applies in the case of other treaties—for example, the European Convention on Human Rights. Though undesirable, it would not have prevented the Communities from functioning; consequently, its undesirability cannot be regarded as indicating that the authors of the Treaties intended them to be directly effective as a matter of Community law.

Direct Effect of Directives

Let us now consider measures adopted by the Community. The two most important kinds of Community act for which provision is made in the EC Treaty[9] are regulations and directives.[10] The former are clearly legislative; the latter may result in legislation, but were not intended themselves to be legislation. The relevant provisions are the second and third paragraphs of Article 189 {249} EC. The second paragraph states:

> A regulation shall have general application. It shall be binding in its entirety and directly applicable in all Member States.

This contrasts with the position regarding directives, as set out in the third paragraph of Article 189 {249}. This states:

> A directive shall be binding, as to the result to be achieved, upon each Member State to which it is addressed, but shall leave to the national authorities the choice of form and methods.

The statement in the second paragraph that a regulation is "directly applicable" means that it is directly effective, as defined above. The second paragraph of Article 189 {249} is the only provision in the EC Treaty dealing with direct effect, and the fact that it expressly

---

[9] The position under the Euratom Treaty is largely the same as that under the EC Treaty; that under the ECSC Treaty is somewhat different. We will restrict our discussion to the EC Treaty, since it is by far the most important of the three.

[10] Decisions constitute a third kind of Community act. They usually deal with individual cases and are of an administrative nature: Art. 189 {249} EC states merely that a decision is "binding in its entirety upon those to whom it is addressed".

states that regulations are directly effective makes it even more sig-nificant that it fails to say the same with regard to Treaty provisions.

Can directives be directly effective? There are three reasons which suggest that the authors of the Treaty did not intend them to be. The first is the omission to state expressly that they are directly effective, an omission made all the more striking by the fact that an express statement is found in the very same Treaty provision with regard to regulations.[11] The second is that a directive is not binding "in its entirety", as is a regulation, but is binding merely "as to the result to be achieved". The third is that Member States, on whom alone directives are binding, are given "the choice of form and methods". The inescapable implication of these provisions is that directives were not intended to be directly effective: Member States were intended to take action themselves to attain the result envisaged by the direc-tive.

In spite of this, the European Court held in *Van Duyn* v. *Home Office*[12] that directives can be directly effective as a matter of Community law. It put forward three arguments to justify its ruling. The first was that it would be incompatible with its binding effect if a directive was not capable of being directly effective as a matter of Community law. This argument is wrong: an obligation can be legally binding on the international level without being directly effective. As was pointed out above, prior to the European Court's judgment in the *Van Gend en Loos* case, no international instrument

---

[11] The Court tried to meet this objection by stating in the *Van Duyn* case (n. 12 below) (para. 12 of the judgment), "If . . . by virtue of the provisions of Art. 189 {249} regulations are directly applicable and, consequently, may by their very nature have direct effects, it does not follow from this that other categories of acts mentioned in that Article can never have similar effects". This implies that direct effect is not the same as direct applicability, but is the natural consequence of it. Exponents of this approach do not always make clear what they think direct applicability is, but it usually boils down to the fact that regulations, being directly applicable, do not have to be transposed into the national legal system by any national measure of incorporation (implementing measure). However, this formulation puts the cart before the horse: it is *because* regulations are directly effective that they do not have to be transposed by national measures of incorporation. When the authors of the Treaty said that regulations were directly applicable they meant that they were what is sometimes called "self-executing"—what we have termed "directly effective"—namely that they were to be part of the law of the land in the Member Sates without the need for any national act of incorporation. This is common usage in international law: see, for example, Jackson, "Status of Treaties in Domestic Legal Systems: A Policy Analysis" (1992) 86 Am.Jo.Int.L 310, n. 1. Direct effect is not a consequence of direct applicability: it is an essential element of it. The failure of the Treaty to say that directives are directly applicable, which was surely deliber-ate, meant that they were not intended to be directly effective.

[12] Case 41/74, [1974] ECR 1337.

was directly effective *as a matter of international law*; moreover, in "dualist"[13] countries such as the United Kingdom, international obligations were never directly effective.

The second argument was that the practical effectiveness (*"effet utile"*, in French) of directives would be greater if they were directly effective. This is true. The Community has always had difficulty in getting Member States to implement directives on time: if they were directly effective, individuals could claim rights under them even if they were not implemented. This, therefore, is an argument for saying that directives *ought* to be directly effective; it is not, however, an argument for saying that they *are* directly effective: the Community system could function if directives were not directly effective; it just would not function so well.

The third argument was based on Article 177 {234} EC. This permits national courts to ask the European Court to give preliminary rulings on the validity and effect of acts of the institutions of the Community. The European Court argued that, since this covers directives, it must mean that the authors of the Treaty intended them to be directly effective. However, national courts might need a ruling on the validity or interpretation of a directive even if it was not directly effective. If a national court was called upon to interpret the national measure giving effect to the directive, it might well want to know the correct interpretation of the directive so it could interpret the national measure in harmony with it. The European Court itself has said that national courts must do this.[14] A ruling on the validity of a directive might be needed in order to determine the validity of the national measure transposing it into the national legal system: in some circumstances—for example, in the United Kingdom when the national measure is a statutory instrument under section 2(2) of the European Communities Act 1972—the validity of the national measure might depend on the validity of the directive. For these reasons, no inferences can be drawn from the terms of Article 177 {234} EC.

A fourth argument, which was not mentioned in the *Van Duyn* case but which achieved prominence in later cases, is that if the European Court had not declared directives capable of being directly effective, Member States would have been able to benefit from their

---

[13] On the meaning of this term, see n. 33, below.
[14] *Von Colson and Kamann v. Land Nordrhein-Westfalen*, Case 14/83, [1984] ECR 1891.

own wrongdoing in not implementing them on time.[15] Though this argument applies only where rights under a directive are claimed against the State, it reinforces the "effectiveness" argument mentioned above. There is, however, no reason to believe that it was present in the minds of the authors of the Treaty—the European Court itself did not think of it until some time after the *Van Duyn* case— and it must again be regarded as an argument as to what the law ought to be, rather than as to what it is.

We may conclude, therefore, that none of these arguments justifies the Court's ruling. The authors of the Treaty did not intend directives to be directly effective. The Court's judgment in *Van Duyn* v. *Home Office* is contrary to the Treaty.[16]

The ruling in the *Van Duyn* case evoked considerable opposition in France[17] and Germany;[18] so in the first *Marshall* case[19] the European Court made a concession by limiting the direct effect of directives to rights against the State,[20] as distinct from rights against private persons,[21] a limitation which fits in with the argument that the State should not be able to benefit from its own wrongdoing. The neatness of this fit has, however, been spoilt by the wide definition given to the "State" for this purpose: it includes, for example, local authorities[22] and nationalized industries,[23] neither of which can be regarded as responsible if the Government fails to transpose a directive.

The limitation in turn gave rise to anomalies: for example, a directive giving rights to employees against their employer could be

---

[15] The first case in which the European Court used the argument appears to be *Ratti*, Case 148/78, [1979] ECR 1629 (para. 22 of the judgment). It was derived from the principles of Equity in English law (though similar principles exist in other legal systems) and was first put forward by Advocate General Warner in *ENKA*, Case 38/77, [1977] ECR 2203 at 2226.

[16] For a grudging recognition of this over twenty years later by a current member of the European Court (Judge Mancini), see Mancini and Keeling, "Language, Culture and Politics in the Life of the European Court of Justice" (1995) 1 Columbia JEL 397, where it is said (at p. 401) that *Van Duyn* v. *Home Office* "perhaps goes beyond the letter of Art. 189".

[17] *Cohn-Bendit, Conseil d'Etat*, 22 December 1978, Dalloz, 1979, p. 155.

[18] *Bundesfinanzhof*, 16 July 1981, [1982] 1 CMLR 527; *Bundesfinanzhof*, 25 April 1985 (VR 123/84), *Entscheidungen des Bundesfinanzhofes* 143, at 383.

[19] *Marshall* v. *Southampton & South West Hampshire Area Health Authority (Teaching)*, Case 152/84, [1986] ECR 723.

[20] Sometimes termed "vertical" direct effect.

[21] Sometimes called "horizontal" direct effect.

[22] *Fratelli Costanzo* v. *Comune di Milano*, Case 103/88, [1989] ECR 1839.

[23] *Foster* v. *British Gas*, Case C-188/89, [1990] ECR I-3313.

directly invoked by those working in a nationalized industry, but not by those in a private firm. As a result, there were calls for the direct effect of directives to be extended to rights against private persons, a development which would have obliterated the distinction between directives and regulations for most practical purposes;[24] nevertheless, it was supported by no fewer than three advocates general.[25] However, when the point arose for decision in *Faccini Dori* v. *Recreb*,[26] the Court refused to extend the principle, arguing that to make directives directly effective against persons other than the State would conflict with the statement in Article 189 {249}, third paragraph,[27] that a directive is binding on each Member State to which it is addressed, a statement from which the Court inferred that a directive cannot be binding on private persons. This is surely correct, but it is strange that the Court did not see that *any* form of direct effect of directives is contrary to Article 189 {249}.

The decision in *Faccini Dori* is noteworthy because it shows that circumstances exist in which the Court is prepared to stand by the words of the Treaty. Its determination to do so in the *Faccini Dori* case may have been due to the opposition evoked by the *Van Duyn* case, opposition which had died away by the time *Faccini Dori* was decided,[28] and to the objections of the Member States to any extension to the direct effect of directives;[29] in spite of this, however, *Faccini Dori* must be recognized as a contrary example in our examination of judicial activism.

---

[24] Member States would still have been obliged to transpose directives, but their failure to do so would not have affected rights claimed under them.

[25] Advocate General van Gerven in the second *Marshall* case, *Marshall* v. *Southampton & South West Hampshire Area Health Authority* (*Teaching*), Case C-271/91, [1993] ECR I-4367; Advocate General Jacobs in *Vaneetveld*, Case C-316/93, [1994] ECR I-763; and Advocate General Lenz in *Faccini Dori* v. *Recreb* (n. 26 below) itself.

[26] Case C-91/92, [1994] ECR I-3325.

[27] Quoted above.

[28] For France, see the *Rothmans* and *Arizona Tobacco* cases, *Conseil d'Etat*, 28 February 1992, [1993] CMLR 253 (discussed in T C Hartley, *The Foundations of European Community Law* (4th ed. 1998) at pp. 246–247); for Germany, see *Bundesverfassungsgericht*, decision of 8 April 1987, [1987] RIW 878 (discussed *ibid.*, at pp. 238–239).

[29] Written or oral submissions were put before the Court by Denmark, France, Germany, Greece, Italy, the Netherlands and the United Kingdom. All except Greece were opposed to extending the direct effect of directives. There are also arguments of a practical nature against such an extension: see Hartley, "Five Forms of Uncertainty in European Community Law" [1996] CLJ 265 at pp. 281 *et seq.*

Preliminary References

Article 177 {234} EC gives the European Court jurisdiction to make preliminary rulings on a reference from a national court. According to Article 177 {234}, this may be done in three cases:

    (a) the interpretation of this Treaty;
    (b) the validity and interpretation of acts of the institutions of the Community and of the ECB;[30]
    (c) the interpretation of the statutes of bodies established by an act of the Council where those statutes so provide.[31]

The first question is whether these provisions give the European Court jurisdiction to rule on the interpretation of international agreements with third countries. In the *Haegeman* case,[32] the Court held that they cover agreements between the Community and one or more non-member States. Such agreements are concluded by the Council, usually by means of a decision or regulation, and the Court seized on this as justification for holding that they fall under paragraph (b), above. However, the Court was not asked to interpret the instrument by which the Council signified its assent to the agreement, but the agreement itself. The Court's judgment could only be justified, therefore, if the agreement had no effect in the Community legal system as an international treaty, but only as a legislative measure of the Council (dualist[33] position). However, this has never been the position of the European Court, which has consistently adopted the monist[34] point of view.

---

[30] The reference to the ECB (European Central Bank) was added by the Maastricht Agreement and was not part of Art. 177 {234} when the European Court decided the cases discussed below. Its presence or absence has no effect on the points to be considered.

[31] Here "statutes" means the rules governing the activities of the body in question. This provision appears never to have been invoked.

[32] Case 181/73, [1974] ECR 449.

[33] This is the view which, in broad terms, treats international law and national law as being completely separate, as a result of which there can be no question of international treaties ever having direct effect. If their provisions are to apply in the domestic law of the country concerned, they can do so only if incorporated as part of national legislation. They would then apply as part of the national legislation, not as international law. This contrasts with the monist view, according to which international law and national law are ultimately part of one greater unity, which means that direct effect is in principle possible. Where it occurs, the provisions of an international treaty can apply in the domestic legal system as international law.

[34] See previous note.

If, on the other hand, one takes the view that the agreement itself constituted an act of the Council, one is faced with the question whether the word "acts" in Article 177 {234} was intended to cover bilateral (or multilateral) acts (agreements) or only unilateral acts. Certainly, the list in Article 189 {249} of acts that may be adopted by the Council, Commission and Parliament is confined to the latter, though the Court has held that this list is not exhaustive.[35] In any event, Advocate General Trabucchi has expressed the opinion that only unilateral acts are covered by Article 177 {234}[36] and this seems to be borne out by the decision of the Court in *France* v. *Commission*.[37] In this case, France brought proceedings under the first paragraph of Article 173 {230} EC to annul an international agreement concluded by the Commission with the United States. The relevant part of Article 173 {230} is set out below:[38] it gives the Court jurisdiction to annul (amongst other things) acts of the Commission. Could an agreement with a third country constitute such an act? The Commission argued that it could not, since, in its view, "act" covers only a unilateral act. The Court seemed to agree: it held that France's application, which had been directed against the agreement itself, should be regarded as having been directed against the Commission decision to conclude the agreement.[39]

Another objection to the view that an international agreement is an act of the Council is that, where the Community enters into an agreement with a non-member State, the party to the agreement on the Community side is the Community itself—the EC, the ECSC or Euratom, as the case may be—and not any *institution* of the Community.[40] The regulation or decision by which the Community expresses its assent to the agreement may be an act of the Council, but the agreement itself is not. For all these reasons, therefore, the decision in *Haegeman* is dubious, to say the least.

Whatever one may think about the *Haegeman* case, there can be no dispute that the *SPI*[41] case goes beyond what is permitted by Article 177 {234}. In this case, the European Court held that

---

[35] *Commission* v. *Council (ERTA)*, Case 22/70, [1971] ECR 263.
[36] *Bresciani*, Case 87/75, [1976] ECR 129 at 147.
[37] Case C-327/91, [1994] ECR I-3641.
[38] See p. 35.
[39] See paras 13–17 of the judgment.
[40] This was made clear by the Court in *France* v. *Commission* (n. 37 above), at para. 24 of its judgment.
[41] Cases 267–9/81, [1983] ECR 801.

Article 177 {234} gave it jurisdiction to interpret the (old) GATT, an agreement to which all the Member States were parties, but to which the Community had not formally acceded: there was no act of the Council by which the latter gave its assent to the agreement; consequently, even the dubious rationale of the *Haegeman* case was inapplicable. In spite of this deficiency, the Court held that the GATT was covered by Article 177 {234}. It did not specify which of the sub-paragraphs quoted above was the relevant one, in the circumstances no doubt a prudent omission, nor did it seriously argue that the words used in Article 177 {234} were intended to cover the GATT; instead, it argued that it would be desirable if the GATT were covered, since, if the national courts had the final word on its interpretation, it might be interpreted differently in different Member States, something which could produce distortions of trade. Of course, whether the GATT *ought* to be covered is a different thing from whether it *is* covered. The European Court's failure to make any genuine attempt to address the latter question, or rather its attempt to deduce "is" from "ought", could be regarded as a tacit admission that its judgment was not founded on the Treaty.

In a later case, *Sevince*,[42] the Court went even further and held that, where an agreement with a non-member State provides for the establishment of an international institution (*in casu*, a Council of Association), decisions of that institution are also covered by Article 177 {234} EC. Now, there is no way in which the phrase "acts of the institutions of the Community" in Article 177 {234} can cover acts of a Council of Association: the institutions of the Community are listed in Article 4 {7} EC and they do not include a Council of Association, nor has anyone ever seriously suggested otherwise. The only argument the Court could come up with was that the decisions of a Council of Association are "directly connected with the Agreement to which they give effect",[43] hardly a telling point. The judgment in *Sevince*, therefore, is also contrary to the Treaty.

The provisions of Article 177 {234} EC quoted above are not found in the ECSC Treaty. The nearest equivalent is Article 41 ECSC, which states:

---

[42] Case C-192/89, [1990] ECR I-3461.
[43] Para. 9 of the judgment.

>   The Court shall have sole jurisdiction to give preliminary
>   rulings on the validity of acts of the High Authority
>   [Commission[44]] and of the Council where such validity is in
>   issue in proceedings brought before a national court or tribunal.

This differs from Article 177 {234} EC in several important respects,
two of which are of concern to us. The first is that it gives jurisdiction to rule only on the *validity* of acts, not their interpretation, and
the second is that it gives the European Court *sole* jurisdiction in this
regard. Article 177 {234} EC, on the other hand, gives the European
Court jurisdiction to rule on both the validity *and* interpretation of
Community acts, but it does not provide that this jurisdiction is
exclusive.

The European Court has obliterated both these differences. In
Foto-Frost[45] it held that its jurisdiction to rule on the validity of
Community acts under the EC Treaty is exclusive[46] and in *Busseni*[47]
it held that it has jurisdiction to rule on the interpretation of measures
adopted under the ECSC Treaty.[48] Neither of these rulings is justified by the Treaties.

In the *Foto-Frost* case, the Court tried to justify its ruling by arguing that, if national courts had the power to declare Community acts
invalid, divergences could develop between courts in different
Member States and this could "place in jeopardy the very unity of the
Community legal order and detract from the fundamental requirement of legal certainty".[49] However, this argument can hardly have
escaped the attention of the drafters of the EC Treaty. They had the
ECSC Treaty, signed some six years previously, before them; nevertheless, they chose not to follow it. No doubt, they had their reasons.
In these circumstances, the Court's statement is hardly a serious argument for the contention that Article 177 {234} *actually means* that the

---

[44] Art. H {9} of the Maastricht Agreement amends Art. 7 ECSC to provide that the
High Authority will be referred to as "the Commission".

[45] Case 314/85, [1987] ECR 4199.

[46] It held that, while a national court may declare a Community act valid, it may not
declare it invalid: only the European Court can do this.

[47] Case C-221/88, [1990] ECR I-495.

[48] Its reasoning was that both Art. 41 ECSC and Art. 177 {234} EC have the same function, that interpretation and appraisal of validity are related matters and that it is just as necessary for the European Court to fulfil its role in the case of the ECSC as in the case of the
other Communities.

[49] Para. 15 of the judgment.

Court's power is exclusive; all it does is to support the view that it would have been good if it *had meant* that.

The arguments given in *Busseni* were no better. One argument was that interpreting a legal act and determining its validity are related matters, since a Court might have to interpret a measure before it could decide if it was valid. In some situations this is true and it clearly justifies the Court's having the power to interpret an act *in order to determine its validity*; but it does not justify the Court's having the power to interpret an act when there is no question of determining its validity.

The second argument in *Busseni* was even weaker. The Court said that it would be contrary to the objectives and coherence of the Treaties if it had the power to promote the uniform application of Community acts under the EC and Euratom Treaties, but not under the ECSC Treaty. This implies that differences cannot exist between the Treaties as regards the Court's powers to promote the uniform application of Community law, clearly an untenable position.

Annulment Actions

Proceedings to annul Community acts are dealt with by Article 173 {230}, the first paragraph of which, as it existed at the time of the cases we are about to discuss, read as follows:

> The Court of Justice shall review the legality of acts of the Council and the Commission other than recommendations or opinions. It shall for this purpose have jurisdiction in actions brought by a Member State, the Council or Commission on grounds of. . . .

Two things are clear from this provision: it permitted a challenge to be made only to acts of the Council or Commission; and such a challenge could be brought only by a Member State, the Council or Commission.[50] Despite this, the European Court held in *Parti Ecologiste "Les Verts"* v. *European Parliament*[51] that it permitted a challenge to acts of the European Parliament that were intended to have legal effects *vis-à-vis* third parties, a decision that was clearly contrary

---

[50] Subsequent paragraphs of Art. 173 {230} permitted actions to be brought in certain limited cases by private applicants, but these are not germane to the cases we are about to discuss.

[51] Case 294/83, [1986] ECR 1339.

to the text. Moreover, it held in the *Chernobyl* case[52] that proceedings could also be brought *by* the Parliament[53] under Article 146 Euratom, which at the time was identical to Article 173 {230} EEC (EC).

This latter decision is of particular interest because, in an earlier case,[54] the Court had expressly held that the Parliament did *not* come within the terms of Article 173 {230}.[55] In the *Chernobyl* case, the Court accepted this, but held that the Parliament could nevertheless bring the action. Its reasoning is so illuminating that it must be quoted in full:[56]

> The absence in the Treaties of any provision giving the Parliament the right to bring an action for annulment may constitute a procedural gap, but it cannot prevail over the fundamental interest in the maintenance and observance of the institutional balance laid down in the Treaties establishing the European Communities.
>
> Consequently, an action for annulment brought by the Parliament against an act of the Council or the Commission is admissible provided that the action seeks only to safeguard its prerogatives and that it is founded only on submissions alleging their infringement.

This passage states explicitly what is implicit in some of the other cases discussed, namely that the Treaty provides no authority for the judgment the Court is about to give. It also makes clear that the Court is prepared to go against the Treaties where it feels that the constitutional development of the Community so requires.

The Treaty-Making Power

Our final example concerns the power of the European Community (in the strict legal sense)[57] to enter into treaties with non-member

---

[52] *European Parliament* v. *Council*, Case C-70/88, [1990] ECR I-2041.

[53] The Court, however, restricted this to actions brought by the Parliament for the limited purpose of protecting its prerogatives.

[54] *European Parliament* v. *Council* (*Comitology*), Case 302/87 [1988] ECR 5615.

[55] It held that it was not covered by the first paragraph of Art. 173 {230}—the provision quoted earlier in the text—and also that it was not a "legal person" within the meaning of what is now the fourth paragraph, the result being that it could not enjoy even the limited standing given to private persons.

[56] Paras 26 and 27 of the judgment.

[57] The phrase "European Community" ("EC") is used today in two senses: in the strict legal sense it refers to one of the three Communities, the other two being the European Coal

States. This is dealt with in Article 228 {300} EC, which begins, "Where this Treaty provides for the conclusion of agreements between the Community and one or more States or international organizations . . ." and goes on to say that the agreement will be negotiated by the Commission and concluded by the Council. On the basis of this, one might suppose that the EC's treaty-making power is limited to cases for which provision is made by specific Articles of the EC Treaty, the most important being Article 113 {133} and Article 238 {310}.

This supposition is confirmed when one compares Article 228 {300} EC with the equivalent provision under the Euratom Treaty, Article 101 Euratom, which states that the European Atomic Energy Community (Euratom) has the power to enter into international agreements "within the limits of its powers and jurisdiction". This empowers Euratom to enter into treaties whenever the subject-matter falls within the general area of its jurisdiction, even if there is no express authorization. The contrast in wording between these two provisions is striking. Since the EC Treaty (originally the EEC Treaty) and the Euratom Treaty were negotiated and concluded at the same time, the difference must have been deliberate:[58] if the authors of the EC Treaty had wanted the EC to have the same powers as Euratom, they would have used the language of Article 101.

In spite of this, the European Court has held, in a series of cases beginning with the *ERTA* case,[59] that the European Community can also make treaties in any area in which it has internal legislative power, thus putting it in substantially the same position as the European Atomic Energy Community. In the *ERTA* case, the Court held that this implied treaty-making power comes into existence only when the internal power is exercised;[60] subsequently, however, it

and Steel Community (ECSC) and the European Atomic Energy Community (Euratom), each of which has separate legal personality and is therefore a separate legal entity; in more general language, however, it is also used to refer to the whole European enterprise in a political sense. In the past, the EC in the first sense was called the EEC (European Economic Community), but the Maastricht Agreement changed the name of this Community to the EC.

[58] The reason for Euratom's greater powers was no doubt that international agreements seemed destined to play a dominant role in all areas of Euratom's activities but only in particular areas of the EC's activities.

[59] *Commission* v. *Council*, Case 22/70, [1971] ECR 263.

[60] See, in particular, para. 84 of the judgment.

held that the mere *existence* of such internal power is sufficient.[61] This doctrine is sometimes called "parallelism".[62]

In the *ERTA* case the Court tried to justify its ruling by arguing that, if internal legislative power in a given area is vested in the Community but treaty-making power belongs to the Member States, the latter will be unable to adopt the necessary legislation to give effect to any treaty they conclude. In view of this, reasoned the Court, the Community must be regarded as having implied treaty-making power in all areas in which it has internal legislative power.[63]

Though attractive at first sight, this argument is not convincing. In international affairs, it frequently happens that treaty-making power is vested in one entity, while the power to adopt any legislation needed to give effect to the treaty is vested in another. Thus treaties are normally concluded by the Executive, while only the Legislature may be empowered to pass the necessary legislation. In such a situation, the Executive will not normally ratify the treaty until it is satisfied that any necessary legislation will be passed.

In federal States the position is more complex. The federal Executive normally has treaty-making power in all areas, even those in which internal legislative power belongs to the units (States, provinces, etc.). What happens if the subject-matter of the treaty falls into one of these areas and legislation is needed to give effect to it? In the United States, the federal Legislature (Congress) can pass the necessary legislation, thus encroaching on the normal jurisdiction of the States.[64] This could be regarded as a sort of "reverse parallelism". In Canada, on the other hand, the federal Legislature cannot do this; so the Government of Canada has to ask the Provinces to adopt the legislation.[65] The result is awkward, but it does not preclude Canada from playing its part in international affairs.

In the case of the Community, there would be no difficulty if the Member States acted in unison: they could conclude the treaty in their capacity as Member States and adopt the legislation in their capacity as members of the Council. The Commission would have to

[61] See *Laying-up Fund for Inland Waterway Vessels*, Opinion 1/76, [1977] ECR 741, at para. 4 of the judgment.

[62] The Court itself does not use the term.

[63] See paras 16–22 of the judgment.

[64] *Missouri v. Holland*, 252 US 416 (1920).

[65] *Attorney-General for Canada v. Attorney-General for Ontario* (Labour Conventions Case) [1937] AC 326 (PC); for discussion and criticism, see Peter W Hogg, *Constitutional Law of Canada* (3rd ed. 1992), Vol. 1, pp. 11–10 to 11–19.

co-operate by making the necessary proposal. There is no practical reason why this could not be done; the European Court's judgments in the *ERTA* case and those following it cannot, therefore, be justified on this ground. They must be regarded as contrary to the EC Treaty.

The case of *France* v. *Commission*[66] (discussed above) throws further light on these questions. In this case, the Commission had concluded an agreement with the United States on co-operation in competition (antitrust) matters. This was challenged by France, which argued that only the Council could have concluded the agreement. The Court agreed. It first ruled that only the Community as such—the EC, the ECSC or Euratom—can be a party to an international agreement, not an institution of the Community.[67] Could the Commission, acting alone, bind the European Community? The Court held that it could not, since Article 228 {300} EC provides that international agreements, though negotiated by the Commission, are concluded by the Council.

The Commission tried to use the doctrine of parallelism: it argued that, since it had internal executive power in the field of competition law, it should by implication be regarded as having treaty-making power in that field. This was an interesting variant of the argument adopted by the Court in the *ERTA* case. It was rejected by the Court in one terse paragraph:[68]

> Even though the Commission has the power, internally, to take individual decisions applying the rules of competition, a field covered by the Agreement, that internal power is not such as to alter the allocation of powers between the Community institutions with regard to the conclusion of international agreements, which is determined by Article 228 of the Treaty.

In other words, the doctrine of "parallelism" applies only between the Community and the Member States, not between the Council and the Commission. One wonders why not, since the allocation of powers between the Community and the Member States is also determined by Article 228 {300}.

In *France* v. *Commission*, the Court also accepted the validity of arguments based on a comparison between the provisions of the EC

---

[66] Case C-327/91, [1994] ECR I-3641.
[67] See paras 24–25 of the judgment.
[68] Para. 41 of the judgment.

and Euratom Treaties. It will be remembered that, while Article 228 {300} EC permits the European Community to enter into treaties only where "this Treaty provides for the conclusion of agreements . . .", Article 101 Euratom permits the European Atomic Energy Community to do so "within the limits of its powers and jurisdiction", an express acceptance of "parallelism". Another difference between the two Treaties is that, while under the EC Treaty the agreement is concluded by the Council, under the Euratom Treaty it is concluded by the Commission. This is normally done with the approval of the Council, but such approval is not needed if the implementation of the treaty does not require action by the Council and can be effected within the limits of the relevant budget. In *France* v. *Commission*, the Commission argued that it was entitled to conclude the Agreement with the United States because its implementation did not require action by the Council. This would have put the Commission in substantially the same position under the EC Treaty as it is in under the Euratom Treaty. The Court rejected the argument:

> [T]he EEC and the Euratom Treaties were negotiated simultaneously and signed on the same day; accordingly, if those negotiating the two Treaties had intended to grant the Commission the same powers, they would have done so expressly.

It is surprising that the Court did not see that the same argument could be used to reject the whole doctrine of "parallelism". If one simply substitutes the word "Community" for the word "Commission", the above quotation would perfectly express the argument set out previously as to why the Court's ruling in the *ERTA* case is contrary to the EC Treaty.

CONCLUSIONS

We began this chapter by advancing the contention that words in a legal document are capable of an objective meaning. We then sought to ascertain whether the European Court ever gave judgments contrary to the objective meaning of the Treaties. To do this, we chose a number of cases in which the European Court had been called upon to interpret Treaty provisions, tried to determine whether those provisions had an objective meaning and, if they did, to ascertain what it was. Our conclusion was that in certain cases the Court had given judgment contrary to the Treaty. Indeed, the arguments advanced by the Court in support of its ruling were often not even concerned with the objective meaning of the provision it was called upon to interpret, but rather with what the law ought to be. Thus the Court itself seemed implicitly to recognize that its judgment was not based on an objective interpretation of the Treaty. In *Chernobyl*, moreover, it recognized this explicitly by acknowledging that the Treaty did not give it the jurisdiction it was about to exercise.

The cases also make clear that the departures from the objective meaning of the Treaty were not the result of inadvertence, or a misunderstanding of the text, but were deliberate. The Court realized that its judgment was not based on the text, but went ahead all the same. It should also be noted that the general trend of the judgments was to enhance the powers of the Community in general and those of the Court itself in particular.

The legislative character of certain judgments has been implicitly recognized by the Court in another way as well. This has occurred whenever the Court has applied the *Defrenne* doctrine, so called because it was first enunciated in *Defrenne* v. *Sabena*.[69] Under this doctrine, which applies only when the European Court expressly so declares, rulings handed down by the Court operate only prospectively—that is, they apply only to rights and obligations based on facts arising after the Court's judgment—except with regard to the parties to the case itself and to any others who had instituted legal proceedings, or made equivalent claims, before the date of the judgment. Such a doctrine is justifiable only on the assumption that the Court's ruling is constitutive—legislative—rather than declaratory: if the Court is merely stating what the law always was, there would be no reason for its ruling to be limited in this way.[70] It need hardly be said that there is no basis for the doctrine in the Treaties themselves.

---

[69] Case 43/75, [1976] ECR 455.

[70] In the *Defrenne* case itself, the Court suggested a different reason for the doctrine: it said that several of the Member States had not transposed Art. 119 {141} into their national legal systems, and the Commission had taken no steps to force them to do so; in particular, it had not instituted proceedings under Art. 169 {226} EC. It is hard to see why this should be relevant, however, since the whole point of direct effect is that the Community provision is binding on individuals *without* any national measure. The general belief that Art. 119 {141} was not directly effective was not the result of the Commission's failure to institute proceedings under Art. 169 {226}. As was said above, the authors of the Treaty almost certainly did not intend any of its provisions to be directly effective. The Court ruled

Some readers may feel that the point has been sufficiently— perhaps excessively—elaborated and be eager to move on to the next chapter, where the rights and wrongs of the Court's attitude will be discussed. Obvious as it may seem, however, it is by no means universally accepted that the Court gives judgments contrary to the Treaty. Though this has been pointed out over the years by a number of writers,[71] their conclusions have evoked loud and often anguished protest.[72] In such a climate, anyone so bold as to make assertions of this kind must ensure that they are fully supported.

otherwise in the *Van Gend en Loos* case, decided some thirteen years before *Defrenne*. However, in the *Van Gend en Loos* case the Court indicated that a Treaty provision can be directly effective only if it is "not qualified by any reservation on the part of states which would make its implementation conditional upon a positive legislative measure enacted under national law" ([1963] ECR at 13). Art. 119 {141} *is* so qualified: it does not say "Men and women have the right to equal pay"; it says (italics added) *"Each Member State shall . . . ensure and subsequently maintain* the application of the principle that men and women should receive equal pay . . .".* For this reason, the Court's ruling that it was directly effective involved an extension of the law. The generally-held view that Art. 119 {141} was not directly effective followed from the wording of the provision itself, and was not the consequence of anyone's being misled by the Commission or the Member States. The Court's judgment was legislative. It was this fact, coupled with the serious economic consequences which would otherwise have ensued, that made it necessary to declare the judgment non-retroactive.

[71] See, among others, the following: A H Hermann, "British President is against the Rule of Judges", *Financial Times*, 12 April 1984, p. 43; Hjalte Rasmussen, *On Law and Policy in the European Court of Justice* (1986); Gavin Smith, "Judicial Function of European Court", letter printed in *The Times*, 12 October 1991; André Bzdera, "The Court of Justice of the European Community and the Politics of Institutional Reform" (1992) 15 West European Politics 122, at p. 124; Martin Howe, *Europe and the Constitution after Maastricht* (1993), pp. 35 *et seq.*; Aidan O'Neill and Jason Coppel, *EC Law for UK Lawyers* (1994), pp. 21–24; De Witte, "Rules of Change in International Law: How Special is the European Community?" (1994) 25 Neth.Yb.Int.L 299, at p. 323; Sir Patrick Neill, *The European Court of Justice: A Case Study in Judicial Activism* (published in the House of Lords Select Committee on the European Communities, Minutes of Evidence, 18th Report, p. 218 (HL Paper 88, 1994–95)); Bill Cash, "Dissenting Judgment", Law Soc. Gaz., 18 October 1995, p. 20; Ian Ward, *A Critical Introduction to European Law* (1996), Chapter 2 (especially pp. 64–77).

[72] See, for example: Cappelletti, "Is the European Court of Justice 'Running Wild'?" (1987) 12 ELRev. 3; Weiler, "The Court of Justice on Trial" (1987) 24 CMLRev. 555; Lord Howe, "Euro-Justice: Yes or No?" (1996) 21 ELRev. 187; Tridimas, "The Court of Justice and Judicial Activism" (1996) 21 ELRev. 187; Arnull, "The European Court and Judicial Objectivity: A Reply to Professor Hartley" (1996) 112 LQR 411 (criticizing an article by the present author in (1996) 112 LQR 95). See also the critical comments on Sir Patrick Neill's paper by two members of the European Court, Advocate General Jacobs and Judge Edward, quoted by Lord Howe, above, at p. 190. For an assessment of the two points of view which reaches a conclusion favourable to the Court, see House of Lords Select Committee on the European Communities, 21st Report, *The 1996 Inter-Governmental Conference*, para. 256 (HL Paper 105, 1994–95).

3

Judicial Objectivity—Does it Matter?

> Whoever hath an absolute authority to interpret any written or spoken laws, it is he who is truly the lawgiver, to all intents and purposes, and not the person who first spoke or wrote them.
>
> Bishop Hoadly's Sermon preached before the King in 1717 (quoted in Lockhart, Kamisar, Choper, Shiffrin and Fallon, *Constitutional Rights and Liberties* (8th ed. 1996), p. 1).

Does it matter that the European Court gives judgments contrary to the Treaties? The view that it does is based mainly on arguments of a moral, constitutional and political nature.[1] The moral argument is that the Court ought not deliberately to give judgment contrary to the law it was created to uphold since this involves a breach of good faith both towards the Member States (who created the Community legal system) and towards the parties to the case. The constitutional argument is that it is a violation of the rule of law.

The political argument applies only where the effect of the judgment is to increase the powers of the Community at the expense of the Member States, but all the cases discussed in the previous chapter could, to a greater or lesser extent,[2] be regarded as falling into this category. The argument is that when the Member States signed the Treaties they agreed to transfer only certain powers to the Community; if the Court, an institution of the Community, takes additional powers for itself or for the Community in general, it could be regarded as taking more from the Member States than they agreed

---

[1] As we shall see in the next chapter, there is also the more practical argument that it leads to uncertainty.

[2] The Court's judgment in *Parti Ecologiste "Les Verts"* v. *European Parliament*, Case 294/83, [1986] ECR 1339, might be regarded as an exception, though even here the judgment had the incidental effect of increasing the jurisdiction of the Court.

to give, a justifiable cause for complaint.[3] The Court could also be accused of being influenced in its judicial decision-making by its interests as a Community institution and thereby failing in its duty of impartiality.[4]

Since courts are not supposed to give judgments contrary to the law, supporters of the Court try to justify its conduct by advancing various arguments, most of which are based on the premise that it somehow occupies a special position. These arguments will now be considered.

GAPS

The first argument is that Community law contains more gaps than most legal systems and that the European Court is obliged to fill them by laying down new rules. It is true that where a gap exists in a legal text such as a statute, code or treaty, a court may have to act creatively in order to fill it. However, a true gap exists only where there is reason to believe that the authors of the text *intended* a given topic to be covered. This occurs where a provision of the text cannot be applied, or does not make sense, unless a rule is created to cover another question. For example, if the EC Treaty had said that the Community could enter into international agreements with non-member States but had not stated how such agreements were to be concluded, a gap would exist which—in the absence of some other solution—the Court would have to fill before the Community could exercise the power it had been granted.

---

[3] See the judgment of the *Bundesverfassungsgericht* (German Constitutional Court) in the German *Maastricht* case, *Brunner* v. *European Union Treaty*, decision of 12 October 1993, [1994] 1 CMLR 57, and the judgment of the Danish Supreme Court in the Danish *Maastricht* case, decision of 6 April 1998, Case I 361/1997, *Carlsen* v. *Rasmussen* (not yet reported: English text available from the Danish Foreign Ministry), both of which are discussed in Chapter 8.

[4] It is of interest to note that whenever there has been any threat of a rival court appearing on the scene, the European Court has used its judicial power to protect its own position. Thus it objected to the creation of a tribunal under the Agreement establishing a European Laying-up Fund for Inland Waterway Vessels (Opinion 1/76, [1977] ECR 741); it blocked the creation of the proposed EEA Court (Opinion 1/91, [1991] ECR 6079) and it held that the Community has no competence to adhere to the European Convention on Human Rights, a move which would have given the European Court of Human Rights jurisdiction to decide on human rights violations by the Community, a task at present performed by the European Court (Opinion 2/94, [1996] ECR 1759).

A gap does not, however, exist simply because a topic is not covered—even if it would be convenient if it were. If the Treaty had made no mention of international agreements, one could not say that this constituted a gap: the normal assumption would be that the authors of the Treaty had not intended the Community to enter into them.

None of the cases in the previous chapter concerns a gap in the true sense. The only case in which the Court suggested that a gap existed was *Chernobyl*,[5] where it said that the absence in the Treaties of any provision giving the European Parliament the right to bring an action for annulment constituted a procedural gap. However, there was no gap since there was no reason to believe that the authors of the Treaty intended the Parliament to have this right: no other provision of the Treaty required it.

TELEOLOGICAL INTERPRETATION AND EFFECTIVENESS

Another argument is that the Court's decisions are justified by the principles of teleological interpretation and effectiveness. According to the principle of teleological interpretation, a court should try to ascertain the purpose of the provision and interpret it in such a way as to give effect to that purpose. The principle of "effectiveness" (*"effet utile"* in French) is similar: it means that provisions should be interpreted in such a way as to ensure their effectiveness in practice, so that their purpose is actually attained. These approaches can be good, provided the Court bases its reasoning on the purpose which the authors of the measure actually had, rather than the purpose which the Court thinks they *ought* to have had. Account must also be taken of the fact that the authors of legislative texts often have several (possibly conflicting) purposes, one of the problems of legislation being to reconcile them.

The decision of the European Court in *The Queen* v. *The Immigration Appeal Tribunal, ex parte Antonissen*[6] may serve as an illustration of what happens when these methods are misapplied. The case concerned EC immigration law and the question before the Court was whether a Community worker without a job has the right

---

[5] See above, p. 36.
[6] Case C-292/89, [1991] ECR I-745.

to immigrate to another Member State in order to look for work. The relevant Treaty provision is Article 48(3) {39(3)} EC, which provides:

> [Freedom of movement for workers] shall entail the right . . .
>   (a) to accept offers of employment actually made;
>   (b) to move freely within the territory of the Member States for this purpose . . .

It seems clear that the phrase "for this purpose" in subparagraph (b) refers back to subparagraph (a) and indicates that immigration rights under Article 48(3) {39(3)} are limited to persons who already have a job offer.[7] Thus no immigration rights are conferred on persons who want to look for a job.

However, when proposals for two Community measures[8] intended to implement Article 48(3) {39(3)} were before the Council in 1968, a declaration was made by the Member States and recorded in the Council Minutes[9] which stated that migrants without jobs would be admitted for three months in order to look for work, provided they did not become a burden on public welfare. The implementing measures did not themselves give this right, but national legislation passed to transpose the Community rights into national law did do so.[10] It is probable, therefore, that the declaration was intended to record an agreement that the right would be granted by national law, and was not intended to constitute a direct source of rights or to indicate the correct interpretation of the implementing measures.

This is the background to the *Antonissen* case.[11] In it, the Court stated that the Council declaration had no legal significance;[12] it

---

[7] Pabon, "Het Vrije Verkeer van Werknemers binnen de Europese Gemeenschap Definitief tot Stand Gebracht!" (1968) 23 Sociaal Maandblad Arbeid 754 at p. 756; Smit and Herzog, *The Law of the European Economic Community* (loose-leaf), pp. 2-484 to 2-485 (§ 48.04).

[8] Regulation 1612/68, OJ (Special Ed.) 1968 (II), p. 475 and Directive 68/360, *ibid.*, p. 485.

[9] Since Council meetings are held behind closed doors and Council Minutes are not published, the existence of the declaration would not have been publicly known had it not been leaked and published by a press agency: see *Europe*, 30 July 1968, p. 5.

[10] For the United Kingdom, see the Immigration Rules for Control on Entry (EEC and other non-Commonwealth nationals), HC Paper 81 of 1972–73, para. 52.

[11] There was also a *dictum* in a case decided in 1974, *Royer*, Case 48/75, [1976] ECR 497 (para. 31 of the judgment), in which the Court said that workers did have a right to migrate to look for a job, but omitted to say what the foundation of the right was.

[12] Para. 18 of the judgment. This aspect of the case is considered further in Chapter 4.

rejected the interpretation given above of Article 48(3) {39(3)} EC, which it characterized as "strict", and it ruled that Article 48(3) {39(3)}, properly interpreted, gave Community citizens a right to migrate to other Member States to look for work. To reach this conclusion, the Court assumed that the purpose of Article 48(3) {39(3)} was to promote the free movement of workers; it then argued that, since it would be more difficult to attain this objective if workers could not travel to another Member State to look for employment on the spot, the "strict" interpretation of Article 48(3) {39(3)} would make that provision ineffective;[13] therefore, it concluded, the "strict" interpretation must be rejected. Thus the principle of effectiveness and the teleological method were used to justify an interpretation of Article 48(3) {39(3)} that was contrary to the plain words of that provision.

The objection to this is that it fails to recognize the possibility that, though the authors of the Treaty may have wished to make it easier for Community nationals to work in another Member State, *this might not have been the only consideration they had in mind.* Another objective that the Member States presumably had was to avoid an influx of unemployed migrants who might be unable to support themselves. The wording of Article 48(3) {39(3)} reflects the balance struck by the Member States when they signed the Treaty in 1957. No doubt the situation changed as the years passed, and by 1968 the Member States were willing to take a further step. They could have done this by granting a right of entry in the legislation they adopted that year. They did not do this. Instead, they made the declaration. The purpose of this was apparently to ensure that the right was granted under national law, rather than under Community law, thus allowing the Member States to decide its precise extent. This may have represented a compromise between those Member States that wanted to give further rights to migrant workers and those that were concerned about the economic and social consequences.

The effect of the Court's judgment was, therefore, to convert a right based on national law into a right based on Community law, thus giving the European Court, rather than the national courts, the final say on its interpretation. In the *Antonissen* case, the Court immediately proceeded to exercise its jurisdiction by forbidding the application of a strict time limit: it ruled that a migrant cannot be deported

---

[13] See para. 12 of the judgment.

just because he fails to find a job after six months—the United Kingdom had increased the three-month limit to six months—provided he produces evidence that he is continuing to seek employment and has a genuine chance of being engaged. This ruling will make it more difficult to enforce any limit, since it replaces a clear-cut criterion with one that will be difficult to monitor.

The principle of effectiveness was also invoked by the Court in *Van Duyn* v. *Home Office*[14] (discussed in the previous chapter[15]), the case in which the Court held that directives can be directly effective. In this case, the Court tried to justify its interpretation of Article 189 {249} EC by arguing that it would make individual directives more effective. This too was a misapplication of the principle, since the Court again failed to take account of the fact that the authors of the Treaty had more than one purpose: although they wanted Community measures to be effective (in the sense of attaining their objective), they also wanted to limit the intrusiveness of Community law in the national legal systems. The compromise they reached was to make provision for two kinds of Community instruments—regulations (which were intended to be directly effective) and directives (which were not). Regulations were to be adopted in some instances and directives in others. One assumes that, where they considered effectiveness to be paramount, they chose regulations; where they thought that flexibility was more important, they chose directives. In the latter instance, they were willing to sacrifice a certain degree of effectiveness in order to give the national authorities more room for manœuvre. By putting excessive emphasis on effectiveness, the Court prejudiced the maintenance of flexibility.[16]

It may be concluded that, though teleological interpretation and effectiveness are valid principles, they do not justify the departures from the Treaty in the judgments under consideration.

---

[14] Case 41/74, [1974] ECR 1337.

[15] See pp. 27–29.

[16] Interestingly, one of the arguments used by the Court in *Faccini Dori* v. *Recreb*, Case C-91/92, [1994] ECR I-3325, to reject the proposal that directives should be given "horizontal" direct effect, was that this would give the Community a power which it possesses only in those cases where it is able to adopt regulations: see para. 24 of the judgment. The Court was not, however, prepared to recognize that "vertical" direct effect is open to the same objection.

AN EVER CLOSER UNION

The first clause in the Preamble to the EC Treaty states that the governments signing the Treaty were determined to "lay the foundations of an ever closer union among the peoples of Europe". This provision has sometimes been used as the basis for an argument that the Member States intended the Court to interpret the Treaty in such a way as to promote that union.

This argument was given forceful expression by Judge Federico Mancini, one of the most intellectual and articulate members of the Court, who replied as follows to accusations[17] that the Court always opted for the "European" solution:

> The preference for Europe is determined by the genetic code transmitted to the Court by the founding fathers, who entrusted to it the task of ensuring that the law is observed in the application of a Treaty whose primary objective is an "ever closer union among the peoples of Europe".[18]

This passage combines Article 164 {220} EC, which requires the Court to ensure that "in the interpretation and application of this Treaty the law is observed"—a provision that might be thought to lay a duty on the Court to respect the words of the Treaty—with the "ever closer union" clause of the Preamble. The phrase "genetic code" suggests that the Treaty is organic—capable of growth and development through its own inherent capacities—and that its growth is predetermined to be in the direction of an "ever closer union". The adjective "organic" is in fact often applied by legal writers to constitutions and other legal texts to indicate just this.

The vividness of Mancini's metaphor should not, however, blind us to the fact that Treaties are not living organisms, but merely words on paper, and their meaning cannot really change, though they may come to be understood differently with the passage of time, especially if courts and other authorities interpret them differently. The "ever closer union" clause in the Preamble cannot have been intended as an invitation to the Court to ignore the words of the Treaty to which

[17] See the article entitled "*Im Zweifel für Europa*" ("When in doubt, opt for Europe") in the *Frankfurter Rundschau* of 7 December 1992.

[18] Mancini and Keeling, "Democracy and the European Court of Justice" (1994) 57 MLR 175, at p. 186. Keeling was a legal secretary at the European Court.

the Member States had just agreed: it was merely a statement of political intent to move towards the goal of further integration by means of subsequent Treaties, something that has in fact taken place. It cannot, therefore, justify the Court's giving judgments contrary to the clear words of the Treaty.

DIFFICULTIES OF AMENDMENT

It is sometimes argued that the European Court has to give "legislative" judgments because the Community's own legislature does not function properly: instead of taking decisions by a simple majority like most Parliaments, it must follow the qualified majority procedure (which requires a majority of approximately two-thirds), or even be unanimous. Whatever the merits of this argument, however, it cannot apply to the cases considered in the previous chapter, since they all concern the Community Treaties, not Community legislation. The true analogy, therefore, is with national constitutions,[19] rather than with legislation.

It could of course be argued that, since the Community constitution (the Treaties) is difficult to amend, the Court is obliged to adopt a more "activist" stance in interpreting it. It is true that the Treaties can be amended only if the Member States are unanimous; moreover, amendments must be ratified according to the constitutional requirements of each Member State and this can sometimes cause problems. However, that is the *whole point* of the Community system as it exists at present. The Community was created by a set of Treaties and this is the foundation on which it rests. It was *intended* that its constitution could be amended only with the unanimous consent of all the Member States: this was the basis on which the Member States joined the Community.

It should also be noted that the constitutions of States, when in written form, are also difficult to amend, though, in the case of federal States, they do not normally need the consent of each constituent unit. Moreover, if one looks at the matter from a practical point of view, it seems that the Community constitution is actually easier to amend than those of major federations such as the United States,

---

[19] By this is meant formal, written constitutions, such as those found in the United States, Canada or Germany, not the unwritten constitution of the United Kingdom.

Canada or Germany. Certainly, it has been amended far more often. If one takes the period between 1951, when the ECSC Treaty was signed, and 1998 (when this book was written), there have been major[20] amendments or new Treaties at intervals of, on average, less than five years, namely in 1951,[21] 1957,[22] 1965,[23] 1970,[24] 1972,[25] 1975,[26] 1979,[27] 1985,[28] 1986,[29] 1992,[30] 1994[31] and 1997.[32] With such frequent amendments to the Community constitution, it can hardly be maintained that judicial legislation is needed: if the Member States want to make an amendment, they have ample opportunity to do so. All that is needed is the unanimous consent of the national governments and ratification according to the constitutional provisions of each Member State: these are the requirements laid down in Article N {48} of the Treaty on European Union.

GOOD RESULTS

Is a court justified in giving judgment contrary to the law if the final result is good? This is an important question since, in many of the examples in the previous chapter, the rule created by the European Court had much to be said for it. Is this enough to excuse the transgression of the Treaty?

This view is attractive, especially to the non-lawyer; nevertheless, it is open to serious objection. Who is to decide whether the result is good? If it is the Court, there would no longer be any limit to judicial activity: the Court would become a super-legislature, non-elected and responsible to no one, which could overrule the actual legislature at will.

---

[20] Minor instruments are omitted.
[21] ECSC Treaty.
[22] EEC (now EC) Treaty and Euratom Treaty.
[23] Merger Treaty.
[24] First Budgetary Treaty.
[25] First Accession Treaty.
[26] Second Budgetary Treaty.
[27] Second Accession Treaty.
[28] Third Accession Treaty.
[29] Single European Act.
[30] Treaty on European Union.
[31] Fourth Accession Treaty.
[32] Treaty of Amsterdam.

ACCEPTANCE

The "good results" theory can be improved by arguing that a court is justified in giving judgments contrary to the law if it is *generally accepted* that the result is good. This, however, raises two vital questions: *who* must accept it and *what constitutes acceptance*? In the case of the Community Treaties, the answer to the first question must surely be that the judgment must be accepted by the Member States. They were the authors of the Treaties and it is they who have the right to amend them. If the Member States accept the rule laid down by the Court, it may be argued, that justifies what the Court has done.

With regard to the second question, it must first be said that obedience is not equivalent to acceptance. The rule of law requires the Member States to obey judgments of the Court even if they think they are wrong. The mere fact that a judgment is contrary to the Treaty does not make it invalid. It is still binding; consequently, the fact that the Member States obey it does not prove that they accept it, much less that they approve of it. In order to constitute a justification for the judgment, acceptance by the Member States must be positive and clear.

Express Acceptance

By "express acceptance" is meant some positive act that unambiguously indicates acceptance. The best way of doing this is to amend the relevant Treaty to bring it into line with the interpretation adopted by the Court.[33] The Member States have adopted such amendments in the case of two of the judgments discussed above, *Parti Ecologiste "Les Verts"* v. *European Parliament*[34] and the *Chernobyl* case.[35] In the former, it will be remembered, the Court held that "an action for annulment may lie against measures adopted by the European

---

[33] Another way of indicating express acceptance would be for the Member States to adopt a joint declaration approving the judgment; but this would be very unusual and does not appear to have occurred, though the European Parliament, the Council and the Commission adopted a Joint Declaration on 5 April 1979 which could be regarded as endorsing the Court's case law on human rights: see OJ 1979, C103/1. This case law has now been endorsed by a Treaty provision, Art. F(2) {6(2)} TEU.

[34] Case 294/83, [1986] ECR 1339.

[35] *European Parliament* v. *Council*, Case C-70/88, [1990] ECR I-2041.

Parliament intended to have legal effect *vis-à-vis* third parties".[36] The judgment was given in 1986. In the Treaty on European Union (Maastricht Agreement), signed in 1992, Article 173 {230} was amended to cover "acts of the European Parliament intended to produce legal effects *vis-à-vis* third parties".

In the *Chernobyl* case the European Court held that "an action for annulment brought by the Parliament against an act of the Council or the Commission is admissible provided that the action seeks only to safeguard its prerogatives and this is founded only on submissions alleging their infringement".[37] This judgment was given in 1990. In the Treaty on European Union, Article 173 {230} was also amended to permit the Parliament (and the ECB) to bring annulment actions "for the purpose of protecting their prerogatives".

The fact that the Member States have made these amendments (and used almost the exact words of the Court's judgments) indicates two things. First, it indicates that they regarded the decisions of the European Court in *Les Verts* and *Chernobyl* as being contrary to the text of the Treaty. If this were not the case, there would have been no need to amend the text to bring it into line with the judgments. Secondly, it indicates that the Member States regarded the interpretations as acceptable or even desirable. In these two cases, therefore, one can conclude that the judgment was justified *ex post facto* by the amendment. This disposes of two of the cases we have been considering.

Express Rejection

So far, there has been only one instance in which the Member States have adopted a Treaty amendment to reverse a decision of the European Court, though there have been two other cases in which they have come close to doing so. The one clear reversal concerned the Court's decision in *Kalanke* v. *Bremen*,[38] a case on sex discrimination in the civil service of the German City State (*Land*) of Bremen. Under the Bremen sex-equality statute, a woman whose qualifications were equal to those of a man had to be given preference as

---

[36] Para. 25 of the judgment.
[37] Para. 27 of the judgment.
[38] Case C-450/93, [1995] ECR I-3051.

regards appointment to a post in the Bremen civil service if fewer than half the persons in the relevant grade were women. The case concerned the post of section manager in the Bremen Parks Department. Two candidates were short-listed, a man and a woman. The man, Mr Kalanke, was chosen, but the woman challenged this decision on the ground that the sex-equality statute required that the job be given to her. The case wound its way up through the German court system and eventually arrived in the European Court on a reference from the *Bundesarbeitsgericht* (Federal Labour Court).

The question put to the European Court was whether the Bremen statute was contrary to Article 2 of an EC directive on sex discrimination, the Equal Treatment Directive.[39] Article 2(1) of this Directive states that the principle of equal treatment means that "there shall be no discrimination whatsoever on grounds of sex either directly or indirectly". The European Court held that the Bremen statute involved discrimination against men, which was contrary to Article 2(1). The equal-treatment rule was, however, subject to Article 2(4), which permitted national measures "to promote equal opportunity for men and women, in particular by removing existing inequalities which affect women's opportunities". The Court, however, held that this does not cover national rules which give women absolute and unconditional priority: such rules go beyond equality of opportunity and seek to attain equality of representation in all grades.

This judgment caused outrage in certain circles in Germany, and German politicians openly boasted that it would be reversed next time the Treaty was amended. It was. An amendment to the EC Treaty brought in by the Treaty of Amsterdam states, in Article 119(4) {141(4)}, that the principle of equal treatment does not prevent Member States from providing for advantages to make it easier for the "under-represented sex" to pursue a vocational activity. This will presumably permit provisions such as that in the Bremen statute.[40]

This seems a fairly explicit reversal of a judgment, though the new rule will not apply retroactively to deprive Mr Kalanke of his job. There are two other instances in which the Member States have come close to reversing the Court's judgments. The first also con-

---

[39] Directive 76/207.

[40] Interestingly, the decision in *Kalanke* was substantially modified even before the Treaty of Amsterdam was ratified: see *Marschall* v. *Land Nordrhein-Westfalen*, Case C-409/95, [1997] ECR I-6363, a decision of the Full Court (13 judges).

cerned discrimination against men, obviously a delicate matter. This was *Barber* v. *Guardian Royal Exchange Assurance Group*,[41] in which the European Court held that Article 119 {141} EC applies to occupational pension schemes and that it prohibits men from being given less favourable retirement terms than women. The Court, however, invoked the *Defrenne* doctrine[42] and stated that the ruling would not apply to claims to "entitlement to a pension, with effect from a date prior to this judgment", except in the case of claimants who before that date had initiated legal proceedings or raised an equivalent claim. This limitation could clearly mean several very different things: it could mean that pensioners could not contest pension payments made before the judgment; it could mean that no claims at all could be made by claimants who had retired before the judgment; it could mean that the judgment did not apply to pension rights resulting from contributions made before the judgment; and it could mean that the judgment did not apply to individuals who had joined a pension scheme before the judgment. It need hardly be said that the practical consequences of these different interpretations vary enormously; the question was, therefore, crucial both for many individuals and for the pensions industry. The Member States were not, however, content to allow the European Court to clarify its judgment when opportunity next arose, which, in the nature of things, was bound to be soon: they decided to do the job themselves by means of a Treaty amendment brought in by the Maastricht Agreement (Treaty on European Union).[43] This states that the third of the interpretations set out above is the correct one.[44]

The second instance concerns *SPUC* v. *Grogan*,[45] a case on abortion. It arose when students in the Republic of Ireland tried to publicize the names and addresses of abortion clinics in England so that female students needing an abortion would know where to go. Since abortion is prohibited by Article 40.3.3 of the Irish Constitution, a private society, the Society for the Protection of Unborn Children

---

[41] Case C-262/88, [1990] ECR I-1889.

[42] Case 43/75, [1976] ECR 455.

[43] The Protocol Concerning Article 119 {141} of the Treaty Establishing the European Community, a Protocol annexed to the EC Treaty.

[44] Interestingly, the question came before the European Court after the Treaty on European Union had been signed but before it came into force. Theoretically, the Court was free to adopt a different interpretation, but it tactfully followed that in the Protocol: *Neath* v. *Hugh Steeper Ltd*, Case C-152/91, [1993] ECR I-6935.

[45] Case C-159/90, [1991] ECR I-4685.

(SPUC), brought proceedings before the Irish courts. The students claimed that abortion constituted a service and that Community law gave them a right to publicize services lawfully available in another Member State. This raised the question whether the Community rules on freedom to provide and receive services applied to abortion. The Society for the Protection of Unborn Children argued that they did not, because abortion, in their view, is grossly immoral. The European Court, however, held that it could not substitute its judgment for that of the legislature in those Member States where abortion is practised legally. It therefore held that abortion, performed in accordance with the law of the state where it is carried out, constitutes a service for the purpose of Community law. It nevertheless ruled that the students could not claim the protection of Community law because they were not acting at the request of the abortion clinics.

This judgment upset anti-abortionists in Ireland. As a result, the Maastricht Agreement annexed Protocol No. 17 to the EC Treaty. This provides that nothing in any of the Treaties affects the application in Ireland of Article 40.3.3 of the Constitution.[46] It is doubtful whether the Protocol affects anything the Court said in *SPUC* v. *Grogan*, but it was apparently intended to guard against possible future rulings by the Court.

We can sum up these three cases by saying that the first is a fairly clear-cut reversal of a judgment; the other two are not reversals, but they indicate that the Member States were concerned that the judgments in question might have been interpreted in an unacceptable way: the purpose of the amendments was to forestall this. It must, however, be said that none of the Court's judgments in any of these three cases can fairly be regarded as being contrary to the words of the provisions it was interpreting. Irrespective of whether or not one agrees with the results, the meanings given to the provisions were ones which the words *could* have had.

---

[46] Subsequently, a declaration was made by the Member States on 1 May 1992 which states that it was their intention that the Protocol would not limit freedom to travel between Member States or, in accordance with conditions which may be laid down, in conformity with Community law, by Irish legislation, to obtain or make available in Ireland information relating to services lawfully available in Member States. A subsequent amendment to Art. 40.3.3 now makes clear that the Irish Constitution does not limit the freedom of Irish women to travel to other Member States.

Conclusions

What conclusions can we draw from these cases? Can one say that failure by the Member States to reverse a judgment constitutes implicit acceptance? This would be unjustifiable because a Treaty amendment must be accepted *unanimously* by the Member States: failure to amend the Treaty proves no more than that *one* Member State accepted the judgment. To regard failure to reverse a judgment as tacit acceptance would be just as unreasonable as to regard failure to amend the Treaty to confirm a judgment as tacit rejection. No inference can be drawn from a failure to amend the Treaty.

Is there any other way in which a judgment could be implicitly accepted? It seems there is not: it could hardly be argued that implicit acceptance is indicated by the fact that a Member State has not left the Community in protest. Apart from this, there seems to be nothing—other than verbal criticism, which has certainly not been lacking—that a Member State can do if the Court gives a judgment it regards as contrary to the Treaty. The theory of "general acceptance" is not, therefore, valid except where the judgment is expressly affirmed in a Treaty amendment.

CONSTITUTIONAL NECESSITY

It is sometimes said that the European Court is a "constitutional court" and as such it is entitled—perhaps even obliged—to take constitutional necessity into account in interpreting the "constitution" of the Community. There is no doubt that a court that is called upon to decide fundamental constitutional questions, such as the relationship between the Legislature and the Executive or that between federal (Community) law and state (national) law, must take into account the political consequences of what it decides. Moreover, if the vital interests of the nation are at stake, a court could be justified in departing from the strict wording of the law: *salus populi est suprema lex*.[47] Such a departure, however, is justified only where the continued existence

---

[47] For a discussion of cases in various countries in which the doctrine of necessity (or some similar consideration) was regarded as justifying a departure from the letter of the law in situations of constitutional crisis, see de Smith, "Constitutional Lawyers in Revolutionary Situations" (1968) 7 Western Ontario Law Review 93.

of the State or some equally fundamental value is at stake: mere governmental convenience can never suffice.[48]

Can it be said that any of the cases considered in the previous chapter has raised issues of this importance? The only two which come anywhere near this requirement are the *Van Gend en Loos* case[49] (in which the European Court held that provisions of the EC Treaty can be directly effective as a matter of Community law) and *Van Duyn* v. *Home Office*[50] (in which it held that directives can be directly effective as a matter of Community law). However, neither of these cases can be regarded as raising issues of constitutional necessity. Both rulings were important in strengthening the Community and making it operate more effectively, but it cannot realistically be maintained that the Community would have collapsed without them. At the time in question, the aspirations of the Community were limited to a common market and a few common policies (most notably in agriculture), and it was perfectly possible to attain these objectives without the new doctrines introduced by the Court. The Treaties contained provisions for directly effective instruments in the form of regulations and, if these had proved insufficient, the Member States could always have amended the Treaties. Constitutional necessity cannot, therefore, justify these decisions.

Of course, those who consider that the Community should aspire to something more than a common market and a few common policies may take a different view. If one day a United States of Europe is created, the actions of the European Court will no doubt come to be regarded as justified: like victory in war, the successful creation of a new State retrospectively legitimates the means used to attain it. The leading European judges of our time may then be seen as heroes whose boldness and singleness of mind helped to lay the foundations of the European State. Those who believe that the coming into existence of such a State is both inevitable and desirable may even now consider that the Court's decisions are justified by virtue of some such doctrine as constitutional necessity. But this is constitutional necessity of a very different kind from that described above.

---

[48] Necessity of this latter kind was roundly rejected over two centuries ago by Lord Camden CJ in *Entick* v. *Carrington* (1765) 19 State Trials 1030, 1073, when he said ". . . with respect to the argument of State necessity . . . the common law does not understand that kind of reasoning . . .".

[49] Case 26/62, [1963] ECR 1.

[50] Case 41/74, [1974] ECR 1337.

CONCLUSION

The conclusion to which this chapter leads is that, except in two cases, the judgments under consideration cannot be justified by the arguments normally put forward. It might be argued that in practice they did not cause much harm. In some respects, this is true; however, they reveal a disquieting streak in the character of the Court that could have serious consequences in future. Moreover, there is at least one set of cases that *does* have unfortunate results. These are the cases on liability in tort of Member States for breach of Community law.

If the government takes action which turns out to have been unlawful, it is possible in most countries for individuals who were harmed by the action to sue the State for damages in tort. In most countries, however, the conditions that must be fulfilled are so restrictive that such proceedings are rarely successful. This is justified on the ground that public authorities would be unduly fettered in their activities if they could be sued for acts done in good faith in the public interest.

As far as the Community is concerned, the second paragraph of Article 215 EC provides for Community liability "in accordance with the general principles common to the laws of the Member States". The European Court has used this provision as the basis for the rules it has created on the liability of the Community for harm caused by action contrary to Community law. This is not the place to discuss the details of these rules,[51] but their most striking feature is that it is extremely difficult in practice for claimants to obtain damages against the Community. Indeed, Advocate General Tesauro, speaking in 1995, said that only eight awards had ever been made.[52]

Prior to the *Francovich* case,[53] the liability of Member States for violations of Community law was determined by national law. Consequently, the same rules applied where it was alleged that action by a national government was contrary to Community law as where it was alleged that it was contrary to national law. This seems reasonable in principle: from the Community point of view, it would be

---

[51] For such a discussion, see T C Hartley, *The Foundations of European Community Law* (4th ed. 1998), pp. 226 *et seq*.

[52] *Brasserie du Pêcheur* v. *Germany*, Cases C-46/93 and C-48/93, [1996] ECR I-1029, at p. I-1101, n. 65, of his Opinion.

[53] N. 54 below.

wrong if it was more difficult to obtain damages where Community law was violated, while, from the national point of view, it would be wrong if it was more difficult to obtain damages where national law was violated.

All this changed with the decision of the European Court in *Francovich* v. *Italy*,[54] in which it held that the liability of Member States for a violation of Community law is determined by *Community* law, not national law.[55] The main ground the Court gave was pure policy:[56]

> The full effectiveness of Community rules would be impaired and the protection of the rights which they grant would be weakened if individuals were unable to obtain redress when their rights are infringed by a breach of Community law for which a Member State can be held responsible.
>
> . . .
>
> It follows that the principle whereby a State must be liable for loss and damage caused to individuals as a result of breaches of Community law for which the State can be held responsible is inherent in the system of the Treaty.

As legal reasoning, this is not impressive. It starts with the proposition that a Community rule would be desirable, and deduces from this that such a rule must therefore be inherent in the Treaty, a confusion of "ought" and "is" that no ordinary lawyer would make. Moreover, the statement that the principle is inherent in the "system of the Treaty" is a tacit admission that it is not to be found in any particular provision of the Treaty.

In a subsequent paragraph,[57] the Court came up with Article 5 EC, which it referred to as "a further basis" for its ruling. Article 5 states:

> Member States shall take all appropriate measures, whether general or particular, to ensure fulfilment of the obligations arising out of this Treaty or resulting from action taken by the institutions of the Community. They shall facilitate the achievement of the Community's tasks.
>
> They shall abstain from any measure which could jeopardize the attainment of the objectives of this Treaty.

---

[54] Cases C-6/90 and C-9/90, [1991] ECR I-5357.

[55] For a full analysis of this judgment and its consequences, see Harlow, "Francovich and the Problem of the Disobedient State" (1996) 2 ELJ 199.

[56] Paras 33 and 35 of the judgment.

[57] Para. 36 of its judgment.

At most, this vague provision might require Member States to enact legislation to provide for liability; by no stretch of the imagination can it be regarded as directly creating it. Since the authors of the Treaty made express provision for the liability of the Community, they would hardly have omitted to do the same thing if they had intended Community law to regulate the liability of the Member States. For these reasons, the judgment in the *Francovich* case must be regarded as contrary to the Treaty.

Previously, the European Court itself seems to have taken the view that the Treaty made no provision for the liability of Member States. In the early 1970s, it was asked for its views on the changes in the Treaty that would be needed to create a European Union. One suggestion it made was that "in the event of a failure by a State to fulfil an obligation, persons adversely affected thereby [should be able to] obtain redress before their national courts".[58] Though not entirely clear, this seems to suggest that the Treaty should be amended to give a right of action for damages against Member States under Community law. The Member States did not act on this suggestion. In these circumstances, the subsequent discovery that the principle was inherent in the Treaty all along must have been very gratifying for the Court.

In theory, the liability of Member States for a breach of Community law is based on the same principles as the liability of the Community.[59] However, those principles seem to be interpreted by the Court in a very different way, so that liability seems to be the norm, rather than the exception: in five of the first six cases to come before it, the Court's judgment suggests that the Member State should be liable.[60]

---

[58] Bulletin of the European Communities, Supplement 9/75, p. 18 (1975).

[59] *Brasserie du Pêcheur* v. *Germany*, Cases C-46/93 and C-48/93, [1996] ECR I-1029; [1996] 2 WLR 506 (para. 42 of the judgment).

[60] Since the cases all began in the national courts, the final outcome depends on those courts. The five cases in which the European Court gave rulings that seemed to imply liability were: *Francovich* v. *Italy*, Cases C-6/90 and C-9/90, [1991] ECR I-5357; *Brasserie du Pêcheur* v. *Germany*, Case C-46/93 and *R* v. *Secretary of State for Transport, ex parte Factortame*, Case C-48/93, (joined cases) [1996] ECR I-1029; [1996] 2 WLR 506; *R* v. *Ministry of Agriculture, ex parte Hedley Lomas*, Case C-5/94, [1996] ECR I-2553; [1996] 3 WLR 787; and *Dillenkofer* v. *Germany*, Cases C-178, 179, 188–190/94, [1996] ECR 4845. In *Brasserie du Pêcheur* v. *Germany*, the *Bundesgerichtshof* (German Supreme Court) decided in the end that Germany was not liable: BGH, EuZW 1966, 761. The case in which the European Court indicated that there should be no liability was *R* v. *HM Treasury, ex p. British Telecommunications*, Case C-392/93, [1996] ECR I-1631; [1996] 3 WLR 203.

The best way to illustrate the results of the Court's new doctrine is to give two examples.

Factortame

The origin of the series of cases that goes under the name *"Factortame"* was a decision by the Community to adopt fish conservation measures. To achieve this objective, limits were laid down to the total number of fish of various species that could be caught in a given period. Quotas were allotted to each Member State. Certain Spanish fishermen, however, thought that they could obtain a share of the British quota by the expedient of registering companies in the United Kingdom and transferring the ownership of their boats to those companies. They claimed that, since their boats were owned by British companies, they were entitled to fly the British flag and therefore take fish from the British quota, rather than the Spanish quota. Understandably, the British fishermen objected to this manœuvre, and the British Government passed legislation to prevent it.[61] The Spaniards immediately challenged the legislation in the British courts and a reference was made to the European Court. The latter ruled that the British legislation was contrary to Community law, especially the principle of freedom of establishment and the prohibition against discrimination on grounds of nationality.[62] The fact that this ruling undermined the whole idea of national quotas appeared to be of no concern to the Court.[63]

The effect of the judgment was that the boats could fish again, but there had nevertheless been an interim period (while proceedings

[61] The Merchant Shipping Act 1988, Part II; the Merchant Shipping (Registration of Fishing Vessels) Regulations 1988 (SI 1988 No 1926). The purpose of this legislation was to ensure that boats could not fly the British flag unless they had a genuine link with the United Kingdom. This was to be achieved by laying down new requirements for registration—for example, that boats owned by a company could not be registered unless 75 per cent of the shares in the company were held by British citizens resident and domiciled in the United Kingdom.

[62] *R v. Secretary of State for Transport, ex parte Factortame*, Case C-221/89, [1991] ECR I-3905; [1992] 1 QB 680; [1992] 3 WLR 288; [1991] 3 All ER 769. For earlier proceedings resulting in the grant of interim relief, see *R v. Secretary of State for Transport, ex parte Factortame*, Case C-213/89, [1990] ECR I-2433; [1991] 1 AC 603; [1990] 3 WLR 818; [1991] 1 All ER 70.

[63] See the Court's answer to the third question asked by the English court. For the background to the case and a critical comment on the judgment, see Noirfalisse, "The Community System of Fisheries Management and the *Factortame* Case" (1992 12 YEL 325.

were pending) during which they had been precluded from doing so. The owners of the boats then brought further proceedings against the British Government to obtain damages for the profits lost during this period.

Since the United Kingdom Government had, in apparent good faith, been trying to deal with an obvious injustice, one might have thought that no damages would be awarded, even though it turned out in the end that the means it had used were not permitted by Community law. The European Court, however, said that Britain was liable.[64] It is not yet clear what the final outcome will be,[65] but newspaper estimates put the damages payable at some £20 million.

Hedley Lomas

The second illustration, the *Hedley Lomas* case,[66] concerns animal welfare. This excites strong feelings and riots have occurred over the export of live animals for slaughter on the Continent. The British Government has always maintained that it is powerless to prevent such exports—however much the animals may suffer in transit—because Community law ties its hands: Article 34 EC prohibits quantitative restrictions on exports or "any measures having an equivalent effect".

In 1990, however, it did ban live exports to Spain. This was not because of suffering during transport, but because it believed there was a significant risk that the animals would suffer unnecessarily in Spanish abattoirs. This problem had been around for some years and in 1974 the Community had adopted a directive[67] to deal with it. The directive, which was supposed to be the first step towards a general Community policy against cruelty, required Member States to ensure that animals were stunned before slaughter. In Spain, the Government gave effect to this by adopting legislation making stunning obligatory, but there was no provision for any penalty if stunning did not take place.

---

[64] *R* v. *Secretary of State for Transport, ex p. Factortame*, Case C-48/93, (joined with *Brasserie du Pêcheur* v. *Germany*, Case C-46/93) [1996] ECR I-1029; [1996] 2 WLR 506.

[65] The case went back to the English courts to apply the law laid down by the European Court. They held that the British Government must pay compensation, though the amount has not yet been assessed: *R* v. *Secretary of State for Transport, ex parte Factortame (No 5)*, *The Times*, 28 April 1998 (CA).

[66] *R* v. *Ministry of Agriculture, ex parte Hedley Lomas*, Case C-5/94, [1996] ECR I-2553.

[67] Directive 74/557, OJ 1974 L316/10.

On the basis of information obtained from various sources— including an animal welfare organization in Spain—the British Ministry of Agriculture concluded that the directive and the Spanish legislation were being ignored in a significant number of abattoirs in Spain. Some abattoirs did not even possess stunning equipment. It was for this reason that the ban on live exports to Spain was adopted. The ban entered into force in April 1990 and was based on Article 36 EC, which permits Member States to restrict exports on grounds of, *inter alia*, public morality, public policy and the protection of the health and life of animals, grounds that might have appeared wide enough to cover the case.

As a result of complaints addressed to it in 1990, the Commission had entered into discussions with the Spanish authorities on the lack of enforcement of the directive. The latter gave certain assurances; the Commission then dropped the matter.

This was the background to the British ban.[68] Although Britain had no proof that every abattoir in Spain was violating the directive, it considered that there was a significant risk that animals exported live from Britain to Spain would suffer. It regarded the risk as sufficient to justify the ban. This might have seemed reasonable, since the prevention of unnecessary suffering during slaughter was a recognized objective of Community law.

If this is what the British Government thought, however, it was making a serious mistake. Instead of making the export ban legitimate in Community eyes, the directive made it illegitimate. The reason, according to the European Court, was that when a problem is recognized by the Community and dealt with in a Community measure, it is taken out of the hands of the Member States and becomes a Community matter. Member State action is no longer permitted; only the Community can take action. The fact that the Community action is totally ineffective does not seem to make any difference. Britain had no right to act. Member States, said the Court, must trust each other. The result was ironic: the directive, which was supposed to benefit animals, actually made things worse. If it had not existed, the ban might have been upheld under Article 36.

[68] Britain did not let the matter rest at this point: meetings were held between the Chief Veterinary Officer of the United Kingdom and his opposite number in Spain to devise a procedure to ensure that all animals exported from Britain went only to abattoirs certified by the Spanish authorities as operating in conformity with the directive; once this procedure was in place, Britain lifted the ban.

This was not the end of the matter. The exporter had claimed damages for the profits it would have gained if the shipment had been allowed, and the European Court, though it acknowledged that it was for the English courts to take the final decision, made clear that Britain should pay.[69]

It is hard to see how the award of damages could be justified in either of these two cases: they show that, at least in this instance, the European Court's "legislative" judgments *can* have unfortunate consequences.

---

[69] One fact in favour of the claimant was that it had specified a particular abattoir in Spain as the destination of the animals and the British Government had no proof that this particular one was guilty of unnecessary cruelty; nevertheless, it is easy to see why the Government was not willing to make an exception. The application for the export licence had moreover been made in October 1992 and the ban was lifted on 1 January 1993; so Hedley Lomas did not have long to wait before it could resume exports.

The Uncertainty Problem in Community Law

Imagine a man who has bought a council house and is in dispute with the local authority over the sale: he thinks that the terms of the agreement are unfair. He wants to know whether he can benefit from the EC Directive on Unfair Contract Terms.[1] He goes to a solicitor. The solicitor says it is impossible to tell whether he can benefit or not: the law is too uncertain. The solicitor he consults is perfectly competent: the problem lies in the vagueness and uncertainty of Community law.

Absolute certainty is impossible in any legal system. In some situations, the objectives of the law require a measure of flexibility. It would be impossible, for example, to list exhaustively, in complete detail and with full precision each and every act which constitutes dangerous driving; the law must, therefore, content itself with a phrase such as "dangerous driving" or "driving without due care and attention" and leave it to the courts to determine in any particular case whether a given manœuvre falls within the terms of the law. The result is a degree of uncertainty, but there is no way round this. For this reason, uncertainty is found in all legal systems; however, it is far more prevalent in Community law than in English law. In some cases, this is because the problem in question is incapable of being solved by a simple legal rule; more often, however, uncertainty is not the result of the problem, but of the character of the Community itself and the way it operates.

THE CAUSES OF UNCERTAINTY

There are a number of reasons why the level of uncertainty is so high in Community law. The most important are: the result-oriented

---

[1] Directive 93/13/EEC, OJ 1993, L95/29.

character of many rules of Community law; multilingualism; poor drafting; the deliberate use of ambiguity in Community measures; the existence of secret agreements between the Member States; and, last but not least, the way the European Court interprets Community provisions. Some of these factors follow from the very nature of the Community and cannot be changed; others could be changed, though it is unlikely that they will be. Each presents its own particular difficulties.

Result-Oriented Rules

Many legal rules are concerned with specified forms of conduct: a motorist, for example, may be prohibited from driving above a specified speed or parking in a specified place. Some rules, however, are not concerned with specified conduct but with a specified *effect*. Thus, for example, any act that results in the death of another person, if done deliberately, constitutes the crime of murder. In this case, it is not *what* you do that counts, but what the *result* is. Such rules may cause uncertainty because when one performs the act one cannot be sure what the result will be. However, if the law attaches consequences to the act only if it is done with the deliberate intention of causing the result in question, there can be no objection on this score: if a murderer does something with the intention of bringing about the death of another person, he cannot complain that he could not be certain at the time whether it would have this result. If, on the other hand, the law attaches the consequences to the act irrespective of intention, the position is different. Here the person might justifiably complain that he did not know at the time he performed the act what the result would be. Even here, however, result–oriented rules cannot always be avoided. If the person *ought* to have foreseen the result, one could say that he was negligent and should therefore be responsible for any ensuing harm.

Result-oriented laws, even where the element of intention is lacking, are therefore an unavoidable feature of most legal systems, including English law. What is special about Community law is not that it has result-oriented rules, but that they are so numerous and play so large a part in the system. To take just one example, Article 30 {28} EC prohibits quantitative restrictions on imports and "all measures having equivalent effect". The European Court has interpreted this as prohibiting all trading rules which "are capable of hindering, directly or indirectly, actually or potentially, intra-Community trade".[2] The area covered by this provision is potentially enormous, as may be illustrated by the fact that it was claimed to apply to British Sunday-trading legislation. It might have been thought that legislation prohibiting shops from opening on Sundays could not affect trade between Member States of the Community; this, however, would have been to ignore the ingenuity of well-paid lawyers. The argument was that if shops were allowed to open on Sundays, they would sell more goods; and, since some of these goods would have been imported from other Member States, intra-Community trade would increase. Consequently, it was argued, legislation prohibiting shops from opening on Sundays was a restriction on intra-Community trade contrary to Article 30 {28}. As we shall see below,[3] this argument was taken seriously by the European Court, and was unequivocally rejected only on the second occasion on which it was put to the Court.[4] Before this, there was great uncertainty: shopkeepers did not know whether they had to obey the Sunday-trading laws or not, and local authorities did not know whether they had to enforce them or not.

Multilingualism

Every item of Community legislation is promulgated in each of the working languages of the Community. At present there are 11 of these—Danish, Dutch, English, Finnish, French, German, Greek, Italian, Portuguese, Spanish and Swedish.[5] Unfortunately, the text of a given provision is not always the same in each of these languages. The Unfair Contract Terms Directive, mentioned above, is an example. The Directive provides that "unfair terms" in contracts between

---

[2] *Procureur du Roi* v. *Dassonville*, Case 8/74, [1974] ECR 837 (para. 5 of the judgment). There is of course a great deal of case law and much scholarly writing as to what exactly this means; in spite of this, however, there is still considerable uncertainty.

[3] See 78–79.

[4] The first occasion was *Torfaen Borough Council* v. *B & Q plc*, Case C-145/88, [1989] ECR 3851 (discussed below); the second was *Stoke-on-Trent City Council* v. *B & Q plc*, Case C-169/91, [1992] ECR I-6635; [1993] 2 WLR 730.

[5] Irish has a lesser status.

a seller (or supplier)[6] and a consumer[7] are not binding on the latter.[8] This is a provision of major importance for business people, since they can no longer rely on consumers being bound by all the terms of the contract.

The hypothetical house-buyer mentioned above wanted to know whether the Directive applies to sales of land. Since the English text refers to sales of "goods",[9] and since "goods" in English does not cover land,[10] one might assume that it does not. This is probably the conclusion that the average English barrister or solicitor would have reached if asked to advise a client when the Directive first appeared;[11] it also seems to have been the conclusion of the drafters of the United Kingdom implementing measure, The Unfair Terms in Consumer Contracts Regulations.[12]

However, if we turn to the French text, we see that wherever the English text uses the word "goods", the French refers to "*biens*". One might have thought that this meant the same thing, but it does not. Article 516 of the French Civil Code makes clear that "*biens*" can be either movables ("goods" in the English sense) or immovables (land).[13] "*Biens*", therefore, does not mean "goods": it means "property", and includes land.[14] On the basis of the French text, one would conclude that land *was* covered.

---

[6] The Directive defines "seller" or "supplier" as anyone acting for purposes relating to his trade, business or profession: Art. 2(c).

[7] Defined as any natural person (i.e. not a company) acting for purposes outside his trade, business or profession: Art. 2(b).

[8] This is subject to certain exclusions: see, for example, Art. 1(2).

[9] See Art. 4(1). The word also appears nine times in the preamble: it is accepted practice in Community law to use the preamble to a measure as an aid to its interpretation.

[10] See, for example, the Sale of Goods Act 1979, s. 61(1).

[11] The position might be different now, since the question has subsequently received some publicity: see Bright and Bright, "Unfair Terms in Land Contracts: Copy Out or Cop Out?" (1995) 111 LQR 655; Attew, "Teleological Interpretation and Land Law" (1995) 58 MLR 696.

[12] SI 1994 No. 3159. Regulation 2(1) defines "seller" as a person who sells *goods* for purposes relating to his business; so the seller of land cannot be a "seller" under the Regulations. The "Guidance Notes" issued by the Department of Trade and Industry in July 1995 are, however, equivocal on the point. Para. 3.4 states that the Directive's provisions appear to be limited to contracts concerning the sale of goods or supply of services, and in para. 3.19 it is said: "As to land, it is arguable that since it is neither a good nor a service, it does not fall within the scope of the directive". After referring to counter-arguments, however, para. 3.20 concludes that the matter is by no means free from doubt and that it would be prudent to assume that the Directive could extend to transactions in land.

[13] It states: "*Tous les biens sont meubles ou immeubles*".

[14] I would like to thank Professor Marc Fallon for the help he has given me on French legal terminology.

If one went further and looked at other language-versions of the Directive, one would discover that the German text refers to "*Waren*" and the Danish to "*varer*", both of which mean "goods"[15] in the English sense. The Italian speaks of "*beni*", which means the same as "*biens*",[16] and the Spanish has "*bienes*", which probably means this as well.[17] The Dutch text uses the word "*goederen*", which is ambiguous: in ordinary language, it means the same as "goods" in English and it had this meaning in the old Dutch Civil Code; however, in the new Civil Code, which came into force in 1992, it has a much wider meaning and could cover land.[18] One could continue with the versions in other languages, but enough has been said to demonstrate that a clear conflict exists on the point.

In these circumstances, it might be thought that the English text would apply in England, the French in France and the Danish in Denmark, etc. However, this solution has been rejected by the European Court because it would lead to the fragmentation of the Community legal system.[19] Instead, the Court has said that all language-versions are equal:[20] they must all be taken into consideration when the provision is interpreted. There is no question, however, of the majority prevailing. According to the Court, the text must be interpreted on the basis of "the real intention of its author and the aim he seeks to achieve".[21] This phrase must not, however, be taken entirely literally, since the Court seems less interested in ascertaining the actual intention of the author—the author of major Community measures is usually the Council, the members of which may have had conflicting intentions—than in interpreting the provision on the basis of the intention which *it thinks the author ought to have had*. This creates considerable uncertainty.

The particularly unfortunate feature of linguistic uncertainty is that it is not normally apparent that a problem *even exists* until the case

---

[15] I would like to thank Professor Ole Lando for information on Danish terminology.

[16] Arts 810 and 812 of the Italian Civil Code. I am grateful to Mr Andrea Appella for this information.

[17] I would like to thank Mr Jorge Martí for this information.

[18] See Art. 1 of Book 3 of the Code. I am grateful to Mr Harry Duintjer Tebbens for supplying this information.

[19] *Stauder* v. *City of Ulm*, Case 29/69, [1969] ECR 419 (para. 3 of the judgment); see also *Moksel* v. *BALM*, Case 55/87, [1988] ECR 3845 (para. 15 of the judgment).

[20] In practice, the Court seems to give most weight to the French version, though it would not admit to doing so.

[21] *Stauder* v. *City of Ulm* (above) (para. 3 of the judgment).

comes before the European Court. The average English solicitor is unlikely to think of reading a Community directive in any language other than English, and, if he did, would probably find considerable difficulty in obtaining a copy, except perhaps in French. If he did obtain it, he would be unlikely to have sufficient knowledge of the foreign language and the foreign legal system—in many cases a knowledge of the language is not enough[22]—to realize that a discrepancy existed. Linguistic uncertainty thus constitutes a hidden trap into which the average lawyer (and his client) may fall.

Poor Drafting

Another reason for the lack of clarity in Community legislation is the poor standard of drafting. This is partly because all texts but one are translations: the normal procedure is to draft in French—or, today, sometimes in English—and then translate. A translation is never as good as the original because there may not always be a word or phrase in the second language that has precisely the same meaning as that in the first. At best, the result will be clumsy; at worst, misleading. Thus, for example, the French phrase "*le rapprochement des législations*", which appears in several places in the EC Treaty,[23] is translated into English as "approximation of laws", not a normal phrase in present-day English.[24] It appears to mean the lessening of differences between laws in the various Member States without necessarily eliminating them; "unification of legislation" might, therefore, be too strong, though perhaps "harmonization of legislation" would be close enough.

Sometimes simple sloppiness is the cause. One directive, for example,[25] refers to measures taken by the Member States on grounds of public policy, public security or public health and states, "Such grounds shall not be invoked to service economic ends". Clearly, the draftsmen meant, "Such grounds shall not be invoked to *serve* economic ends".

Another reason for the bad drafting found in Community legislation is the procedure under which such measures are adopted. In

---

[22] The meaning of "*biens*" (discussed above) is an example.
[23] For example, in the heading of Title V, Part Three of the Treaty.
[24] But see *The New Shorter Oxford English Dictionary*, s.v. "approximation".
[25] Directive 64/221 (OJ 1963/64, p. 117), Art. 2(2).

Britain, most legislation is introduced by the Government after careful preparation by skilled draftsmen and, since the Government normally has a majority in Parliament, it usually reaches the statute book largely unaltered. Admittedly a back-bench rebellion or trouble in the Lords may lead to amendments, but these are often drafted, after consultation with the rebels, by the same Government draftsmen. Thus, even if the Government has to make a retreat on a point of substance, the structure of the measure will be undamaged: its clarity will not suffer.

In the Community the position is different. Major measures are normally adopted by the Council on a proposal from the Commission.[26] The Commission proposal will be prepared by Commission lawyers, who play a role analogous to that of civil service draftsmen in Britain (though they may do so with less skill, since they will not always be working in their mother tongue). However, the Commission does not have a majority in the Council; in fact, it controls no votes in it at all. Legislation can normally be passed by the Council only if there is a "qualified majority"[27] of votes in favour. Securing agreement from fifteen governments with differing interests is never easy and can take a long time. The final text may be adopted in a bargaining session in which amendments to different provisions are traded off against each other in complicated package deals in which nobody quite knows who has won in the end. Under such a system, the Commission dare not re-open the discussion simply in order to improve the drafting, since the whole deal may then collapse. The specific features of the Community system are, therefore, a major cause of bad drafting.

Deliberate Uncertainty

Deliberate uncertainty occurs when terms are used in a Community instrument precisely *because* they are uncertain. This can happen when the representatives of the Member States are unable to reach agreement. To bridge the gap, a term may be used that could mean either what the one Member State wants or what the other wants.

---

[26] Some are adopted jointly by the Council and the European Parliament: in such cases, all the problems about to be discussed still apply, together with additional problems resulting from the fact that the Parliament must also give its consent.

[27] On the meaning of a "qualified majority", see Chapter 1, pp. 15–16, above.

Thus agreement is reached on a form of words when there is no agreement on what the words mean.

To give an example we must leave the Unfair Contract Terms Directive and consider another Community instrument in the field of private law, the Convention on Jurisdiction and the Enforcement of Judgments in Civil and Commercial Matters, signed in Brussels on 27 September 1968.[28] This concerns (in part) the jurisdiction of courts in civil proceedings. One issue relates to actions in tort. In many countries, such actions may be brought in the courts of the country in which the tort occurred. A problem arises, however, if the defendant acted in one country and the resulting harm was suffered in another. Say, for example, a mining concern pours pollutant into the Rhine in France and this causes harm to a nurseryman in the Netherlands. Where is the tort committed? The drafters of the Convention were aware of this problem, but they abstained from providing a solution:[29] the Convention states merely that jurisdiction may be taken "by the courts for the place where the harmful event occurred", a provision deliberately intended to be vague.[30] It was left to the European Court to give the answer.[31]

It need hardly be said that this practice is undesirable, both because it makes the litigant pay the price for the Member States' failure to agree, and because it requires the European Court to adopt a quasi-legislative role. In spite of this, it seems fairly common, though it is normally impossible to be certain whether it has occurred. The Brussels Convention is a special case, since the official reports on it reveal what went on behind the scenes.[32]

---

[28] OJ 1972, L299, p. 32. The United Kingdom became a party on joining the Community, and it was put into effect by the Civil Jurisdiction and Judgments Act 1982.

[29] See the official report on the Convention, the Jenard Report, OJ C59/1 at p. 26.

[30] See *per* Advocate General Capotorti in *Bier* v. *Mines de Potasse*, Case 21/76, [1976] ECR 1735 at p. 1751, where he said, "The imprecision [of the provision] is not fortuitous. . . [T]he authors of the Brussels Convention . . . intended to leave open the question concerning the meaning to be conferred upon these words, clearly preferring to charge the courts with their interpretation".

[31] See *Bier* v. *Mines de Potasse* (n. 30 above).

[32] Another example from the Brussels Convention is whether Art. 21 of the Convention can apply where a court takes jurisdiction under a convention on a "particular matter" in terms of Art. 57: see the Schlosser Report, OJ 1979 C 59/71 at pp. 139–140 (paras 239–240), in which it is said that it was decided to leave the solution to "legal literature and case law". The answer was given by the European Court in *The Maciej Rataj* (*The Tatry*), Case C-406/92, [1994] ECR 5439. For comments, see Briggs [1995] LMCLQ 161 (attacking the judgment) and Hartley, (1995) 20 ELRev. 409 (attempting to defend it).

Secret Agreements

When Community legislation is before the Council, the Member States sometimes enter into secret agreements, usually recorded as declarations in the Council Minutes,[33] which specify how the legislation is to be interpreted and applied or what parallel action is to be taken by national governments when it is put into operation. The effect of these declarations obviously depends on whether they eventually become known. The Rules of Procedure of the Council provide that its deliberations are secret, though the Council may make exceptions in particular cases.[34] It is expressly stated that the Council may authorise production of an extract from its Minutes for use in legal proceedings.[35] The result is that secret declarations may remain secret, or they may become public either as a result of an official decision by the Council or through a leak.

If they remain secret, lawyers and courts will be unaware of their existence; nevertheless, they could create uncertainty in a number of ways. First, they might affect the way the Commission applies the legislation and whether or not it decides to bring enforcement proceedings under Article 169 {226} EC. Secondly, they might affect the way the legislation is applied by national governments: this might be their very purpose. Thirdly, they might affect the terms of national legislation, where the adoption of such legislation is necessary in order to apply the Community measure within the national legal system. Fourthly, they might affect statements made by government ministers in national legislatures when implementing legislation is introduced. In the United Kingdom, the rule in *Pepper* v. *Hart*[36] per-

---

[33] We are concerned here with unpublished declarations, not with the published declarations that are officially annexed to many of the Community Treaties.

[34] Rules of Procedure of the Council, Decision 93/662, OJ 1993 L304/1, Art. 5(1); see also the Code of Conduct concerning public access to Council and Commission documents (6 December 1993), OJ 1993 L340/41, and Decision 93/731, OJ 1993 L340/43, as amended by Decision of 6 December 1996, OJ 1996 L325/19. See further Curtin and Meijers, "The Principle of Open Government in Schengen and the European Union: Democratic Retrogression?" (1995) 32 CMLRev. 391 at pp. 417–442. For a legal challenge by a British journalist to a refusal by the Council to disclose certain documents (including the Minutes of a particular meeting), see *Carvel* v. *Council*, Case T-194/94, [1995] ECR II-2767. The challenge was successful because the Council had adopted a policy of automatically refusing such requests, instead of weighing up the considerations involved in each particular instance.

[35] Rules of Procedure (n. 34 above), Art. 5(2).

[36] [1993] AC 593.

mits the courts to take account of ministerial statements when interpreting a provision in British legislation if that provision is ambiguous or obscure, or if its literal meaning would lead to an absurdity. It
has recently been held that where British legislation is adopted to give
effect to an EC directive, such ministerial statements may also be used
to ascertain the general purpose of the legislation.[37]

Where secret declarations eventually become known, they could
have a wider effect. In *The Queen* v. *The Immigration Appeal Tribunal,
ex parte Antonissen*,[38] the European Court said that, where no reference is made in the Community legislation to the content of the
declaration, the declaration cannot be used to interpret the legislation. In such a case, said the Court, the declaration "has no legal significance".[39] This means that a secret declaration—even if it is
eventually published—cannot be cited by a court as the basis for its
interpretation of the provision. It does not, however, mean that, if its
existence becomes known, it may not *in fact* influence a court called
upon to interpret the provision. Indeed, if it represents the opinion
of the Member States on how the measure should be interpreted, it
is hard to see how it could not influence the European Court, especially since the Court tries to interpret Community provisions in
such a way as to give effect to their purpose.

This may be illustrated by the *Antonissen* case itself. This case was
discussed in Chapter 3, and it will be remembered that it concerned
the rights of workers from other Community countries to immigrate
to a Member State in order to look for work. The relevant Treaty
provision, Article 48(3)(b) {39(3)(b)} EC, seems to cover only those
migrants who already have job offers.[40] However, when proposals for
two Community measures[41] intended to implement Article 48(3)(b)
{39(3)(b)} were before the Council in 1968, a secret declaration was
made by the Member States and recorded in the Council Minutes.
According to this, migrants without jobs would be admitted for three
months in order to look for work, provided they did not become a
burden on public welfare. The Community measures did not themselves give this right, but national legislation passed to transpose the

---

[37] *Three Rivers District Council* v. *Bank of England (No 2)* [1996] 2 All ER 363.
[38] Case C-292/89, [1991] ECR I-745.
[39] Para. 18 of the judgment.
[40] See pp. 45–46, above.
[41] Regulation 1612/68, OJ (Special Ed.) 1968 (II), p. 475 and Directive 68/360, *ibid.*,
p. 485.

Community rights into national law did do so.[42] It is probable, therefore, that the declaration was intended to record an agreement that
the right would be granted by national law, and was not intended to
constitute a direct source of rights or to indicate the correct interpretation of the Community measures.[43] The distinction is important
because in the first case the European Court would have no jurisdiction to rule on the extent of the right; in the latter two cases, it
would.

The secret declaration did not remain secret for long: it was
revealed almost immediately by a press agency[44] and was subsequently referred to by various writers.[45] Therefore, when the matter
was first considered by the European Court in 1975, the existence
and content of the declaration must have been known to it, though
it did not refer to it directly. This was in the *Royer* case,[46] where the
Court indicated that Community law *did* give immigration rights to
persons looking for work, though it failed to say whether this was
on the basis of Article 48(3)(b) {39(3)(b)} or on the basis of the
Community measures mentioned above. Given the fact that neither
the Treaty nor the Community measures expressly grant the right,
and that most writers at the time assumed that it followed from the
declaration,[47] it is hard to avoid the conclusion that the Court was at
least *influenced* by the declaration in reaching its conclusion.

The first time the declaration was mentioned by a member of the
Court was in *R* v. *Pieck*,[48] where Advocate General Warner referred
to it in conjunction with the *dictum* in the *Royer* case.[49] The full text

---

[42] For the United Kingdom, see the Immigration Rules for Control on Entry (EEC and
other non-Commonwealth nationals), HC Paper 81 of 1972–73, para. 52, where the three-
month period was increased to six months.

[43] This view has not, however, been accepted by all the writers: see Smit and Herzog,
The Law of the European Economic Community (loose-leaf), pp. 2-484 to 2-485 (§ 48.04);
Maestripieri, *La Libre Circulation des Personnes et des Services dans la CEE* (1971), pp. 15–16;
Mégret, *Le Droit de la Communauté économiqe européenne* (1971), vol. 3, p. 21, n. 29.

[44] *Europe*, 30 July 1968, p. 5.

[45] Pabon, "Het Vrije Verkeer van Werknemers binnen de Europese Gemeenschap
Definitief tot Stand Gebracht!" (1968) 23 Sociaal Maandblad Arbeid 754 at p. 756; Smit and
Herzog, n. 43 above, pp. 2-484 to 2-485 (§48.04); Maestripieri, n. 43 above, pp. 15–16
(quoted in full in French); Mégret, n. 43 above, vol. 3, p. 21, n. 29; ter Heide, "The Free
Movement of Workers in the Final Phase" (1969) 6 CMLRev. 466 at p. 476.

[46] Case 48/75, [1976] ECR 497 (para. 31 of the judgment).

[47] Smit and Herzog, n. 43 above; Maestripieri, n. 43 above; Mégret, n. 43 above. Pabon,
n. 45 above, and ter Heide, n. 45 above, both cite the agreement but do not say clearly that
it creates a legal right.

[48] Case 157/79, [1980] ECR 2171.

[49] At p. 1292.

of the declaration was set out in the Report for the Hearing in the *Levin* case,[50] where it was referred to as an "interpretative declaration", thus suggesting it provided the correct interpretation of the Community measures.[51] The Court itself did not refer to the declaration: it indicated that it accepted the existence of the right, but still did not commit itself on its legal basis.[52] Finally, it was mentioned in the *Lebon* case, where Advocate General Lenz referred to it as an "interpretative declaration".[53]

This, then, was the background to the statement in the *Antonissen* case[54] that the declaration has no legal significance. In that case, the European Court ruled that persons seeking work have a right of entry under Community law and gave Article 48(3) {39(3)} of the EC Treaty as the legal basis. As explained in Chapter 3, this ruling was based on a misapplication of the principles of effectiveness and teleological interpretation; nevertheless, it is hard to avoid the conclusion—the Court's disclaimer notwithstanding—that it *was* influenced by the declaration, either directly or by way of earlier authorities—its own previous *dicta*[55] and the views of the writers mentioned above—which in turn were influenced by it.[56] Moreover, the mere fact that a court *might* be influenced by such a declaration is enough to cause uncertainty: no lawyer who knew of its existence would feel comfortable about advising a client without seeing it.

The immigration declaration is a special case because its existence became publicly known. More insidious are those declarations that remain secret. It is impossible to tell how many of them there are; however, they are sufficiently numerous for the Council's own Legal Service to have drawn up a report on the subject. It is indicative of the climate of secrecy in the Community that this report is *itself*

[50] Case 53/81, [1982] ECR 1035 at p. 1043. It seems that it was put before the Court by the Commission.
[51] The Advocate General in the case, Sir Gordon Slynn (as he then was), pointed out that the question was not relevant to the proceedings. For that reason, and also because he was not satisfied it would in any event be right to have regard to it, he did not consider the declaration: see p. 1056.
[52] See the words "or desirous of so doing" in para. 9 of its judgment.
[53] *Centre Public d'Aide Sociale de Courcelles* v. *Lebon*, Case 316/85, [1987] ECR 2811 at p. 2829.
[54] N. 38 above.
[55] In the *Antonissen* case, Advocate General Damon said that the declaration had been "taken into account" by the European Court in the *Levin* case: see [1991] ECR at p. I-762.
[56] See Hartley, "Five Forms of Uncertainty in European Community Law" [1996] CLJ 265 at pp. 275–278.

secret, but, according to a newspaper article, it deprecated such declarations on the ground that they "threaten to undermine legal certainty".[57]

Judicial Uncertainty

The last cause of uncertainty is the European Court itself. It creates uncertainty in two ways—by its method of interpreting Community provisions and by the lack of clarity in some of its rulings. The former was considered in Chapters 2 and 3, where it was shown that, in order to attain its policy objectives, the Court sometimes "interprets" Community provisions contrary to the words of the text and what may reasonably be regarded as the intention of its authors. This cannot but produce uncertainty, since it is never possible to predict with accuracy what the policy objectives of the Court are, what it will consider necessary to ensure their attainment, and how far it will be willing to go in departing from the words of the provision in order to achieve them.

Lack of clarity in its rulings is a separate cause of uncertainty. To illustrate this, we can return to the question of Sunday trading. The first case in which this came before the European Court was *Torfaen Borough Council* v. *B & Q plc.*[58] The issue was whether the Sunday trading legislation then in force in England and Wales, the Shops Act 1950, was contrary to Community law.[59] The case arose when proceedings were brought in the Cwmbran Magistrates' Court by the Torfaen Borough Council under sections 47 and 50 of the Shops Act. The defendants, a chain of DIY shops, argued that they were not obliged to obey the statute because it was contrary to Community law. The magistrates referred the matter to the European Court. The answer it gave was famously opaque. It will be quoted in full:

> Article 30 of the Treaty must be interpreted as meaning that the prohibition which it lays down does not apply to national rules prohibiting retailers from opening their premises on Sunday where the restrictive effects on Community trade which may result therefrom do not exceed the effects intrinsic to rules of that kind.

---

[57] *The Independent*, 23 June 1995, p. 13.
[58] Case C-145/88, [1989] ECR 3851.
[59] For the details, see p. 68, above.

As might be expected, this caused total confusion. How were magistrates' courts to decide whether the restrictive effects exceeded those intrinsic to rules of that kind? Some believed that a sophisticated economic analysis was necessary. As a result, teams of economists toured the country giving evidence for one side or the other in such cases. The DIY stores requested hearings ranging from one to five weeks. The outcomes varied, but the expense was considerable. Uncertainty existed to a high degree.[60] Nevertheless, it was three years before the matter was clarified in *Stoke-on-Trent City Council* v. *B & Q plc*.[61] In that case, the European Court gave a straight answer: it said the legislation was not contrary to Article 30 {28}.

CONCLUSIONS

Community law has a particularly vague and open-textured character which gives it a flavour quite unlike that of English law: some of its rules prohibit almost anything that might "directly or indirectly, actually or potentially" have a specified effect; its provisions may mean different things in different languages; it may be badly drafted, possibly as a result of a hurriedly-contrived compromise at a Council meeting; it may be couched in language chosen precisely *because* it is uncertain; its application by Community and national authorities may be affected by secret agreements; and it will be interpreted by the European Court, which can take a measure which is clear, and declare that it means something quite different from what it says. As a result of this, the ordinary citizen often does not know where he stands: he does not know what he may do and what he must not do. And, at least until recently, this lack of certainty seems to have been of only limited concern to the Community authorities.

---

[60] See Rawlings, "The Eurolaw Game: Some Deductions from a Saga" (1993) 20 Jo. of Law and Society 309 at p. 317.

[61] Case C-169/91, [1992] ECR I-6635; [1993] 2 WLR 730.

IS THERE A SOLUTION?

Today the problem is beginning to be recognized, both at national level in the United Kingdom[62] and at the Community level. Attached to the Treaty of Amsterdam there is a declaration on the quality of drafting of Community legislation. It states that good drafting is crucial if Community legislation is to be properly implemented by the national authorities and better understood by the public; and it goes on to declare that the European Parliament, the Council and the Commission ought to establish guidelines for improving the draftsmanship of Community measures. Whether this declaration will have any effect is doubtful. As was shown above, the causes of uncertainty are to a large extent embedded in the nature of the Community itself: its multilingual character and its method of legislation by negotiation, for example, are unlikely to change in the foreseeable future.

National Remedies?

Can anything be done at the national level? With regard to most types of Community instruments, there is nothing that can be done. In the case of directives, on the other hand, a possible remedy lies in the fact that they have only limited direct effect. Directives, unlike regulations, must be implemented by the Member States. By "implementation" is meant the passing of national legislation (either a statute or secondary legislation) to attain the result to be achieved under the directive.[63] It follows from this that the individual is faced with two legal measures, the directive and the implementing measure. Thus, for example, the Unfair Contract Terms Directive is mirrored by the United Kingdom implementing measure, The Unfair Terms in Consumer Contracts Regulations.[64] Since there may be differences between them, the relationship between these two instruments is

---

[62] See, for example, the Efficiency Scrutiny Report commissioned by the President of the Board of Trade, *Review of the Implementation and Enforcement of EC Law in the UK* (1993), p. 38, para. 4.4.

[63] This is not, however, necessary if the objective of the directive has already been attained in national law.

[64] SI 1994 No. 3159.

crucial. To explain it, we must consider two doctrines of Community law, "vertical" direct effect and "indirect effect".[65]

According to the doctrine of "vertical" direct effect,[66] a directive can be directly effective only to the extent of conferring rights on an individual[67] against the State: it cannot impose obligations on an individual in favour of the State or another individual. For this purpose, "the State" is widely defined, and covers much more than the Crown or the Central Government. It includes the police, local authorities, public bodies such as the National Health Service, and at least some nationalized industries.[68]

As a result of this, the relationship between directives and national implementing measures depends on the parties involved. If an individual is claiming rights against the State (as defined), he can ignore the implementing measure and go straight to the directive, claiming that the rights given to him by it must be enforced by the national court. In such a case, the terms of the national measure are of little importance: if the individual takes the matter far enough, the case will end up in the European Court, which will interpret the directive without giving much consideration to the national measure.[69] It is for this reason that the hypothetical house-buyer mentioned at the beginning of this chapter was looking to the Unfair Contract Terms Directive as a possible source of rights.

If, on the other hand, one individual asserts a right against another (or the State asserts a right against an individual), the directive is not directly effective; the case must, therefore, be decided on the basis of the national implementing measure. However, this does not mean that the directive is of no account. Under the doctrine of "indirect effect", the directive must be taken into account by the national court when it interprets the national measure, and the latter must be interpreted, "as far as possible, in the light of the wording and the purpose of the directive so as to achieve the result it has in view".[70] Even in an action between two individuals, therefore, the directive can never be ignored.

[65] Neither of these terms is used by the European Court itself.
[66] See Chapter 2, pp. 29–30.
[67] For this purpose, "individual" includes a company; in fact, it covers any legal person other than the State.
[68] See Chapter 2, p. 29.
[69] This is because the European Court considers that a directive must have the same meaning in every Member State.
[70] *Faccini Dori* v. *Recreb*, Case C-91/92, [1994] ECR I-3325, at para. 26 of the judgment.

The key phrase in the above quotation is "as far as possible". It is for the national court to determine whether the national measure is "open to an interpretation consistent with the directive".[71] If the national measure is clear or, though unclear, if it cannot reasonably be interpreted in conformity with the directive, the national court must follow the national measure. In such a case, the directive will not be applied. If, on the other hand, the national measure is open to it, it must be interpreted so as to be consistent with the directive. In this case, the directive remains the dominant provision.

The national implementing measure can, therefore, stand between an individual (though not a public authority) and the directive, thus giving the individual a degree of protection. It can do this, however, only if it resolves the ambiguities of the directive. To what extent do British implementing measures do this? The answer is that they do so only to a limited extent. The reason for this is "copy-out".

"Copy-Out"

"Copy-out" is the term used for the technique of implementing directives by copying out their provisions word for word, or virtually word for word, in the national measure. This was the technique adopted by the DTI when implementing the Unfair Contract Terms Directive. The technique was considered by the authors of an Efficiency Scrutiny Report commissioned by the President of the Board of Trade[72] and was compared with the "elaborative approach", which involves rewriting the directive in the style normally used in domestic legislation and, where legislation already exists in the field, integrating it with the latter.

The Report rejects the contention that the elaborative approach produces greater certainty:[73]

> We think it is misleading to imply that the elaborative approach gives greater certainty. Ultimately courts will base their interpretation on the original directive. If that is ambiguous, greater certainty cannot be added in domestic law without the risk of ECJ action against the Member State.

[71] *Webb* v. *EMO Air Cargo Ltd* [1993] 1 WLR 49, at p. 60 (HL).
[72] *Review of the Implementation and Enforcement of EC Law in the UK* (1993).
[73] Para. 4.19.

If this were correct, it would mean that nothing could be done to remedy the uncertainty of Community directives. However, as was explained above, greater certainty *can* be obtained if those responsible for implementation are prepared to rewrite the directive in order to produce a clear and coherent text. As the Scrutiny Report points out, there might be a price to pay: if the Commission thought that the Government had misconstrued the directive, it might bring action against the United Kingdom in the European Court under Article 169 {226} EC.[74] Moreover, the Government might be liable in tort under the *Francovich* principle[75] to compensate any person who suffered loss as a result of the failure to implement the directive correctly, though this would occur only if the meaning of the directive was reasonably clear: if it was not, and the Government's interpretation was reasonable, there would be no liability.[76]

The elaborative approach therefore involves some risks. The existence of these risks, however, does not justify resort to copy-out where the elaborative approach would make it easier for individuals to know what their rights are.

[74] One way of guarding against this would be to consult the Commission when drafting the implementing measures. It is said that the Commission is reluctant to give an opinion on the meaning of Community legislation; however, if it raised no objection at the time of drafting, it would probably not take action later unless there was a change of circumstances.

[75] See pp. 59–65, above.

[76] *R* v. *HM Treasury, ex p. British Telecommunications*, Case C-392/93, [1996] ECR I-1631; [1996] 3 WLR 203.

5

The Division of Power:
The Member States and the Community

The Prime Minister (Mr John Major): . . . There is a tendency
for the Community to want to legislate over a wide area. That
tendency needs to be curbed. [HON. MEMBERS: "Hear, hear."]
That is the essence of what has become known as subsidiarity. I
am aware that different people view it in different ways, but
what subsidiarity must mean is that, if a problem can be dealt
with at national level, it should be.

Extract from *Parliamentary Debates* (*Hansard*), House of
Commons, vol. 199, col. 279 (20 November 1991).

SUBSIDIARITY

As a matter of principle, how should legislative power be divided
between the Community and the Member States? The answer, it is
suggested, is that power should remain with the Member States
except where there is a good reason why it should be given to the
Community. In other words, Member-State action should be the
norm, Community action the exception—for which clear justification is required in each instance.

In Community parlance, this principle is known as "subsidiarity",
a word imported into English from German[1] so that the concept
could be discussed with reference to the Community.[2] Although the

---

[1] The German word is "*Subsidiarität*": see *The New Shorter Oxford English Dictionary*
(1993), *s.v.* "subsidiarity".

[2] In some Continental countries, subsidiarity is regarded as a principle of constitutional
and social organization, according to which power should, where possible, be given to
lower-level authorities, rather than to higher-level ones. It is said to underlie certain provisions of the German constitution (though it is not expressly mentioned in it) and is usually
traced back to a doctrine of Roman Catholic social philosophy. Thus, the Papal Encyclical,

word is new in English, the idea is well known: Americans claim that it is the principle on which their constitution is based. In the Community context, subsidiarity first began to attract attention about twenty years ago[3] and it was eventually laid down as a principle of Community law in the Maastricht Agreement (Treaty on European Union). This inserted a new provision, Article 3b {5}, into the EC Treaty, the second paragraph of which reads as follows:[4]

> In areas which do not fall within its exclusive competence, the Community shall take action, in accordance with the principle of subsidiarity, only if and in so far as the objectives of the proposed action cannot be sufficiently achieved by the Member States and can therefore, by reason of the scale or effects of the proposed action, be better achieved by the Community.

The justification for the principle is easy to see. The Community covers an area of considerable geographical, economic, political, social, religious and cultural diversity. A policy that works well in, for example, Greece might be unsatisfactory in Denmark. In principle, it makes sense for the Greeks to make laws for Greece and for the Danes to make laws for Denmark: diverse conditions need diverse legislation. Community legislation should be adopted only when there is a specific need.

Though the recognition of subsidiarity in the Maastricht Agreement was hailed by some as a major break-through, its

Pacem in Terris (Pope John XXIII, 1963), states: "Moreover, just as it is necessary in each state that relations which the public authority has with its citizens, families and intermediate associations be controlled and regulated by the principle of subsidiarity, it is equally necessary that the relationships which exist between the world-wide public authority and the public authorities of individual nations be governed by the same principle" (Para. 140, NCWC translation, St Paul Books and Media). An earlier reference is to be found in the Encyclical *Quadragesimo Anno* (1931). See, further, Emiliou, "Subsidiarity: An Effective Barrier against 'the Enterprises of Ambition'?" (1992) 17 ELRev. 383; Van Kersbergen and Verbeek, "The Politics of Subsidiarity in the European Union" (1994) 32 JCMS 215.

[3] See the Commission's *Report on the European Union*, submitted to the Council on 26 June 1975, EC Bull., Supp. 5/75, p. 10. Subsidiarity found a place in the Draft Treaty Establishing the European Union (OJ 1984 C 77/33), a document adopted by the European Parliament in 1984 but never accepted by the Member States. See further Toth, "The Principle of Subsidiarity in the Maastricht Treaty" (1992) 29 CMLRev. 669, at pp. 1088 *et seq.*

[4] There are less detailed references to subsidiarity in other parts of the Treaty: the second paragraph of Art. A {1} TEU states that in Europe "decisions are taken as closely as possible to the citizen", a statement which, in one respect, goes further than Art. 3b {5} EC, since it suggests that, where possible, decisions should be taken at regional or local level, rather than at national level; there is also a reference to subsidiarity in the last paragraph of Art. B {2}.

formulation in Article 3b {5} has major defects. First, Article 3b {5} cannot be used to question the granting of powers to the Community, but only the *exercise* of those powers by the passing of specific pieces of legislation.[5] Secondly, Article 3b {5} applies subsidiarity only in those areas which do not fall within the exclusive competence of the Community: in other words, the test laid down in Article 3b {5} applies only where the Community shares concurrent powers with the Member States. Unfortunately, the Treaty nowhere specifies which those areas are.[6] The Commission has issued a list of areas which it regards as falling within the exclusive competence of the Community and therefore outside the scope of the doctrine.[7] It covers a great deal of ground.[8] Moreover, the Commission considers that it will increase as time goes on.[9]

A third defect is that, while sound in principle, subsidiarity is difficult to apply in practice because different views could be held as to when Community action is necessary.[10] In an attempt to meet this objection, the Member States agreed in the Treaty of Amsterdam to add a Protocol to the EC Treaty, the Protocol on the Application of the Principles of Subsidiarity and Proportionality. This makes clear that *both* requirements in the definition in Article 3b {5} have to be

[5] This follows from the fact that Art. 3b {5} is simply a Treaty provision like any other; consequently, it cannot affect the validity of other provisions of the Treaty. See also Art. 3 of the Protocol on the Application of the Principles of Subsidiarity and Proportionality (annexed to the EC Treaty by the Treaty of Amsterdam).

[6] Commentators have expressed divergent views. Toth considers that *all* the areas of power granted to the Community under the EEC Treaty as originally concluded are exclusive: Toth, "The Principle of Subsidiarity in the Maastricht Treaty" (1992) 29 CMLRev. 669 at pp. 1091 *et seq.*; Steiner, on the other hand, suggests that the only areas in which the Community has exclusive competence for the purpose of Art. 3b {5} are those in which it has already legislated: Steiner, "Subsidiarity under the Maastricht Treaty", in David O'Keeffe and Patrick M Twomey, *Legal Issues of the Maastricht Treaty* (1994), p. 49 at pp. 55–58; see also Emiliou, "Subsidiarity: Panacea or Fig Leaf?", *ibid.*, p. 65 at pp. 74–75; Schilling, "A New Dimension of Subsidiarity: Subsidiarity as a Rule and a Principle" (1994) 14 YEL 203 at pp. 217 *et seq.* (this last analysis is probably the most closely reasoned).

[7] See *The Principle of Subsidiarity*, Com. Doc. SEC(92) 1990, 27 October 1992, p. 5.

[8] The areas are: the removal of barriers to the free movement of goods, persons, services and capital; the common commercial policy; the general rules on competition; the common organization of agricultural markets; the conservation of fisheries resources; and the essential elements of transport policy.

[9] *Ibid.*, p. 8.

[10] Lord Mackenzie-Stuart, a former President of the European Court, has called the definition of subsidiarity in the Treaty a "prime example of gobbledygook": letter to *The Times*, 15 June 1992. This is an over-reaction, but there can be no disguising the fact that it is not easy to apply in practice. See, further, Mackenzie-Stuart's article in *The Times*, 11 December 1992.

met: it must be established that the objectives of the proposed action cannot be sufficiently achieved by the Member States *and* that they can be better achieved by action on the part of the Community.[11] The Protocol also lays down guidelines for determining whether these conditions are fulfilled.[12] They indicate that this is likely to be the case where:

—the issue under consideration has transnational aspects which cannot be satisfactorily regulated by action by Member States;

—actions by Member States alone or lack of Community action would conflict with the requirements of the Treaty (such as the need to correct distortion of competition or avoid disguised restrictions on trade or strengthen economic and social cohesion) or would otherwise significantly damage Member States' interests;

—action at Community level would produce clear benefits by reason of its scale or effects compared with action at the level of the Member States.

These guidelines make the principle easier to apply, but the fact remains that it is really a matter of political judgment whether an issue can be "satisfactorily" regulated by the Member States, whether lack of Community action would "significantly" damage Member States' interests or whether action at Community level would produce "clear benefits".[13]

A fourth defect in the formulation in Article 3b {5} is that, as things stand at present, it is far from certain that the European Court will be prepared to strike down measures which infringe subsidiarity. In view of the Court's centralizing philosophy, it will probably be

---

[11] Art. 5 of the Protocol. This means that if the objectives can be sufficiently achieved by the Member States, the Community is not allowed to act even if it could achieve them better. Moreover, even if they cannot be satisfactorily achieved by the Member States, the Community cannot act unless it is established that it could do better than the Member States.

[12] *Ibid.*

[13] A close reading of the Protocol suggests that some Member States regarded the principle with suspicion and were anxious that it should not restrict Community powers too much. Thus, Art. 2 specifies that the application of subsidiarity must respect the *acquis communautaire*, thereby seemingly preventing it from applying to legislation passed before the Maastricht Agreement came into force, and that it must not affect the rules laid down by the European Court on the relationship between Community law and national law, one such rule being that Community law is supreme over national law. Art. 3 says it must not call into question the powers conferred on the Community by the Treaty "as interpreted by the Court of Justice", apparently a reference to the doctrine of implied powers developed by the European Court.

reluctant to do so. However, if the Court is not willing to act, the principle may in time become a dead letter.[14]

WHEN IS COMMUNITY ACTION JUSTIFIED?

There is little to be gained from further analysis of Article 3b {5}; instead, we will take the general idea of subsidiarity and use it as a yardstick to examine the division of power between the Community and the Member States: when, as a matter of general principle, is it justifiable for decision-making to be given to the Community? Since our inquiry will be unfettered by the limitations of Article 3b {5}, we will discuss both the grant of powers to the Community and the exercise of those powers by the passing of legislation. We will not be concerned with the merits of any particular policy, but solely with the question of jurisdiction (or competence, in European terminology): who should decide on policy—the Community or the Member States?[15] Since our starting point is the principle of subsidiarity, it will be assumed that policy should be made at the national level unless there is a good reason for it to be made at the Community level.

As already explained, it is difficult to formulate a general theory which specifies with precision when a matter should be decided at the Community level. It is, however, possible to suggest four principles which could justify Community jurisdiction. They have some affinity to the "guidelines" laid down in Article 5 of the Protocol, but they give a clearer indication (it is hoped) of when Community action is justified. They are:

1. The principle of mutual concessions, which applies where concessions made by one country are balanced against reciprocal

---

[14] Art. 1 of the Protocol added by the Treaty of Amsterdam provides that, in exercising the powers conferred on it, each institution "shall ensure that the principle of subsidiarity is complied with". Since the European Court is an institution, this appears to require it to use its judicial powers to ensure that the other institutions respect the principle, if necessary by annulling legislation that conflicts with it. See also the *Conclusions of the Presidency*, European Council in Edinburgh (11–12 December 1992), Annex 1 to Part A, p. 4. In view of this, the most likely outcome is that the Court will hold subsidiarity to be justiciable, but will annul measures only in the clearest cases. For more detailed analysis, see Toth, "Is Subsidiarity Justiciable?" (1994) 14 ELRev. 268; and Emiliou, "Subsidiarity: An Effective Barrier against 'the Enterprises of Ambition'?" (1992) 17 ELRev. 383, at pp. 402–405.

[15] In some instances, of course, it might be desirable for a matter to be determined at a higher level than that of the Community, even at a world level; in others, it might be desirable for it to be determined at a lower level than that of the Member States, perhaps at a local level. These questions will, however, be largely excluded from the discussion that follows.

concessions made by another, so that the whole system is in everyone's interest, even though each separate element may be against the interest of the country required to carry it out;

2. The principle of uniformity as an end in itself, which applies in certain situations, especially where it is necessary for the single European market;

3. The principle that transnational problems need transnational (or supranational) solutions; and

4. The principle of solidarity: joint action against outsiders can achieve more than separate action by individual Member States.

We will consider each of these in turn.

Mutual Concessions

There are many situations in which it is in everyone's long-term interest if each individual follows certain rules, even though the rules in question may be against the short-term interests of the individual concerned. The problem here is that each individual would be better off if he broke the rules, provided everyone else kept them; however, all would be worse off if the system broke down. Unless there is a generally high level of social responsibility in the society in question, it is desirable in such a situation for some central authority to have the power to lay down the rules and to enforce them. One of the problems of international society is that, where the actors are States, there is usually no authority capable of doing this. This is not the case in the Community. In situations of this kind, therefore, it makes sense for Community law to lay down the rules (either in the Treaties or in legislation adopted by the Council) and for the Commission and the Court to ensure that they are obeyed.

Free movement of goods is an example. To allow foreign goods to enter a country and compete with local goods might be regarded as contrary to the interests of the country concerned, since it could lead to the closure of factories and the loss of employment. However, if all countries did the same, the result would be in the long-term interests of everyone, since economic efficiency would increase. As countries are unlikely to liberalize international trade on a unilateral basis, it is desirable to put the matter in the hands of an international authority. The EC Member States have given jurisdiction to the

Community. The result is the single European market, the greatest achievement of the EC. The same result could be, and is being, achieved on a world-wide basis through the World Trade Organization; however, a higher level of trade liberalization has been attained among the EC countries, partly because the Community rules go further and partly because they are more effectively enforced.

The argument presented here is based on the assumption that each country regards the system as a whole as in its interest. Where this is not the case, the principle of mutual concessions does not apply. To illustrate this, we will take the example of immigration. The EEC Treaty originally provided for free immigration of workers, self-employed persons and providers of services,[16] a right later extended to virtually all citizens of the EU.[17] This system could be seen as one of mutual concessions: it is generally regarded as against a country's interests to allow foreigners to enter and compete for employment with its citizens,[18] but this is balanced by the fact that its citizens have a similar right in other Member States. Some Member States may benefit from particular aspects of the system more than other Member States—there are more Italian workers in Germany than German workers in Italy—but all Member States regard the system as a whole as in their interest. It therefore makes sense for the Community to have power to regulate it.

In the 1980s, there was a move to go further and abolish entry controls at frontiers within the Community. The idea was that such controls would remain in place for persons arriving from outside the Community, but would be removed for journeys from one Community country to another. In the latter case, travellers would be able to cross the frontier without any check or control at all: travelling from Germany to France would be the same as travelling from England to Scotland.

This might seem an attractive proposition, but there is a problem. Community immigration rights are enjoyed only by EU citizens (every citizen of a Member State is automatically a citizen of the Union).[19] Citizens of non-member States have no immigration rights under Community law.[20] However, if there are no immigration con-

---

[16] Arts 48 {39} *et seq.* EC.
[17] Art. 8a(1) {18(1)} EC.
[18] This is not necessarily so: if there is a labour shortage, it could be beneficial.

trols at internal frontiers, how can third-country nationals who have entered one Community country be prevented from entering another?[21] It would not be possible to have entry controls for third-country nationals only, since immigration officers cannot tell which migrants are not EU citizens unless *all* are required to show a passport or identity card.

The solution, according to the proponents of the new move, was to shift immigration control to a later stage: instead of checking migrants at the frontier, it would be done after they had entered the country. It is at this point of the argument that a difference appears with regard to the two Member States which are islands—Britain and Ireland. Countries with extensive land frontiers always find it difficult to prevent migrants from crossing the border clandestinely. For them, entry control has never been effective; consequently, they have relied to a considerable extent on control after entry. In many Continental countries, all citizens have an identity card, which must be produced to the authorities on demand; immigrants must show their passport. In such countries, it is easy to identify illegal immigrants, since they will not be able to present either a national identity card or a foreign passport duly stamped with leave to enter. This system is strengthened where, as is often the case, all persons—citizens and immigrants alike—have to register their address with the police. In Britain and Ireland, on the other hand, such measures have never been introduced, since control on entry was thought sufficient.[22] Consequently, it would be much more difficult for these countries to remove entry controls on intra-Community travel: unless they introduced identity cards and other checks, they would have nothing to

[19] Art. 8(1)) {17(1)} EC.

[20] There are certain limited exceptions: for example, third-country nationals who are members of the family of a Community national have immigration rights which allow them to accompany the Community national; and citizens of countries (such as Turkey) which have association agreements with the Community may in some cases obtain immigration rights under them.

[21] Since each Member State decides for itself which third-country nationals to admit to its territory, persons already in one Community country cannot be given automatic immigration rights in other Member States. In this respect, the position is different in the case of goods: there are common Community rules regarding the importation of goods into the Community from outside; consequently, once goods have entered one Member State, they can be allowed to move into other Member States without further controls.

[22] Entry controls have never existed between the Republic of Ireland and the United Kingdom, which (together with the Channel Islands and the Isle of Man) form a common travel area. This is made possible by the fact that these countries have a common policy with regard to migration from third countries and co-operate closely on immigration matters.

fall back on. For this reason, when provision for the abolition of entry controls on intra-Community travellers was eventually written into the EC Treaty,[23] the United Kingdom and Ireland were granted an exemption.[24]

This example shows that the principle of mutual concessions holds good only when the system as a whole is in the interests of all Member States. However, if some Member States are in a fundamentally different situation from the others—they, for example, are islands and the others are not—those Member States may not regard the system as a whole as being in their interests: the drawbacks may outweigh the benefits. The principle of mutual concessions then ceases to be valid and centralized decision-making is no longer desirable.

Uniformity

Where Community-wide uniformity is paramount, it makes sense for the matter to be decided at the Community level. This is especially important with regard to matters which affect the single European market. Technical specifications for manufactured goods are a case in point. All countries have rules laying down specifications for goods of various kinds. In the case of motor vehicles, for example, rules adopted in the interests of safety and non-pollution require cars to be fitted with safety belts, reversing lights, catalytic converters and various other features. If different Member States had different requirements, motor vehicle manufacturers would have to make different models for export to each market, a situation which would be economically inefficient.

In this area, it is easy to see that centralized decision-making at the Community level makes sense. However, the argument is not as clear-cut as it might seem, since a decision to adopt a uniform rule usually involves a balancing of considerations: on the one hand, a single set of product specifications promotes economic efficiency; on the other hand, it means that no account can be taken of local differ-

---

[23] See Art. 73i(1) {61(1)} EC (inserted by the Treaty of Amsterdam). Prior to this, there was a special convention, the Schengen Agreement, with the same aim. Britain and Ireland never became parties.

[24] See Art. 73q {69} EC, and the Protocol on the position of the United Kingdom and Ireland (inserted by the Treaty of Amsterdam).

ences. In the case of motor vehicles, for example, manufacturers still have to make right-hand-drive models for Britain and Ireland and left-hand-drive models for the rest of the Community. Should Britain and Ireland be ordered to drive on the right? Such a move would certainly benefit motor manufacturers, both on the Continent and in Britain; it would also benefit motorists driving abroad. On the other hand, it would result in an enormous bill for British and Irish taxpayers for the redesign of roads and would require British and Irish motorists to learn to drive on the other side of the road. Since the drawbacks of such a scheme would be felt exclusively by two Member States while the advantages would benefit all, decision-making by (qualified) majority vote at the Community level would tend to produce a different result from decision-making at the national level. Thus the decision to decide the matter at the Community level would to a significant extent predetermine the outcome, since it would give preference to the arguments in favour of uniformity over those in favour of taking local differences into account.

Community-wide uniformity is also important in the case of rules which affect the competitive position of producers in different Member States. Member States will not want to take down the barriers to intra-Community trade if producers in other Member States have unfair advantages over local producers. What exactly constitutes an unfair advantage is, however, controversial. Are lower wages or less generous welfare provisions an unfair advantage? Some say they are, though it would be unrealistic to expect every Member State to have the same wage levels. It would also condemn the poorer Member States on the periphery of the Community to perpetual backwardness, since their only hope of catching up is to attract investment by offering lower production costs.

Environmental regulations that affect production costs—for example, rules requiring factories to purify their effluent—are generally regarded as falling into this category. If these regulations are more stringent in some Member States than others, producers located in the former will be at a competitive disadvantage. They might even relocate their plants to more accommodating Member States. There is thus a strong argument in favour of giving jurisdiction to the Community in this regard. Nevertheless, local differences apply here too: a country which is able to satisfy all its power requirements from pollution-free hydro-electricity might have a different attitude towards the pollution caused by coal-fired power stations from a country with few mountains but large coal reserves.

Transnational Activities

If you have an activity that is by its very nature transnational, it often makes sense for legislation dealing with it to be made on an international basis. Safety measures in international air transport are an example. Another example is international road transport: measures to ensure that drivers have sufficient rest periods (so they do not become over-tired and thus a danger to other road-users) would be more effective if adopted on a European, rather than a national, basis. Similarly, conservation of fish stocks in waters outside the jurisdiction of any State can be ensured only if undertaken on an international basis: it would be possible for a country to restrict its own fishermen, but this would do no good unless fishermen from other countries were similarly restricted.[25]

Drug smuggling is a transnational activity, and there is no doubt that in some instances Community measures could be useful in controlling it. However, Community jurisdiction is acceptable only to a certain extent. Assume, for example, that the Netherlands decided to legalize cannabis.[26] If the drug was freely available in the Netherlands, people might buy it there and smuggle it back to, say, France, where it is illegal. In such a situation, France might complain that the Netherlands' action in legalizing the drug made it more difficult for France to prohibit it. The problem is especially acute since (as was explained above) the Community is in the process of abolishing border controls on persons moving between Member States (other than Britain and Ireland). In spite of this, however, it would be wrong to give the Community power to decide whether a particular drug should be legalized.

---

[25] This could also be seen as a "mutual concessions" situation.
[26] In practice, the use of cannabis is already tolerated to a considerable extent.

Joint Action

It has long been recognized that if a number of small countries unite against a common enemy, they will be more successful than if they allow the enemy to deal with each one of them in turn. The same principle applies in politics: a group of countries with similar interests will be more successful in trade negotiations if they present a common front than if they negotiate individually.[27] It is for this reason that the EC Treaty gives exclusive jurisdiction to the Community to enter into international trade agreements.[28]

Conclusions

The purpose of this discussion—which is intended to be no more than a preliminary sketch for a general theory on the allocation of powers—has been to give examples of situations in which Community jurisdiction is beneficial to all Member States. It is clear, however, that each of the principles put forward is subject to exceptions in which the system as a whole is not in the interests of some Member States. In such cases, those Member States should be allowed to opt out, provided this does not defeat the object of the enterprise. Countries opting out should not be allowed to gain unfair advantages, nor should they obtain the benefits of the scheme without making the necessary sacrifices: Britain's opt-out from the project for a border-free Europe means that travellers from the United Kingdom will still have to go through immigration control when they enter other Member States. Subject to this, opt-outs should be accepted: uniformity for the sake of uniformity—or for the sake of administrative convenience—should have no place in a Community based on the free association of its members.

[27] This will not be possible if they have radically different interests.
[28] Art. 113(3) {Art. 133(3)} EC. For exceptions concerning services and intellectual property rights, see Opinion 1/94 (*WTO* case), [1994] ECR I-5267.

COMMUNITY JURISDICTION IN PRACTICE

The legislative powers of the Community are contained in a number of separate provisions, most of which deal with specific topics. Examples of areas in which the Community enjoys extensive powers include: trade between Member States; agriculture; immigration of EU citizens within the Community; intra-Community provision of services; and competition (antitrust) law in so far as it affects trade between Member States. It has less extensive powers in areas such as education, culture, public health, consumer protection and the environment.

In addition to powers dealing with specific matters, there are a number of other powers of a more general nature. One example is that contained in Article 100 {94}, which allows the Community to adopt directives for the approximation (harmonization) of national measures which "directly affect the establishment or functioning of the common market". In the Single European Act 1986, this was supplemented by Article 100a {95} EC, which provides for EC legislation for the approximation of national measures "which have as their object the establishment and functioning of the internal market". An important difference between these two provisions is that, while the former requires unanimity in the Council, thus giving each Member State a veto, the latter provides for qualified-majority voting.

An even wider power is that in Article 235 {308} EC, which provides that if, in the course of the operation of the common market, action by the Community is necessary to attain its objectives and the Treaty has *not* provided the necessary powers, the Council can take the appropriate measures anyway. This provision, which is as near as one can get in constitutional law to a blank cheque, is subject only to the proviso that the Council must be unanimous.[29]

It will be seen from what has been said that the powers given to the Community are wide and ill-defined. The danger exists that they could be gradually expanded so as to deprive the Member States of almost all their functions. Though national powers have been considerably reduced, Community legislation so far has been largely

---

[29] The power may be exercised only on a proposal from the Commission, and the European Parliament must be consulted, though its opinion need not be followed.

consistent with subsidiarity. There are, however, exceptions. We will consider two.

TWO PROBLEM AREAS

Consumer Protection

The Community has adopted a number of directives on consumer protection, the most important being the Product Liability Directive[30] and the Unfair Contract Terms Directive.[31] The former provides that producers are liable for defective products, even in the absence of fault, and the latter provides that consumers are not bound by unfair terms in their contracts with sellers or suppliers.[32] These measures are not limited to transnational situations, such as sales by a producer in one country to a consumer in another, but are concerned with the ordinary, every-day law in the Member States. They have brought about major changes in many countries. What justification is there for allowing the Community to do this?

Three arguments have been put forward to provide such a justification. The first is that the existence of differences between the laws of the Member States can constitute a barrier to trade. Consumer-protection legislation is not regarded as a barrier in itself: it is *differences* between the laws of the Member States that is regarded as the problem.[33] A moment's thought shows this argument to be unconvincing. It may be true that a manufacturer in a country with a low level of consumer protection might hesitate before exporting his

---

[30] Directive 85/374, OJ 1985 L 210/29.

[31] Directive 93/13, OJ 1993 L 95/29. This measure was discussed previously in Chapter 4.

[32] For a fuller discussion, see Stephen Weatherill, *EC Consumer Law and Policy* (1997), Chapter 5 (product liability) and Chapter 4 (unfair terms).

[33] Thus the first paragraph of the Preamble to the Product Liability Directive states that "approximation of the laws of the Member States concerning the liability of the producer for damage caused by the defectiveness of his products is necessary because the existing divergences may distort competition and affect the movement of goods within the common market . . ."; while the second paragraph of the Preamble to the Unfair Contract Terms Directive states that "the laws of the Member States relating to the terms of contract between the seller of goods or the supplier of services, on the one hand, and the consumer of them, on the other hand, show many disparities, with the result that the national markets for the sale of goods and services to consumers differ from each other and that distortion of competition may arise amongst the sellers and suppliers, notably when they sell and supply in other Member States".

product to one with a high level, but this would be remedied only if the Community measure brought the law in all Member States down to a uniformly *low* level. In fact, the policy has been to level up, rather than to level down, and, since the coming into force of the Maastricht Agreement, it is expressly provided in the EC Treaty that this must be done.[34] Moreover, it is expressly provided (both in the directives themselves[35] and, since the coming into force of the Maastricht Agreement, in the EC Treaty[36]) that Member States are free to maintain in force existing measures that give *higher* levels of protection than that laid down by the Community measure. Member States are also entitled to introduce *new* measures that give a higher level of protection, provided they are compatible with the general provisions of the Treaty. As a result, Community measures in this field will not necessarily remove all differences between the laws of the Member States, nor can they ever have the effect of lowering the level of protection, only of raising it. Consequently, a manufacturer who is reluctant to export to another Member State because of the latter's high level of consumer protection will obtain no comfort from a Community directive, because it will not lower the level of protection in that Member State. Such directives cannot, therefore, be justified on the ground that they remove barriers to trade.

The second argument is that differences in consumer-protection legislation can distort competition. This would be justified only if such differences meant that producers established in different Member States were subject to different consumer-protection rules when selling in the *same* market. This, however, will only rarely be the case.

Most of the EC consumer-protection directives (including the Unfair Contract Terms Directive) fall into the field of contract. In the case of these directives, the applicable law will almost always be that of the Member State in which the product is marketed. This follows from Article 5 of the Rome Convention,[37] a Community instrument

---

[34] Art. 129a(1) {153} EC. This provision was recast by the Treaty of Amsterdam, but the obligation to attain a high level of consumer protection remains.

[35] Art. 13 of the Product Liability Directive; Art. 8 of the Unfair Contract Terms Directive.

[36] Art. 129a(3) EC (prior to the Treaty of Amsterdam); Art. 153(5) (after the coming into force of the Treaty of Amsterdam).

[37] Convention on the Law Applicable to Contractual Obligations, 1980.

to which all the Member States[38] are parties.[39] As a result, all competitors in a given market have to comply with the same consumer-protection measures. To give an example, assume that there was a lower level of consumer protection in Portugal than in Denmark: this would not give an unfair advantage to Portuguese producers over Danish ones because both would be subject to the Portuguese provisions when marketing in Portugal and to the Danish provisions when marketing in Denmark; there would, therefore, be no distortion of competition. Moreover, even if this were not so, the EC directives would not solve the problem, since, as was explained above, Member States are allowed to apply national measures so long as they provide for higher levels of protection.

The only directive in the field of tort appears to be the Product Liability Directive. In this field, there is as yet no EC convention, though there is an international (non-Community) one, the 1973 Hague Convention on the Law Applicable to Products Liability, to which five EC States are parties.[40] Under this, the applicable law will normally be that of the place in which the consumer is habitually resident or that of the place of injury.[41] In most cases, these will be in the same country. In Member States which are not parties to the Convention, a similar result will often follow from national choice-of-law rules.[42] In all these situations, there will be no distortion of competition.

In some States, the law of the producer's country may apply.[43] To

---

[38] New Member States are obliged to adhere as soon as possible.

[39] Art. 5 provides for the application of the law of the country in which the consumer has his habitual residence, provided certain other conditions are fulfilled, the purpose of which is to ensure that the producer marketed his goods there. For further discussion, see Morse, "Consumer Contracts, Employment Contracts and the Rome Convention" (1992) 41 ICLQ 1; Plender, *The European Contracts Convention* (1991), Chapter 7.

[40] Finland, France, Luxembourg, the Netherlands and Spain.

[41] The law of the consumer's habitual residence will apply if this is also either the producer's principal place of business or the place where the product was marketed: Art. 5; otherwise, the applicable law is that of the place of injury, provided this is also either the place of the consumer's habitual residence or the producer's principal place of business or the place where the product was marketed: Art. 4. The law of the producer's country applies only if neither of the above rules is operative, an unlikely contingency.

[42] In the United Kingdom, for example, the applicable law is that of the place where the consumer suffered death, personal injury or damage to property: section 11(2)(a) and (b) of the Private International Law (Miscellaneous Provisions) Act 1995.

[43] For a detailed discussion, see Fawcett, "Products Liability in Private International Law: A European Perspective" (1993–I) 238 *Recueil des cours* (Hague Academy of International Law) 13, especially Chapter 8. The section of Fawcett's paper on United Kingdom law is now out of date, since it was written before the 1995 Act was passed.

the extent that this is the case, there might be a distortion of competition. However, this will not necessarily be remedied by the directive, since the directive allows Member States to retain existing legislation, or adopt new legislation, which provides a higher level of protection. In any event, distortions in competition could be more easily remedied by unifying the relevant choice-of-law rules, than by unifying the substantive law. Such a solution would be more in accord with the principle of subsidiarity, which requires Community legislation to take the simplest form possible and to be no more extensive than necessary to achieve the objective.[44]

The third argument is that it is necessary to harmonize consumer-protection law at a uniformly high level in order not to deter people in one Member State from visiting another Member State as tourists. A variant of this argument is that people must not be deterred from moving to another Member State as immigrants. The variant will be discussed further below. Here, we will simply point out three major objections to the argument as regards tourists. The first is that, in the real world, tourists do not normally concern themselves with the consumer-protection law of the country they intend to visit. If they engage in litigation at all, it will be in their home country with their tour operator. The second objection is that it is absurd to say that a country's consumer-protection law should be designed primarily to benefit tourists, rather than the native inhabitants: this is the tail wagging the dog with a vengeance. The third objection is that, if this argument were accepted, large areas of policy would have to be handed over to the Community. Tourists are more likely to be afraid of being robbed or raped than of being cheated by a shopkeeper; therefore, if one takes the argument seriously, criminal law, criminal procedure and the police should be Community matters. A second worry for tourists is falling ill; so health matters, including hospitals and the medical profession should be Europeanized. One could continue in this vein, but enough has been said (it is hoped) to justify the dismissal of the tourist argument.

One can conclude from this that there is no justification for Community jurisdiction in the area of consumer protection.[45]

---

[44] This is laid down by Art. 6 of the Amsterdam Protocol on the Application of the Principles of Subsidiarity and Proportionality.

[45] Whether the Community directives are legally valid is another matter. Prior to the coming into force of the Maastricht Agreement (Treaty on European Union), there was no provision in the EC Treaty specifically empowering the Community to legislate on

Sex Discrimination[46]

There was a provision on sex discrimination in the original EEC Treaty, but it covered only one issue—equal pay for men and women. This was Article 119 {141}: the reason it was put in the Treaty was that, at the time in question, some Member States had national laws giving women the right to equal pay, while others did not. The former took the view that it would give an unfair advantage to manufacturers established in the latter countries if those countries were allowed to continue paying women lower wages. This is why Article 119 {141} covers equal pay, but not other forms of discrimination: it does not prevent a firm from refusing to employ women, from discriminating against them with regard to promotion, or from dismissing them; but if it does employ them, it must pay them the same wages as men.

Article 119 {141} was thus introduced to prevent distortion of competition, not for reasons of social policy. Though not entirely convincing, this justification for Community jurisdiction has a

consumer protection; consequently, resort was had to Art. 100 {94} EC or, after the Single European Act came into force, Art. 100a {95} EC (both discussed above). Resort to the former (under which the Product Liability Directive was passed) is permissible only if the measure directly affects the establishment or functioning of the common market; resort to the latter (under which the Unfair Contract Terms Directive was passed) is permissible only if the measure has as its object the establishment and functioning of the internal market. It is hard to see how either of these conditions is fulfilled in the case of consumer-protection measures. The position changed with the coming into force of the Maastricht Agreement, since this inserted into the EC Treaty a provision, Art. 129a {153}, expressly giving the Council jurisdiction to take action supporting and supplementing the policy pursued by the Member States to protect consumer interests. This gave EC consumer-protection legislation a firmer foundation, though it is open to question whether it should be applied retroactively to validate measures passed before it came into force. In addition, however, the Maastricht Agreement established subsidiarity as a principle of Community law by inserting Art. 3b {5} into the EC Treaty. It is doubtful whether the consumer-protection directives are consistent with subsidiarity, though it seems that subsidiarity cannot apply retroactively to invalidate measures already passed: see Art. 2 of the Amsterdam Protocol on the Application of the Principles of Subsidiarity and Proportionality. For political reasons, the European Court would be reluctant to hold any of the consumer-protection measures invalid. One way in which it could avoid doing so would be to rule that Art. 129a {153} EC applies retroactively to validate them, but that Art. 3b {5} EC does not apply retroactively to invalidate them.

[46] For a general discussion of this topic, see Ruth Nielsen and Erika Szyszczak, *The Social Dimension of the European Union* (3rd ed. 1997), Chapter 4.

certain logic to it.[47] Subsequently, however, the Community went further and introduced a directive to outlaw other forms of discrimination in employment. This is Directive 76/207,[48] usually known as the Equal Treatment Directive. It prohibits discrimination on grounds of sex with regard to matters such as recruitment of staff and promotion.

What justification is there for giving the Community jurisdiction in this area? The fair-competition argument does not apply, unless one takes the view that employing women is detrimental to a firm and therefore harms its competitive position. However, there is no reason to believe that this is so. In any event, the directive does not require firms to hire a given proportion of women, but merely to hire the best applicant irrespective of sex; so compliance with the directive is not economically disadvantageous to a firm. The only possible exception concerns pregnancy and maternity rights.[49] Except in this case, arguments based on fair competition are not applicable.

The directive itself makes no attempt to justify Community jurisdiction, but merely states that sex equality is an objective of the Community. This, however, was not true when the directive was passed: Article 2 {2} EC (as supplemented by Article 3{3}) set out the objectives of the Community, and sex equality was not one of them. This was altered by the Treaty of Amsterdam, which amended Article 2 {2} by inserting the words "equality between men and women", but this took place more than twenty years later. In any event, this leaves unanswered the question whether sex equality *should* be a Community objective: is there any reason why it can be better achieved by Community action than by Member-State action?

The only argument that has been put forward to justify the directive in these terms is that without it women might be deterred from migrating to another Member State in order to work. Since the free movement of workers is an objective of the Community, this is said

[47] The European Court has, however, held that Art. 119 {141} applies to the civil services of the Member States, a case in which the competition rationale is inapplicable: *Gerster* v. *Freistaat Bayern*, Case C-1/95, [1997] ECR I-5253.

[48] OJ 1976 L39/40.

[49] The European Court has interpreted the directive as prohibiting an employer from refusing to hire a woman who is pregnant, even if her absence on maternity leave would cause difficulties for the firm: *Dekker*, Case C-177/88, [1990] ECR I-3941; *Webb* v. *EMO Air Cargo Ltd*, Case C-32/93, [1994] ECR I-3567.

to justify Community jurisdiction. This argument is, however, open to the same objections as the "tourist" argument mentioned above. If women were deterred from working in a foreign country because the law of the country in question did not protect them against sex discrimination, they would be equally deterred if the country's law did not protect their rights to the custody of their children, to a fair divorce and reasonable maintenance and to abortion if they should need one. If one accepts the "immigrant" argument, therefore, all these matters should be subject to Community jurisdiction. Moreover, all immigrants are concerned about receiving reasonable social welfare benefits, not paying excessive taxes, obtaining satisfactory accommodation and finding good education for their children. If one accepts the argument, all these matters should also be given over to the Community. If this were done, there would be little left for the Member States to do.

The fact of the matter is that, except in the limited circumstances where it might affect a firm's competitive ability, there is no justification for Community jurisdiction in the area covered by the Equal Treatment Directive: no reasonable argument can be advanced that it can be better dealt with at Community level than at national level. Here too Community jurisdiction is unjustified.[50]

Conclusions

In this chapter, we have taken subsidiarity as a general principle and, ignoring the restrictions placed on it under the Treaty, used it as the basis for determining how legislative power ought to be divided between the Community and the Member States. Consumer protection and sex discrimination were taken as examples of areas in which Community jurisdiction is hard to justify. The response of the Member States to the doubts that have been raised in these areas has been to amend the Treaty to provide expressly for Community jurisdiction. This solves the legal problem (at least for future measures), but shows that the Member States do not take subsidiarity seriously, since no convincing arguments have been put forward that the

---

[50] The legal validity of the directive, which was adopted under Art. 235 {308} EC, may depend on whether amendments brought in by the Treaty of Amsterdam to Arts 2 {2} and 119 {141} EC can be applied retroactively to validate it.

Member States could not have attained the objectives perfectly adequately themselves.[51]

It should be emphasized that we are not concerned with the desirability of consumer protection and sex equality, but with the question of *jurisdiction*: where should power lie to legislate in these areas—with the Community or with the Member States? Giving jurisdiction to the Community has a number of undesirable consequences: first, it means that legislation in areas that directly affect private individuals will be adopted under the undemocratic machinery of the Community, when it could be adopted with greater democratic participation by the Member States;[52] secondly, it will make it more difficult to take account of local circumstances in different countries; thirdly, it means that Europeans will have to accept the shoddy, badly-drafted measures that are all too often the output of the Community legislative process;[53] finally, it means that the European Court will become the ultimate arbiter in these matters. Why should the European Court be the body to decide whether Cornwall County Council may lawfully dismiss one of its employees because he intends to undergo a "gender reassignment"?[54] Why should it be the body to decide whether, in pursuance of its policy of affirmative action, the German State of Bremen may lawfully give preference to women when promoting its civil servants?[55] Why should it be the body to decide whether the German State of Bavaria may lawfully apply a rule that, for determining seniority among its civil servants, a year's full-time work counts as more than

---

[51] An argument sometimes put forward at an unofficial level is that, for reasons of national character, the southern Member States are unlikely, if left to their own devices, to adopt satisfactory legislation on these matters. (A similar argument is sometimes used to justify Community jurisdiction regarding animal rights.) Even if the assumption on which it is based is correct, this argument is contrary to the principle of subsidiarity, which permits Community jurisdiction only where, *by reason of the transnational dimension of the matter*, the Community is better able to act than the Member States.

[52] The lack of democracy in the Community was discussed in Chapter 1.

[53] This problem was discussed in Chapter 4.

[54] *P v. S and Cornwall County Council*, Case C-13/94, [1996] ECR I-2143. The gender reassignment began with a "life test", a period during which he dressed and behaved as a woman, followed by a sex-change operation. The European Court ruled that the County Council was guilty of discrimination on grounds of sex, contrary to the Equal Treatment Directive.

[55] *Kalanke v. Freie Hansestadt Bremen*, Case C-450/93, [1995] ECR I-3051. The Court held that this constituted discrimination contrary to the Equal Treatment Directive. For later developments, see pp. 53–54, above.

a year's part-time work?[56] In all these cases, the national courts would have been the appropriate forum.

---

[56] *Gerster* v. *Freistaat Bayern*, Case C-1/95, [1997] ECR I-5253. The Court held that, since the majority of part-time employees were women, such a rule would constitute sex discrimination contrary to the Equal Treatment Directive, unless it was justified by "objective criteria".

6

Enforcing Community Law

> Britain has an almost depersonalized concept of the law in that they blindly obey the law even when it doesn't suit them politically. Almost nobody else in the world does that, and certainly no other Member States do.
>
> Unnamed official at the European Court quoted in the *Wall Street Journal* of 4 October 1994.

It is sometimes said that Britain has to be more careful than other Member States about agreeing to Community measures because, once they are enacted, Britain always enforces them, while other countries turn a bind eye to violations. Is there any truth in this, or is it just jingoistic cant? To answer this question, we must first consider how Community law is enforced.

In theory, directly effective Community law is self-enforcing: it is supposed to be part of the law of the land in each Member State and must be enforced by national courts and officials just like national law. Only if there is a dispute concerning its interpretation is the European Court brought into the picture; otherwise, it is the duty of the Member States to see it is obeyed. However, since things do not always work out like this in practice, and since some Community provisions are not directly effective, there is a procedure laid down in Articles 169–171 {226–228} EC for the Commission to bring a Member State before the European Court if it has failed to fulfil an obligation under Community law. It is this latter procedure that we consider in this chapter.

THE ENFORCEMENT PROCEDURE

One of the tasks of the Commission is to ensure that the Treaties and Community legislation are applied.[1] To do this, the Commission monitors the application of Community law by the Member States. Suspected infringements are recorded and investigated. If the investigation leads the Commission to believe that the Member State in question has failed to fulfil its obligations, the Commission will take the matter up with the government concerned. In the beginning, these discussions are confidential: it is thought that a settlement is more likely if publicity is avoided. However, if the Member State fails to convince the Commission, and if it refuses to fall into line, the Commission will commence formal proceedings.

The first step in the formal proceedings is to send the Member State a document—usually referred to as a "169-letter"[2]—specifying precisely what it is alleged to have done wrong (or failed to do) and inviting it to submit its observations. The Member State is given a period of time in which to respond. Unless it decides to comply, it will give a reply setting out its case. If the Commission is not convinced, it will issue a reasoned opinion formally stating in what way the Member State has infringed the law. The reasoned opinion will give the Member State a period of time in which to comply. If it fails to do so, the Commission will commence proceedings before the European Court. It usually takes between a year and a half and two years for the European Court to give judgment. Under the Treaty, the Court cannot actually order the Member State to take action: all it can do is to declare that it has failed to fulfil its obligations. However, Article 171 {228} EC states that the Member State must take the necessary measures to comply with the judgment.

Until amendments adopted under the Maastricht Agreement (Treaty on European Union) came into force, there was no provision under the EC Treaty for sanctions if a Member State failed to obey the judgment.[3] Now, however, there is the possibility of imposing

---

[1] Art. 155 {211} EC.

[2] So called because it is required by Art. 169 {226} EC.

[3] As regards infringements of the ECSC Treaty, on the other hand, there has always been provision (under Art. 88 ECSC) for the imposition of sanctions: money payable to the delinquent Member State may be withheld, or other Member States may be authorized to take action to correct the effects of the infringement. These sanctions are authorized by the

fines.[4] The Commission takes the initiative: if it considers that the Member State has not complied, it issues another reasoned opinion specifying how it has failed to comply and laying down a time limit for compliance. If the Member State still does not comply, the Commission brings the case back to the European Court. In doing so, it specifies the fine which it thinks should be imposed. Such fines[5] come in two forms: a lump sum and a periodic penalty. The former is a one-off payment; the latter is a continuing penalty of a specified sum for each day that the Member State remains in default. It is the general policy of the Commission to choose the latter: the Commission thinks that this is more likely to ensure compliance.[6] The final decision rests with the European Court. At the time of writing (July 1998), no penalties have yet been imposed by the Court.[7]

In a small number of cases, problems have arisen with regard to the enforcement of judgments: for example, a judgment delivered against Italy in 1973[8] was not complied with for more than ten years.[9] The most notorious case was the so-called "*Sheepmeat*" affair, in which France openly and defiantly banned the import of lamb from Britain and continued to do so despite a judgment from the European Court under Article 169 {226} EC.[10] The Commission then brought a new

Commission, but the assent of the Council (acting by a two-thirds majority) must be obtained. No sanctions have ever been imposed.

[4] Arts 171 {228} EC and 143 Euratom as amended. The initiative for these amendments apparently came from Britain. For the ECSC Treaty, the existing procedure under Art. 88 continues to apply.

[5] The word "fine" is not actually used by the Treaty.

[6] See Commission Memorandum 96/C 242/07, OJ 1996 C242/6, para. 4. On 8 January 1997, the Commission announced the method it would use to calculate penalties (OJ 1997 C63/2). It will start with the sum of 500 ECU per day. This is multiplied by two coefficients, the first (on a scale of 1 to 20) reflecting the seriousness of the infringement, and the second (on a scale of 1 to 3) reflecting its duration. To achieve deterrence, the result will be multiplied by a factor reflecting the ability of the Member State to pay (based on its GDP) and the number of votes it commands in the Council. This factor ranges from 1 for Luxembourg to 26.4 for Germany. As a result, a daily penalty payment at the top of the scale for both seriousness and duration would range from 30,000 ECU for Luxembourg to 791,293 ECU for Germany.

[7] According to the Commission's *Fifteenth Annual Report on Monitoring the Application of Community Law* (1997), COM(98) 317, published in May 1998, the Commission took eight decisions to propose fines to the Court; two of them were actually referred to the Court (see p. I).

[8] *Commission v. Italy*, Case 79/72, [1973] ECR 667.

[9] H A H Audretsch, *Supervision in European Community Law* (2nd ed. 1986), pp. 395–396.

[10] *Commission v. France*, Case 232/78, [1979] ECR 2729.

action under Article 169 {226}. This time the provision alleged to have been violated was Article 171 {228}: this is the provision which says that judgments of the European Court must be obeyed. Since these proceedings would have taken at least a year, the Commission asked the Court for an interim order requiring France to allow British lamb to be imported on a temporary basis until the Court had given a final ruling. Such interim orders are an accepted part of proceedings under Article 169 {226} and had been used against the United Kingdom on an earlier occasion,[11] though they had not previously been used in cases in which a Member State had defied a judgment of the Court. In its judgment on the application,[12] the Court stated that such orders could be given in cases of defiance, but declined to give one in the case before it on the somewhat spurious ground that the order would merely repeat the original judgment, a ground which would obviously apply in all such cases.[13] Obviously, its decision was motivated by political expediency, rather than legal considerations.

This put France in a strong position: it could use its successful defiance, and the harm it was doing to the Court's authority, as a bargaining counter in its bid to obtain a Community support system for its sheep farmers. The other Member States eventually gave in, though Britain did so only after concessions were made on its bid for a rebate on its financial contributions to the Community. Once the support system was in place, France lifted the ban. The outcome of this case, which must be regarded as a victory for France, shows that, in certain situations, defiance of the Court can pay dividends.

If France were to do the same thing again today, the Commission could ask for a substantial daily penalty to be imposed. However, this would cause almost as many problems as it solved. France would refuse to pay, and it is not clear how it could be forced to do so. One solution would be for the Commission to withhold money payable to France, but France could retaliate by withholding money payable to the Community. When a final settlement was agreed, France would demand, as part of the deal, that all accrued penalties be cancelled. This would cause problems because it is not clear that either the Commission or the Member States have the power to do this. The only certain way of ensuring that no fines would have to be paid

[11] *Commission* v. *United Kingdom*, Cases 31, 53/77R, [1977] ECR 921.
[12] *Commission* v. *France*, Cases 24, 97/80R, [1980] ECR 1319.
[13] Moreover, in one respect, there was a new issue: France argued that it had not had sufficient time to comply with the earlier judgment. The Court could have ruled on this.

would be to amend the Treaty. This would be cumbersome; moreover, once one Member State had been let off, it would be difficult to impose fines on other Member States. For these reasons, if the "*Sheepmeat*" scenario were re-enacted today, the European Court might refuse to impose a fine, no doubt citing some seemingly appropriate ground for so doing.

The paradoxical conclusion that one can draw from this analysis is that fines are unlikely to work in the most serious cases. Where a Member State's national interest is not seriously affected, the threat of a fine may be sufficient to bring it into line; but, if the stakes are so high that it is willing to incur the odium of openly defying the Court, a fine may be counter-productive. If a Member State is sufficiently determined to have its way, the matter passes out of the hands of the Community institutions and becomes politicized. Then, the only alternatives open to the other Member States are either to make a deal, or to threaten to drive the recalcitrant Member State out of the Community. The latter might be feasible in the case of one of the more peripheral countries, but it is hardly a serious option in the case of France or Germany. Such a country, therefore, can always get what it wants if it is willing to pay the political price.

INDIVIDUAL MEMBER STATES: COMPLIANCE RATES

Every year since 1984, the Commission has published a report to the European Parliament on its monitoring of the application of Community law by the Member States.[14] The reports contain statistics, some of which are broken down according to the Member State involved and can therefore be used to obtain some idea of the extent to which compliance with Community law varies from one Member State to another. We will first consider the ten-year period from 1980 to 1989, and then we will look at the period from 1990 to 1997.

The 1980s

In considering the figures for the 1980s, we will restrict ourselves to the nine oldest Member States. Greece joined in 1981 and Spain and

---

[14] These are listed in the Select Bibliography, below.

Portugal in 1986; however, when a country joins the Community, the whole body of Community law is not applicable to it all at once: it comes into force in stages; consequently, it is some years before figures for infringements reach their normal level. For these reasons, we exclude Greece, Spain and Portugal from consideration at this point.

Three sets of figures are available: for 169-letters, for reasoned opinions and for references to the European Court. They are broken down by Member State and by year. We give the total for the entire decade. It should be remembered that a 169-letter is sent to a Member State only if informal contacts lead the Commission to believe that an infringement has occurred, and the Member State has not agreed to end it. They are probably the best indicator of the extent to which a Member State complies in general with Community law. This is the case, however, only if the following assumptions are correct. The first is that the number of cases in which the Commission commences investigations with regard to any Member State is proportionate to the number of cases in which it infringes Community law. The Commission investigates all cases in which it becomes aware of a possible infringement. This may result either from its own activities or as a result of complaints from members of the public or from Members of the European Parliament. There is no reason to believe that these are skewed in favour of, or against, any particular Member State. The second assumption is that the Commission investigates suspected infringements equally carefully in the case of all Member States. There is no reason to believe that it does not. The third assumption is that there are no significant variations in the willingness of particular Member States to give in and accept the Commission view prior to the 169-letter. It is not known whether this assumption is correct.

Once the 169-letter has been sent, the matter is out in the open. A reasoned opinion will not invariably follow, since in some cases the Member State may convince the Commission, and in others the Member State may concede. Only if neither of these occurs will the Commission give a reasoned opinion. In fact, these additional factors do not seem to affect the figures very much: the ranking of the various Member States is much the same at this point. This is also true with regard to references to the European Court. The Commission is not legally obliged to refer all cases to the Court, but will normally do so if the Member State does not fall into line within the time-limit set in the reasoned opinion. Here too the ranking is only slightly different.

In the Tables below, the Member States are ranked in the order of their presumed willingness to obey Community law: the country ranked first has the best record and that ranked last has the worst.

Table 1.[15]

169-LETTERS: 1980–1989

Ranking	Member State	Number of Letters
1.	Denmark	240
2.	United Kingdom	306
3.	Luxembourg	310
4.	Netherlands	333
5.	Ireland	346
6.	Germany	360
7.	Belgium	476
8.	France	639
9.	Italy	731

Several comments may be made about these figures. The first is that the ranking for each year during the period is not very different from that for the whole decade. Italy, for example, ranked ninth in six of the years and eighth in the remaining four years, France being ninth on those occasions. At the other end of the scale, Denmark was first on eight occasions. Thus the overall figures have not been distorted by an especially bad year for any particular country.

The second comment is that the ranking does not seem to be closely related to size. Admittedly, the top-ranking country (Denmark) is the second-smallest and the smallest, Luxembourg, ranks third. However, the United Kingdom, one of the largest countries, ranks in second place and Belgium, a fairly small country, ranks third last.

[15] Sources: the Commission's *Fifth Annual Report* (1987), COM(88) 425, Table 1; combined with its *Sixth Annual Report* (1988), COM(89) 411, Table 1; its *Seventh Annual Report* (1989), COM(90) 288, Table 1; its *Ninth Annual Report* (1991), COM(92) 136, Table 1; its *Tenth Annual Report* (1992), COM(93) 320, Table 2.1; and its *Eleventh Annual Report* (1993), COM(94) 500, Table 2.1. There are discrepancies between some of the figures in different Reports; in such cases, the figures in the later Reports have been preferred.

The third, and most important, comment is that there is a clear North-South bias in the distribution, a trend which will be more evident below when we include Greece, Spain and Portugal.

We now give the figures for reasoned opinions, set out in the same way. It will be seen that the numbers are smaller, since most cases are settled before a reasoned opinion is given.

Table 2.[16]

	REASONED OPINIONS: 1980–1989	
Ranking	*Member State*	*Number of Opinions*
1.	Denmark	47
2.	United Kingdom	89
3.	Netherlands	92
4.	Luxembourg	110
5.	Ireland	122
6.	Germany	143
7.	Belgium	222
8.	France	262
9.	Italy	388

What was said previously regarding 169-letters applies equally here.

Our third Table (set out on page 114, below) gives references to the European Court. The numbers here are even smaller still.

One can conclude from these figures that during the 1980s Denmark had the best record for compliance with Community law. The United Kingdom ranked second, but it was grouped so closely with Luxembourg, the Netherlands, Ireland and Germany that one should regard these five countries as more or less in the same position. The six Member States in the northern part of the Community (of which four are small countries) thus have the best record. On the other hand, Belgium, France and Italy—the three more southern Member States—have a consistently less good record. The extent of the gap is

---

[16] The sources for this Table are the same as those for Table 1. The comment regarding discrepancies applies here too.

Table 3.[17]

REFERENCES TO THE EUROPEAN COURT: 1980–1989		
Ranking	*Member State*	*References*
1.	Denmark	15
2.	United Kingdom	22
3.	Netherlands	28
4.	Luxembourg	30
5.	Ireland	35
6.	Germany	52
7.	France	91
8.	Belgium	102
9.	Italy	189

Table 4.[18]

169-LETTERS: 1990–1997		
Ranking	*Member State*	*Number of Letters*
1.	Denmark	384
2.	Netherlands	492
3.	Luxembourg	544
4.	Ireland	552
5.	United Kingdom	595
6.	Belgium	665
7.	Germany	703
8.	Spain	762
9.	France	776
10.	Greece	820
11.	Italy	885
12.	Portugal	887

[17] Sources: the same as for Table 1.
[18] Sources: the Commission's *Twelfth Annual Report* (1994), COM(95) 500, Table 2.1, combined with its *Fifteenth Annual Report* (1997), COM(98) 317, Table 2.1.

indicated by the fact that there were three times more 169-letters sent to Italy than to Denmark, a significant difference.

The 1990s

In the present decade, figures are available only for the eight years 1990–1997. We now include Greece, Portugal and Spain, but not the three newest Member States—Austria, Finland and Sweden. Table 4 (set out on page 114, opposite) is for 169-letters.

The North-South gradient is now quite apparent. The only clear exception is that Spain ranks above France. It is not certain whether this indicates a long-term trend.[19]

Table 5 shows reasoned opinions for the same period.

Table 5.[20]

REASONED OPINIONS: 1990–1997		
Ranking	*Member State*	*Number of Opinions*
1.	Denmark	31
2.	United Kingdom	103
3.	Netherlands	125
4.	Ireland	183
5.	Luxembourg	189
6.	Spain	235
7.	France	246
8.	Germany	250
9.	Belgium	284
10.	Portugal	318
11.	Greece	359
12.	Italy	429

[19] France's record was significantly better for the first five years of the period under consideration and would have been better for the whole period had there not been a particularly large number of letters in 1997.

[20] Sources: the Commission's *Twelfth Annual Report* (1994), COM(95) 500, Table 2.1, combined with its *Fifteenth Annual Report* (1997), COM(98) 317, Table 2.1.

The extremely low number of reasoned opinions regarding Denmark, and the higher ranking enjoyed by the United Kingdom, suggest that these two countries are more willing than most to concede to the Commission once they have received a 169-letter.

Our next Table shows references to the Court.

Table 6.[21]

REFERENCES TO THE EUROPEAN COURT: 1990–1997

Ranking	Member State	References
1.	Denmark	4
2.	United Kingdom	11
3.	Netherlands	28
4.	Portugal	34
5.	Ireland	43
6.	Spain	46
7.	France	53
8.	Luxembourg	54
9.	Germany	57
10.	Greece	83
11.	Belgium	88
12.	Italy	124

The relatively high position of Portugal and the relatively low positions of Belgium and Luxembourg probably indicate the contrasting policies of these countries as regards willingness to fight cases in the European Court.

It should finally be said that those cases that go to judgment are mostly decided in favour of the Commission. This is shown by the following Table, which lists cases commenced in the years specified which were decided for the Commission and for the Member State.[22]

[21] Sources: the Commission's *Twelfth Annual Report* (1994), COM(95) 500, Table 2.1, combined with its *Fifteenth Annual Report* (1997), COM(98) 317, Table 2.1.

[22] It is based on figures in the Commission's *Annual Reports* (see following footnotes). At the time when the Reports were drawn up, some cases were still pending: these are excluded from the figures.

Table 7.

OUTCOME OF CASES COMMENCED IN 1988–1994

Year Commenced	For Commission	For Member State
1988[23]	35	7
1989[24]	31	2
1990[25]	21	0
1991[26]	21	1
1992[27]	41	4
1993[28]	40	3
1994[29]	31	1
TOTAL	220[30]	18 (7.5 per cent)

The 18 Member-State victories were distributed as follows: Italy—4; Belgium, Germany and France—3 each; Greece and Spain—2 each; and the Netherlands—1. This suggests the unsurprising conclusion that the countries that fight the most cases gain the most victories; the success *rate*, however, is probably similar for all the Member States, though the numbers are too small for reliable conclusions to be drawn.

THE NORTH–SOUTH GRADIENT

We can now answer the question posed at the beginning of this chapter. The answer is that, though one of a group of Member States that has a good record for complying with Community law, Britain is far from unique in this regard. The Netherlands, Luxembourg and Ireland are better, and Denmark is considerably better. The quotation

---

[23] Source: *Tenth Annual Report* (1992), COM(93) 320, Table 2.2.

[24] Source: *Eleventh Annual Report* (1993), COM(94) 500, Table 2.3.

[25] Source: *Twelfth Annual Report* (1994), COM(95) 500, Table 2.3.

[26] Source: *Thirteenth Annual Report* (1995), COM(96) 600, Table 2.3.

[27] Source: *Fourteenth Annual Report* (1996), COM(97) 299, Table 2.3.

[28] Source: *Fifteenth Annual Report* (1997), COM(98) 317, Table 2.3.

[29] Source: *Fifteenth Annual Report* (1997), COM(98) 317, Table 2.4.

[30] It must be stressed that these figures are incomplete as they do not include cases pending when the relevant Report was drawn up. It is not known what the outcome of these cases was.

at the beginning of this chapter is therefore incorrect: it would have been more apt with regard to Denmark.

A more important conclusion that can be drawn from the figures is that there is a clear North-South gradient as regards respect for Community law. Though the figures given above are aggregates for fairly lengthy periods, the ranking of the different Member States is not substantially different on a year-by-year basis. Table 8 shows the ranking for each Member State with regard to 169-letters for each year from 1990 to 1997.

Table 8.[31]

169-LETTERS: RANKING 1990–1997

Member State	1990	1991	1992	1993	1994	1995	1996	1997
Denmark	1	1	1	1	1	1	1	2
Netherlands	5=	5	2	2	4=	2	2	1
Luxembourg	2	7	4=	3=	2	4	3	3
Ireland	4	3	3	3=	3	3	4	4
United Kingdom	3	6	4=	5=	4=	5	5	6
Belgium	7	8	7	5=	6	6	10	5
Germany	5=	4	4=	10	8=	8	9	10
Spain	10	9	11	8	7	7	8	7
France	8	2	9	7	8=	9	12	12
Greece	11	11	8	11=	10=	10	7	8
Italy	9	12	12	9	12	11	11	11
Portugal	12	10	10	11=	10=	12	6	9

It is remarkable how consistent these figures are. Denmark occupies first place for every year except one, while Italy is last or second last for every year except two. The Upper Bloc, consisting of the leading five countries[32]—all in the northern half of the Community—occupy places in the top half of the rankings on every occasion but one.[33] On the other hand, the Lower Bloc, consisting of the five southern countries, occupy places in the lower half of the rankings on

[31] Sources: the Commission's *Twelfth Annual Report* (1994), COM(95) 500, Table 2.1, combined with its *Fifteenth Annual Report* (1997), COM(98) 317, Table 2.1.

[32] Denmark, the Netherlands, Luxembourg, Ireland and the United Kingdom.

[33] Luxembourg was seventh in 1991.

all occasions but two.[34] This consistency proves that the rankings are not due to chance, but must reflect underlying factors, presumably culturally-conditioned attitudes towards the law.

Support for this idea is given by surveys published by two non-governmental organizations, Transparency International, based in Berlin, and an English firm of accountants, Grant Thornton. The former, which is derived from various opinion polls and covers the three years 1995–1997, deals with perceptions of governmental corruption in different countries around the world.[35] It is based on the opinions of business people, political analysts and the general public. The Grant Thornton survey covers the years 1993–1996 and deals with late payment of debts by private businesses in different countries in Europe.[36] If we take the data in both these surveys and rank the 12 EC Member States we have been considering, the results are remarkably similar to those in the Tables given: in both the corruption survey and the late payment survey, Denmark comes top and Italy bottom. Since the figures in these two surveys come from unofficial sources, it would be a mistake to read too much into them; nevertheless, it is significant that such a similar pattern emerges.

ORGANIZED DEFIANCE OF COMMUNITY LAW BY INDIVIDUALS

Another problem is organized disobedience to Community law by private individuals. This occurs mainly in France. Although French farmers export their produce all over the Community, they object when foreign products are imported into France. They way-lay the trucks bringing it into the country, force them to stop and destroy their goods. Another tactic is to block the roads with their tractors. The French police are notoriously reluctant to intervene. Although the importers may obtain compensation, this does not solve the problem because many producers simply do not export to France for fear

---

[34] France was second in 1991 and Portugal was sixth in 1996.

[35] Transparency International Corruption Perception Index for 1995, 1996 and 1997, obtainable from Transparency International, Otto-Suhr-Allee 97–99, D-10585 Berlin, Germany.

[36] *Good Payment Practice*. The report is not dated, but is based on the *European Business Survey for 1996* (Grant Thornton International and Business Strategies Ltd). It is obtainable from Grant Thornton, Grant Thornton House, Melton Street, Euston Square, London NW1 2EP.

of violence. Thus, the French tactics have succeeded in keeping imports out of the country.

That this state of affairs was allowed to continue for many years without action by the Community lends weight to the idea that France somehow occupies a favoured position and is allowed to get away with things that would not be tolerated if done by other Member States. In 1985, the Commission finally sent a formal letter to France; but then it let the matter drop. In the 1990s, the situation became worse: a number of organizations, including one called "*Coordination rurale*", began a campaign to prevent wholesalers and retailers from stocking foreign produce. The campaign was based on intimidation and violence. In July 1993, Spanish strawberries were the target; in August, it was Belgian tomatoes.

Violent incidents, including attacks on foreign trucks, continued in 1994. The police took no action. Finally, in July 1994, the Commission sent a 169-letter to France. In reply, the French Government said it strongly condemned the attacks, but was powerless to prevent them. Further attacks followed in 1995, many directed against Spanish produce. In May 1995, the Commission issued a reasoned opinion. France again protested that it was doing all it could. Further attacks took place, with the French police continuing their policy of passivity. In August 1995, the Commission commenced proceedings before the European Court.[37] Britain, and subsequently Spain, intervened on the side of the Commission. In view of its importance, the case was heard by a Full Court of 13 judges. Judgment was given in December 1997, almost two-and-a-half years after the action had begun.

In its judgment, the Court stated that Article 30 {28} EC[38] not only requires Member States to refrain from doing anything which could hinder imports from other Community countries, but also requires them to take all necessary and appropriate measures to ensure that the principle of free trade is respected in their territory.[39] It conceded that the national governments alone are responsible for the maintenance of law and order, and that in doing so they enjoy a margin of discretion in determining what measures are most appro-

---

[37] *Commission v. France*, Case C-265/95, [1997] ECR I-6959.

[38] For the text of this provision, and the wide interpretation given to it by the European Court, see Chapter 4, pp. 67–68, above.

[39] Para. 32 of the judgment.

priate.[40] The Community institutions cannot substitute their judgment for that of the national governments;[41] however, after it has taken into account the Member State's margin of discretion, the Court nevertheless has the power to determine whether the Member State has acted properly.[42]

In applying these principles to the case before it, the Court first held that the acts of the French farmers clearly constituted a barrier to imports. Had the French Government taken sufficient action to prevent this? It had been established by the Commission that the organized defiance of Community law in France had continued for more than ten years. On numerous occasions, the Commission had reminded the French Government of its duty. Although France claimed that it had taken all possible measures to prevent them, the incidents continued year after year. In many cases, the French police had kept away despite advance knowledge of possible trouble; in others, they had been on the spot, but had taken no action even when they outnumbered the trouble-makers. In certain cases, the incidents had been filmed by television cameras, and the identities of the persons concerned were often known to the authorities; however, only a small number were prosecuted. In view of these facts, the Court concluded that the measures taken by the French Government were insufficient to guarantee freedom of trade. It rejected the argument that French farmers had been particularly hard hit by cheap imports from Spain, and that more determined intervention might have caused an even more violent reaction. Judgment was given against France.

At the time of writing (July 1998), it is too soon to know whether this judgment will have any effect. If France continues with its policy of inaction, it could in theory be subjected to a fine. It is doubtful whether a daily penalty would be appropriate, since the abandonment of a policy of non-intervention is something which, by its very nature, cannot easily be pin-pointed as occurring at a particular moment. An official statement or decision would not be enough: the Commission would want to be satisfied that the policy had been abandoned in reality as well as in rhetoric. As the Court pointed out, the violence was episodic, reaching a peak at certain times and then

---

[40] Para. 33.
[41] Para. 34.
[42] Para. 35.

dying away. During periods of comparative tranquillity, it might not be clear whether the French Government had adopted a new policy or not: this would become apparent only when a new peak of violence occurred. For these reasons, a lump sum might be more appropriate than a periodic penalty; unless it was extremely large, however, it would be more of an irritant than a deterrent. One cannot be confident, therefore, that importers will be able to sell their produce in France any more freely in future: things may well continue as before.

CONCLUSIONS

It will be seen from what has been said that Community law does not apply evenly in all the Member States: a Danish company doing business in Italy is likely to face more illegitimate barriers than an Italian company in Denmark; British agricultural produce is likely to encounter more obstacles in France than French produce in Britain. There is no easy solution to this problem. The introduction of fines for States that disobey the European Court, though a step in the right direction, will have only limited impact. As we saw in Chapter 3, the European Court's solution has been to create a right of action for damages in the national courts. The problem with this is that it is the national courts that will find the facts and apply the law to them; the role of the European Court will be limited to laying down general principles. This means that the effectiveness of the system depends on the willingness of the national courts to make it effective. However, those countries that do not have a good record of respecting Community law in general are unlikely to show greater respect for it in the context of these proceedings; consequently, the countries where an effective remedy is most needed are likely to be those in which it is least likely to be found.

7

The Question of Sovereignty—I

By creating a Community of unlimited duration, having its own
institutions, its own personality, its own legal capacity of representation on the international plane and, more particularly, real
powers stemming from a limitation of sovereignty or a transfer
of powers from the States to the Community, the Member
States have limited their sovereign rights, albeit within limited
fields, and have thus created a body of law that binds both their
nationals and themselves.

The European Court, *Costa* v. *ENEL*, Case 6/64, [1964] ECR
585 at p. 593.[1]

In some ways, the question of sovereignty is the most important of
all: is Britain still sovereign, despite membership of the European
Union, or did she give up her independence on joining the
Community? As might be expected, a question as big and controversial as this cannot be answered in a few words. Indeed, it cannot
be answered at all without considering some preliminary issues.

First, we must give some indication of what we mean by sovereignty. In one sense, sovereignty means no more than practical
power: if the United Kingdom as a State decides on a certain course
of action, is it free to carry that out or is it subject to constraints? In
this sense, sovereignty means something akin to national independence or autonomy, the extent to which a State has freedom of action

---

[1] The phrase, "limitation of sovereignty" in this quotation appears in French (the language in which the European Court wrote the judgment) as "*limitation de compétences*", perhaps more accurately translated as "limitation of powers"; however, the phrase "sovereign
rights", which appears in the quotation shortly afterwards, is a correct translation of "*droits
souverains*" in the French text: see Rec. 1964, p. 1141 at 1159. For the argument that a limitation of sovereign rights is different from a limitation of sovereignty, see Bruno de Witte,
"Sovereignty and European Integration: The Weight of Legal Tradition" in Anne-Marie
Slaughter, Alec Stone Sweet and Joseph H H Weiler, *The European Courts and National
Courts—Doctrine and Jurisprudence* (1998), p. 277 at pp. 281–287.

internationally. Since it is clear that Britain's freedom of action is limited by membership of the European Union, her sovereignty in this sense has been diminished, though not eliminated. However, even before joining the Community, Britain's freedom of action in the international sphere was subject to many constraints. Some of these flowed from membership of international organizations such as NATO and the United Nations, as well as treaty commitments such as those under the GATT (and now the World Trade Organization). Restrictions of this kind have both a legal component (under international law) and a political component. In practice, the latter is usually more important. For example, when Britain and France invaded Egypt in 1956, they were forced to withdraw as a result of pressure from the United States. The invasion was a violation of international law,[2] but it was not for this reason that the invaders pulled back. Since America's domination of the world is now virtually unchallenged, Britain's freedom to do almost anything of significance on the international stage depends to a considerable extent on American approval.

Thus, even if Britain had not joined the European Union, her freedom of action would have been subject to many constraints. Indeed, it could be argued that, in some respects, membership of the EU has *increased* Britain's power and influence in the world. If Britain had remained outside, the Community would still have been a major trading partner. Britain would almost certainly have wanted to enter into some sort of trade agreement with it and would have had to negotiate on a large range of issues. Many of the matters which at present cause friction in Britain's relations with the Community would have been equally contentious if Britain had not joined; the only difference is that Britain would have lacked the leverage which comes from being a Member State. A second way in which Community membership puts Britain in a stronger position is that, in negotiations with third countries such as the United States or Japan, Britain is more likely to secure a favourable outcome if she has the backing of the European Union. One can conclude, therefore, that the effect of Community membership on Britain's freedom of action is not entirely negative: the undoubted restrictions must be balanced against less obvious, but equally real, benefits.

[2] The British Foreign Office was told this by its own Legal Adviser, but the invasion went ahead nevertheless: see Marston, "Armed Intervention in the 1956 Suez Canal Crisis: The Legal Advice Tendered to the British Government" (1988) 37 ICLQ 773.

Sovereignty in this sense is not, however, the subject of this chapter. What we are concerned with is sovereignty in the legal sense: as a matter of law, where does ultimate power lie? It is trite law that, before Britain joined the Community, the British Parliament was sovereign. As far as the law and constitution of the United Kingdom were concerned, there were no restrictions on what Parliament could do, except that it could not limit its own future powers.[3] What this meant is that, under United Kingdom law, Parliament could pass any statute it wanted: there were no limits to its law-making powers. The fact that such a statute, or governmental action taken under it, might have been contrary to international law (or the law of another country) would not have affected its validity and lawfulness in the United Kingdom.[4] The courts and police forces of the United Kingdom, as well as the British Army, would have recognized this. In practice, of course, all sorts of political and other considerations meant that there were many things that Parliament would not have tried to do (because the consequences would have been unacceptable), but this did not affect the *legal* position.

The question we address in the remaining chapters of this book is whether the position has been changed by membership of the European Union. To answer this, we must turn our attention to the Community legal system. If Britain has lost sovereignty to the Union, it will be on the basis of Community law that this has taken place. We first consider the nature of the Community legal system.

IS COMMUNITY LAW A SEPARATE LEGAL SYSTEM?

Is Community law a separate legal system, distinct from both international law and the legal systems of the Member States? This is not the place to consider the various theories on what constitutes a legal system,[5] since they shed little light on this

---

[3] For a general discussion, see Stanley de Smith and Rodney Brazier, *Constitutional and Administrative Law* (7th ed. 1994), Chapter 4.

[4] The fact that something can simultaneously be lawful under United Kingdom law and unlawful under international law indicates that international law is a separate legal system from United Kingdom law.

[5] See, for example, Hans Kelsen, *Pure Theory of Law* (1967) (translated by Max Knight from *Reine Rechtslehre* (2nd ed. 1960)); H L A Hart, *The Concept of Law* (2nd ed. 1994); J Raz, *The Concept of a Legal System* (2nd ed. 1980).

question.[6] Nor will we enter this territory ourselves by attempting to formulate a theory of our own; however, a general indication of what is meant will be helpful to the reader.

A legal system is a set of legal propositions—rules, if one understands the term widely—which have a relationship with one another.[7] The rules must be consistent: they must not contradict each other, though an apparent conflict may be resolved by a "super-rule" which is part of the system. For example, a conflict between provisions in two statutes enacted by the same legislature may be resolved by the "super-rule" that the later provision prevails over the earlier. Further characteristics, which are desirable but not essential, are a reasonable comprehensiveness (at least within certain areas) and the possession of institutions of a judicial, executive and legislative nature. These institutions make it possible to determine authoritatively what the law is, to enforce it and to change it.

If it is to be serviceable, the concept of a legal system must be flexible, since its use is largely a matter of convenience. Most people would regard English law and Scots law as separate legal systems (in so far as they are distinct from United Kingdom law), even though for many years neither has had *exclusive* possession of a legislature. On the other hand, one would not normally regard the bye-laws of a county council as a legal system, though such a "system" could be said to have its own legislature and executive. International law is generally regarded as a separate legal system, though the International Court of Justice has only limited jurisdiction, and there is no real legislature to change it or any satisfactory executive to enforce it.

On this basis, it is easy to conclude that Community law is a legal system. It consists of a set of rules which are fairly comprehensive within particular areas and are reasonably consistent with each other. The Community possesses two courts, the European Court of Justice and the Court of First Instance, which are devoted exclusively to the interpretation and application of Community law; Community law is also interpreted and applied by the national courts of the Member States. The European Court has been discussed at length in earlier

---

[6] For an attempt to apply these theories to the Community, see Dowrick, "A Model of the European Communities' Legal System" (1983) 3 YEL 169. Professor Dowrick concludes that Kelsen's theory is of little assistance (p. 185) and that Hart's theory, while illuminating some aspects of EC law, does not accommodate its most prominent features (p. 205).

[7] For a legal theorist whose work *is* of practical use in analysing the nature of legal rules, see W N Hohfeld, *Fundamental Legal Conceptions* (1923).

chapters and, though criticisms of it were made, the zeal with which it develops Community law as a legal system is not open to doubt. There is a Community legislature, the Council (in some instances, the Parliament and the Council acting jointly). Some indication of its powers is given in Chapter 5. As shown in Chapter 6, the Community itself cannot enforce Community law through the application of physical force: there are no Community bailiffs or sheriffs, nor is there any Community police force or army. The Member States, however, are under a duty to enforce Community law and in general they comply with this duty.

Community law is, therefore, a legal system; but is it *separate* from the legal systems of the Member States and from international law?

Separate from Member-State Law?

It is hard to deny that Community law is separate from, say, British law. Community law can cover the same ground as British law and is often inconsistent with it. As mentioned in Chapter 2, the European Court has laid down a rule that directly effective Community law prevails over national law in the event of a conflict. This rule is accepted in large measure by the courts of the Member States, but, as we shall see below, it is not *entirely* accepted. The fact that the "super-rule" in Member-State law is not exactly the same as that in Community law itself indicates that they constitute two separate legal systems. Moreover, some rules of Community law are not directly effective. They remain valid rules of Community law, but national courts are not required to apply them.[8] If such a rule conflicts with a rule of Member-State law, the European Court applies the former and the national courts apply the latter.[9] The fact that two inconsistent rules can both be valid indicates clearly that they must belong to separate legal systems.

The separateness of the two systems is equally evident if we look at the institutions. National legislatures can amend national law but

---

[8] A rule contained in a directive can, as was shown in Chapter 2, be directly effective in so far as it confers rights on individuals against the State, but not otherwise; consequently, it would prevail over an inconsistent Member-State rule in some cases but not in others.

[9] Where such a conflict exists, the Member States are under an obligation to amend their law to bring it into line with Community law; however, this can affect only the *future*: it cannot affect the *past*.

not Community law; the Community legislature can amend Community law but not national law. National courts can interpret Community law but their interpretations can be overruled by the European Court; the European Court cannot give rulings on national law. National courts can declare national law invalid but, according to the European Court,[10] they cannot declare Community law invalid; only the European Court can do this. These things all show that Community law is a separate legal system from the national law of the Member States.

Separate from International Law?

Almost everything so far in this chapter has been fairly uncontroversial; now, however, we must consider a question on which conflicting opinions have been expressed: is Community law no more than a sub-system of international law or is it entirely separate?[11] The argument in favour of the proposition that Community law is a sub-system of international law is that it was created by a set of treaties and owes its continuing existence and validity to them: without the constituent Treaties, there would be no Community legal system. The Community Treaties were clearly intended to be instruments taking effect under international law. The original EEC Treaty, for example, begins by referring to "His Majesty The King of the Belgians, the President of the Federal Republic of Germany, the President of the French Republic . . ." etc. and recites that these Heads of State have decided to create the European Economic Community. Their Plenipotentiaries are then said to have agreed on

---

[10] *Foto-Frost*, Case 314/85, [1987] ECR 4199 (discussed in Chapter 2).

[11] For the various points of view, see Francis G Jacobs, *European Community Law and Public International Law—Two Different Legal Orders?*, Institut für Internationales Recht an der Universität Kiel (Schücking Lecture, 1983); Henry G Schermers and Michel Waelbroeck, *Judicial Protection in the European Communities* (4th ed. 1987), pp. 89-95; Lysén, "The EC as a Self-Contained Regime, as an International Law 'Bubble'" (paper given at a conference in Uppsala in 1997, to be published in 1998 in the first issue of *Europarättslig Tidskrift*, a journal of the Faculty of Law of the University of Stockholm); Pescatore, "International Law and Community Law—A Comparative Analysis" (1970) 7 CMLRev. 167 (further references may be found at p. 168, n. 5, of this article); Plender, "The European Court as an International Tribunal" [1983] CLJ 279; Spiermann, "The Making of the Community Legal Order" (paper given at a conference in Uppsala in 1997, not yet published); Wyatt, "New Legal Order, or Old?" (1982) 7 ELRev. 147.

the text of the Treaty. A close examination of the text establishes that there is nothing in the form of the Treaty suggesting that it is anything other than a treaty under international law. In this respect, it is instructive to compare it with a constitution. That of the United States, for example, begins: "We the People of the United States . . . do ordain and establish this Constitution for the United States of America". The contrast could not be clearer: one is an international agreement between sovereign States; the other is (or purports to be) an act of the people: in form at least, it is not an agreement between the American States. It cannot be disputed, therefore, that the Community Treaties were intended to be, and are, instruments taking effect under international law. Since the Community legislature and the European Court derive their powers from the Treaties, and from nowhere else, it is easy to establish that the validity of the whole Community legal system depends on the Treaties. And the validity of the latter depends on international law.

The fact that one legal system is created by or under another legal system does not, however, mean that it cannot be a separate legal system. On numerous occasions in the past, the British Parliament has enacted legislation granting a constitution, complete with legislature, executive and judiciary, to some dependent territory or other. The validity of the legal system thus created depended on the British statute. But that did not mean that it was not a separate legal system which could pass laws for its territory that were different from the laws in force in the United Kingdom. There is, moreover, no reason why two States should not sign a treaty declaring that some territory subject to their jurisdiction is to become an independent State, or that they are to merge and form a new State.[12] The treaty might contain the constitution of the new State. If the new State came into being, its legal system would be separate from international law, even though it owed its birth to a treaty which in turn derived its validity from international law.[13] Consequently, the fact that the origin of Community law lies in international law does not necessarily means that it is part of international law.

[12] For examples of cases in which this has occurred, see Diarmuid Rossa Phelan, *Revolt or Revolution: The Constitutional Boundaries of the European Community* (Dublin, 1997), at p. 30.

[13] For examples of new States created by international treaties—the German Empire (created in 1870–1871), the abortive United Arab Republic (created by the merger of Egypt and Syria in 1958) and the Republic of Tanzania (created in 1964 by the merger of Tanganyika and Zanzibar)—see Diarmuid Rossa Phelan, n. 12 above, p. 30.

In the above examples, however, it is clear that the intention was to create a separate legal system. Even if this was not stated in so many words, it was implicit in the terms of the statute or treaty. Can the same be said of the Community Treaties? Since there is no express statement in any of them of an intention to create a separate legal system, we must consider whether this was implicit in their general scheme. The main features of this scheme are that three legal entities, the EEC, ECSC and Euratom, were established; each was endowed with legal personality[14] and the capacity to enter into treaties with non-member States and international organizations;[15] and each was given organs (institutions)—the Assembly (subsequently renamed the European Parliament), the Council, the Commission and the Court—through which it could operate.[16] The composition, powers and procedures of these organs were laid down in the Treaties.

These features establish that the Community is an international organization. However, many such organizations exist, and the legal systems under which they operate are generally regarded as part of international law. The United Nations is an example. Most international organizations have legal personality[17] and the capacity to enter into treaties.[18] They have organs—for example, the General Assembly and Security Council of the United Nations—and the treaty establishing the organization normally lays down the composition, powers and procedures of its organs. Organs of a parliamentary nature are unusual, but not unknown.[19] Nor is the European Court unique. Other international organizations also have courts: the

---

[14] For the EEC (now the EC) see Art. 210 {281} EC, a provision which has remained unchanged since the original EEC Treaty. It was probably intended to refer to personality in the legal systems of the Member States; but there is no doubt that the Communities also have legal personality under international law: see Lawrence Collins, *European Community Law in the United Kingdom* (4th ed. 1990), pp. 2–4.

[15] See Arts 113, 228 and 238 EEC as they existed in the original Treaty.

[16] See Art. 4 EEC in its original form. This was subsequently amended to add a fifth institution—the Court of Auditors.

[17] Although there is no express statement in the UN Charter, the International Court of Justice has held that the United Nations has legal personality in international law: see the *Reparations* case, [1949] ICJ Reports 174. See, further, Ian Brownlie, *Principles of Public International Law* (4th ed. 1990), pp. 680–683.

[18] Brownlie, n. 17 above, pp. 683–684.

[19] An example is the Consultative Assembly (subsequently renamed the "Parliamentary Assembly") of the Council of Europe. The members of this are not directly elected, but nor were the members of the European Parliament (Assembly) under the original EEC Treaty: see Art. 138 EEC in its original form. For further details on the Consultative Assembly, see A H Robertson, *European Institutions* (3rd ed. 1973), pp. 42–45.

United Nations has the International Court of Justice;[20] the Council
of Europe has the European Court of Human Rights (to resolve disputes concerning the European Convention on Human Rights);[21]
and the World Trade Organization has its dispute-settlement system.[22] Even if we were to examine the Community system in more
detail, we would see that many of the powers and procedures of the
Community institutions are replicated in other international organizations.[23] Thus the basic scheme of the Treaties is not such as to indicate an intention by the parties to establish a separate system of law.

The best way of arriving at a definitive answer to the question is
to determine what characteristics of the Community most clearly
differentiate it from other international organizations and to see
whether they imply that the parties to the Treaties intended to
create a separate legal system. In doing this, we must restrict ourselves
to the Treaties as they were originally adopted: subsequent developments—amendments to the Treaties by the Member States, or
judgments of the European Court effecting a *de facto* amendment—
cannot be taken into account. Operating on this basis, we can isolate
three features that seem to stand out: the fact that all Member States
are bound to accept the jurisdiction of the European Court to resolve
disputes relating to Community law; the fact that the European
Court has jurisdiction to give rulings on Community law on a reference from a national court; and the fact that the Community can
adopt legislation (by qualified majority voting) that is directly applicable in the Member States. We will consider each of these in turn.

As regards the first, Article 169 {226} EC provides for the
Commission to bring proceedings before the European Court
against a Member State which it considers to have failed to fulfil an

[20] Art. 92 of the United Nations Charter provides that the International Court of Justice
is the "principal judicial organ of the United Nations" and its Statute is annexed to the UN
Charter.

[21] Since Protocol 11 has come into force, the relevant provisions of the Convention are
Arts 19 *et seq*. The Convention was adopted under the aegis of the Council of Europe, an
organization which is completely separate from the European Community and has a wider
membership. For the origins of the Council of Europe, see A H Robertson, *European
Institutions* (3rd ed. 1973), Chapter 2.

[22] See the Understanding on Rules and Procedures Governing the Settlement of
Disputes, which constitutes Annex 2 to the WTO Agreement 1994. See, further,
Schoenbaum, "WTO Dispute Settlement: Praise and Suggestions for Reform" (1998) 47
ICLQ 647.

[23] (Weighted) majority voting, for example, is by no means unique to the Community:
see D W Bowett, *The Law of International Institutions* (4th ed. 1982), pp. 401–408.

obligation under the Treaty; Article 170 {227} gives a similar right to a Member State which considers that another Member State has failed to fulfil such an obligation; and Article 171 {228} EC makes clear that the European Court's judgment is binding.[24] Moreover, Article 219 {292} EC precludes the Member States from submitting any dispute concerning the interpretation or application of the Treaty to any method of settlement other than those provided in it. Taken together, these provisions lay down an impressive system of compulsory dispute resolution by the European Court. Though not unknown,[25] it is unusual for an international court to be in such a position. However, the possession of compulsory jurisdiction of this nature in no way calls into question the character of the European Court as an international court; on the contrary, most international lawyers would regard it as the ideal towards which all systems of international dispute resolution ought to be moving.

The jurisdiction given to the European Court by Article 177 {234} EC is also unusual for an international tribunal. Article 177 {234} provides that any court of a Member State may make a reference to the European Court for a ruling on the interpretation of a provision of Community law (or on the validity of Community legislation) if the national court considers that a decision on the question is necessary for it to give judgment. In general, national courts are not required to make such references; however, if there is no appeal (or other judicial remedy) from its judgment, such a court *must* make the reference. There is no express statement that the national court is bound by the ruling given by the European Court, but this is understood. Indeed, it is much insisted on by the European Court, so much so that if for some special reason the national court would not be bound by the ruling, the European Court will refuse to give it.[26]

---

[24] This procedure is discussed in greater detail in Chapter 6.

[25] Today, there is something similar under the WTO Agreement: see the Understanding on Rules and Procedures Governing the Settlement of Disputes, which constitutes Annex 2 to the WTO Agreement; however, the GATT, the precursor of the WTO Agreement which was in force when the original Community Treaties were drawn up, was significantly different. Since Protocol 11 to the European Convention on Human Rights has come into force, the European Court of Human Rights has been in a similar position; in one respect, indeed, it is in a stronger position than the European Court, since private individuals can bring proceedings against a Contracting State, something which cannot happen under the EC Treaty: see T C Hartley, *The Foundations of European Community Law* (4th ed. 1998), pp. 309–311.

[26] *Kleinwort Benson Ltd* v. *City of Glasgow District Council*, Case C-346/93, [1995] ECR I-615. This case was not under Art. 177 {234} but under an analogous provision on the

The importance of this procedure is that, to a large extent, it gives the European Court the last word on the meaning of any provision of Community law that is in dispute in proceedings before national courts. It thus enables the European Court to penetrate directly into the judicial process of the Member States and, to the extent that it is permitted to do so, to take control of that process. This is an unusual power for an international tribunal to have; nevertheless, it is not a power that would be *inappropriate* for such a tribunal to be given: as long ago as 1929, a man who was then a young lecturer at the London School of Economics suggested that international law might develop to the point where the highest national courts would make references to the Permanent Court of International Justice (the forerunner of the International Court of Justice) for rulings on international law.[27] Earlier still, in 1907, it was proposed that the International Prize Court (which in the end was never set up) should have the power to hear appeals from national courts.[28] Though neither of these proposals was ever put into effect, the fact that they were made shows that jurisdiction of this nature would be entirely proper for an international court to have. Indeed, one writer has said, "From the perspective of public international law, the novelty of the Community's system of references for preliminary ruling lies less in the conception than in the achievement".[29]

The third special feature of the Community is that a Community institution, the Council, was empowered by the EC Treaty to adopt, by qualified majority voting, legislative acts (regulations) which have "general application", are "binding in [their] entirety" and are "directly applicable in all Member States".[30] It was understood that regulations would not merely give rights to one Member State against another, but would also give rights to private individuals against Member States or against other individuals. Moreover, the statement in the Treaty that regulations are directly applicable might reasonably be interpreted (and has been interpreted) as meaning that

interpretation of the Brussels Convention on Jurisdiction and the Enforcement of Judgments in Civil and Commercial Matters. See also the first *EEA* case, Opinion 1/91, [1991] ECR 6079 (paras 61–65 of the Opinion).

[27] H Lauterpacht, "Decisions of Municipal Courts as a Source of International Law" (1929) 10 BYBIL 65 at 94–95.

[28] D W Bowett, *The Law of International Institutions* (4th ed. 1982), pp. 263–264.

[29] Plender, "The European Court as an International Tribunal" [1983] CLJ 279 at p. 284.

[30] Art. 189 {249} EC. This provision remains unchanged from the original EEC Treaty.

regulations can give individuals rights which will be recognized by national courts without the necessity for any measures of transposition or incorporation by the Member States.

In modern international law, it is not unusual for treaties to give rights to individuals—sometimes even against other individuals— which are to be enforced by national courts.[31] It is generally accepted, however, that they will not do this *directly* (i.e. without an act of transposition or incorporation by the State in question) unless the constitutional law of that State so provides. Though the precise relationship between international law and national law is complex,[32] it was said in Chapter 2 that some countries (referred to as "monist") accept that a provision of a treaty that is sufficiently clear and precise ("self-executing") can apply directly in the national legal system without the necessity for any measure of transposition or incorporation; however, in other countries (referred to as "dualist") a treaty provision can never apply as such in the national legal system: national legislation must always be passed to give legal effect to it, in which case it is applied by the national courts as a provision of national law.[33]

The United Kingdom belongs to the "dualist" camp; therefore, when the British Government signs a treaty of this nature, legislation must be adopted to give effect to it in the law of the United Kingdom.[34] When this is done, the British courts will uphold the

[31] One example is the 1924 Brussels Convention for the Unification of Certain Rules of Law relating to Bills of Lading, as amended by the Brussels Protocol of 1968 (establishing the Hague-Visby Rules), which gives rights to the parties to bills of lading for the carriage of goods by sea. The purpose of the Convention is that individuals (for example, cargo-owners) should have rights against other individuals (for example, ship-owners) which will be upheld by national courts, the only courts in which such disputes will normally arise.

[32] For a country-by-country study, see Francis G Jacobs and Shelly Roberts (eds.), *The Effect of Treaties in Domestic Law* (1987).

[33] There are actually a number of different techniques which can be used: one is for the legislation simply to state that the provisions of the treaty (usually set out in a schedule) are to have legal effect; a second is for the words of the treaty to be reproduced in the legislation; a third is for the drafters of the legislation to examine national law to see in what ways it falls short of the requirements of the treaty and to amend it only in those respects. This choice of techniques is, as we saw in Chapter 4, of relevance to the transposition of EC directives. It will be remembered that the second technique is sometimes called "copy-out" and the third the "elaborative approach". It makes a significant difference which method is adopted: the first is more likely to result in individual provisions being interpreted in the context of the whole instrument.

[34] Thus, for example, the Carriage of Goods by Sea Act 1971 gives effect to the 1924 Brussels Convention, as amended by the 1968 Brussels Protocol. This provides, in s. 1(2), that the Hague-Visby Rules, which are set out in a Schedule to the Act, have the force of law in the United Kingdom.

rights in the treaty, not because the treaty is valid under international law, but because the British legislation so requires. If there is no statute, a treaty provision will not be applied by a British court, even if it is valid and binding under international law.[35]

The innovation introduced by the Community Treaties is, therefore, that, while self-executing provisions of ordinary international treaties have direct effect in the courts of the contracting States only if their constitutions so provide, EC regulations have such effect irrespective of the constitutional law of the country concerned (i.e. whether monist or dualist). In the case of a dualist country such as the United Kingdom, the difference is that a provision in an ordinary international treaty will be applied by British courts only if British legislation so provides; directly effective Community law,[36] on the other hand, will be applied even if there is no British legislation specifically so providing. This is an important difference; however, Community law as a whole applies in the United Kingdom only because a British statute, the European Communities Act 1972, so provides.[37] As far as British courts are concerned, therefore, the difference is that, in the case of Community law, a statute has provided in advance for the application of directly effective provisions (including those to be adopted subsequently), while, in the case of ordinary treaties, separate legislation is passed in each case. Though this difference is important both conceptually and practically, it can hardly be taken as a ground for concluding that the parties to the Community Treaties intended to create a separate legal system. In the case of monist countries, the direct applicability of Community law is not very different from the direct applicability of international treaties; in the case of dualist countries, it simply means that, in order to join the Community, they must either amend their constitutions, or adopt a statute along the lines of the European Communities Act 1972.

One can conclude, therefore, that, while the Community Treaties contained novel features, which, especially in combination, show an impressive advance on what had previously been achieved, there is no justification for believing that the parties intended to do more

---

[35] *Cheney* v. *Conn* [1968] 1 WLR 242; *Mortensen* v. *Peters* (1906) 14 SLT 227.

[36] As has already been pointed out, the EC Treaty provides for direct effect (direct application) only in the case of regulations; the European Court, however, has ruled that it also applies to Treaty provisions (*Van Gend en Loos* case, Case 26/62, [1963] ECR 1, discussed in Chapter 2) and to other instruments.

[37] See s. 2(1). See, further, the discussion on the British Parliament in Chapter 9.

than create a sub-system of international law. Indeed, many international lawyers at the time regarded the founding of the Community as a step forward for international law, a new phase in which it could realize its full potential: they took it for granted that Community law was part of international law.[38]

The European Court, however, has taken a different view. Its first pronouncement on the subject was in 1963 in the *Van Gend en Loos* case,[39] in which it said:

> . . . *the Community constitutes a new legal order of international law*[40] for the benefit of which the states have limited their sovereign[41] rights, albeit within limited fields, and the subjects of which comprise not only Member States but also their nationals.

This statement, though unclear, could suggest that the Court favoured the theory that Community law is a sub-system of international law. If this was the European Court's opinion, however, it appeared to change it in the following year. This was in *Costa v. ENEL*,[42] in which it said:

> *By contrast with ordinary international treaties, the EEC Treaty has created its own legal system* which,[43] on the entry into force of the Treaty, became an integral part of the legal system of the Member States and which their courts are bound to apply.[44]

Although not wholly unambiguous, this formulation points towards the view that Community law is a separate legal system; it has certainly been interpreted in this way.[45]

---

[38] See, for example, De Valk, *La signification de l'intégration Européenne pour le développement du droit international moderne* (1962), who wrote (at p. 101), "[L]e droit international moderne s'est réalisé dans le cadre de l'intégration européenne" (quoted in Spiermann, "The Making of the Community Legal Order" (paper given at a conference in Uppsala in 1997, not yet published)).

[39] Case 26/62 [1963] ECR 1 at 12.

[40] Italics added.

[41] The Court appears to be using the word "sovereign" in this passage in the more political sense (freedom of action) discussed at the beginning of this chapter.

[42] Case 6/64, [1964] ECR 585 at 593.

[43] Italics added.

[44] The paragraph immediately following this quotation is set out at the head of this chapter.

[45] See, for example, the judgment of the *Bundesverfassungsgericht* (German Constitutional Court) in the *Internationale Handelsgesellschaft* case, 29 May 1974, [1974] 2 CMLR 540 (para. [19]); and that of the *Corte Costituzionale* (Italian Constitutional Court) in the *Frontini* case, 27 December 1973, [1973] CMLR 372 (para. [12]). See also Pescatore, "International Law and Community Law—A Comparative Analysis" (1970) 7 CMLRev. 167, an article of

Why did the European Court adopt this theory? Since it was not obliged by the facts to do so, it must have been a conscious *choice* by the Court: it chose the "separate-system" theory because it thought that this suited its purposes. Three reasons may be suggested: first, the Court probably regarded international law as a weak and ineffective system, and wanted to distance Community law from it so that it would be possible to develop doctrines, such as direct effect and supremacy, that would make Community law more effective than international law had ever been;[46] secondly, it wanted to avoid having to apply rules of international law in proceedings before it; thirdly, it thought that the methods of "interpretation" criticized in Chapters 2 and 3 could be more easily put into practice if Community law were not regarded as part of international law.[47]

Shortly after its judgment in *Costa* v. *ENEL*, the European Court decided *Commission* v. *Luxembourg and Belgium*,[48] in which two Member States sought to excuse their violation of the Treaty by arguing that the Council had itself failed to carry out its obligations, and that the Community was therefore responsible for the continuance of their infringements (*tu quoque* principle). The European Court dealt with this argument as follows:

> In [Luxembourg and Belgium's] view, since international law allows a party, injured by the failure of another party to perform its obligations, to withhold performance of its own, the Commission has lost the right to plead infringement of the Treaty. However, this relationship between the obligations of parties cannot be recognized under Community law.
>
> In fact the Treaty is not limited to creating reciprocal obligations between the different natural and legal persons to whom it is applicable, but *establishes a new legal order*[49] which governs the powers, rights

---

particular significance since Judge Pescatore was a member of the European Court at the time when the article was published.

[46] It should be remembered that it was in *Van Gend en Loos* and *Costa* v. *ENEL* that the European Court first laid down the doctrines of the direct effect of Treaty provisions and of the supremacy of Community law.

[47] See Pescatore, "International Law and Community Law—A Comparative Analysis" (1970) 7 CMLRev. 167, at 172–174.

[48] Cases 90, 91/63, [1964] ECR 631.

[49] Italics added.

and obligations of the said persons, as well as the necessary procedures for taking cognizance of and penalizing any breach of it.

This is an illustration of the second reason mentioned above.[50]

The consequences of the new theory are more clearly apparent in a case decided much later. This was *Germany* v. *Council* (the *"Banana"* case),[51] in which the Court held that a Community regulation cannot be declared invalid simply because it is contrary to an international treaty (*in casu*, the GATT) which is binding on the Community: the Treaty must be *directly effective* in Community law before the Court will take account of it. Since the GATT was not, in the Court's view, directly effective, the regulation was valid.[52] Now, this is an approach that would be perfectly normal for the court of a *State* to take: even a monist country would do this. However, the Community is not a State. If its legal system were part of international law, it would have been impossible to conclude that the Community regulation was valid despite being contrary to a treaty binding on both the Community and its Member States: international law would not permit such a result. So, although the Court did not repeat its theory that Community law is separate from international law, its conclusion is sustainable only on the basis of that theory.

Conclusions

We have seen that the European Court has chosen to regard Community law as a separate system, separate both from the national law of the Member States and from international law. The former was perfectly correct, but there was no legal justification for the latter. It might of course be argued that, though not based on legal

[50] It is, however, possible that the Court could have reached the same result without jettisoning international law, since under international law the *tu quoque* principle does not apply where it has been expressly or impliedly excluded by treaty. It could be argued that this was done (by implication) by the EC Treaty, since the Treaty provides adequate judicial remedies by which Luxembourg and Belgium could have forced the Council to carry out its obligations: see Wyatt, "New Legal Order, or Old?" (1982) 7 ELRev. 147 at p. 160.

[51] Case C-280/93, [1994] ECR 4973.

[52] Paras 103–112 of the judgment. There are exceptions in two special cases: the first is where the Community act was intended to implement an obligation entered into within the framework of GATT (*Nakajima* v. *Council*, Case C-69/89, [1991] ECR I-2069); the second is where the Community act expressly refers to a specific provision of GATT (*Fediol* v. *Commission*, Case 70/87, [1989] ECR 1781).

principle, the Court's declaration that Community law is separate from international law itself *made it* separate: in other words, it became separate because the Court declared it separate. It might further be argued that, even if there were no valid grounds for considering it separate in the beginning, subsequent developments—including judgments of the Court itself—changed Community law to such an extent that it was no longer reasonable to regard it as a mere sub-system of international law. These views are widely held, and may be correct. However, it is not necessary to reach a final conclusion on the matter: for the remainder of this book, we will *assume* that Community law is separate from international law, and consider the question of sovereignty on this basis.[53] If correct, this means that the Community Treaties are part of *both* international law *and* the Community legal system; Community legislation and the legal principles created by the European Court, on the other hand, are part of the Community legal system alone.[54]

[53] If Community law is separate from international law, it might be asked whether this means that the Community is not an international organization. If it is not, what is it? Since it is not a State, the only possibilities would appear to be either that it is a "State in the process of becoming" (an embryonic State) or that it is a *sui generis* entity which is neither a State nor an international organization of the traditional kind. The first alternative is unacceptable since it assumes something that may never come about. The *Bundesverfassungsgericht* (German Constitutional Court) has opted for the second, and has even coined a new German word, "*Staatenverbund*", to describe the Community: see the German *Maastricht* case, *Brunner v. European Union Treaty, Bundesverfassungsgericht*, decision of 12 October 1993, [1994] 1 CMLR 57 at para. [33], where "*Staatenverbund*" is translated, not entirely happily, as "federation of States"; see, further, the discussion of the German *Maastricht* case in Chapter 8. The Danish Supreme Court, on the other hand, seems to regard the Community as an international organization: see the Danish *Maastricht* case, Danish Supreme Court, judgment of 6 April 1998, Case I 361/1997, *Carlsen v. Rasmussen* (not yet reported: English text available from the Danish Foreign Ministry), also discussed in Chapter 8. The courts in most of the other Member States would probably take the same view as the Danish Supreme Court (for the French *Conseil Constitutionnel*, see Boyron, "The *Conseil Constitutionnel* and the European Union" [1993] PL 30 at 34), though some might follow the *Bundesverfassungsgericht*. The European Court has expressed no opinion on the issue. Perhaps the best solution is to call it an international organization of a special kind. In the future, it is likely that other "enhanced" international organizations will come into existence and it would be useful if they could draw on the conceptual framework established to explain the special nature of the Community: undue emphasis on the uniqueness of the Community would make this more difficult. For this reason, it would be wrong to ignore what the Community has in common with other international organizations (though it would be equally wrong to minimize the differences).

[54] There has been a suggestion in some quarters that the Treaties have ceased to be instruments of international law, a view which draws support from the European Court's statement that they constitute the "constitutional charter" of the Community: *Parti Ecologiste "Les Verts"* v. *European Parliament*, Case 294/83, [1986] ECR 1339 (para. 23 of the

IS COMMUNITY LAW AN INDEPENDENT LEGAL SYSTEM?

Deciding that Community law is a separate system is not the end of the matter. We still have one further question to ask: does Community law owe its existence and validity to some other system of law or is it entirely self-sustaining, owing nothing to any other system? This is what is meant by "independent" in the heading to this section.

As was pointed out above, the origin of Community law is to be found in the Treaties; its coming into existence, therefore, depended on international law. In another sense, it also depended on the national law of the Member States: Community law could not function in the way it does unless it was recognized and applied by the courts of the Member States. As explained previously, when a new Member State joins the Community it has to take the necessary steps to give effect to Community law within its territory. Britain did this by passing the European Communities Act 1972; some other countries adopted a constitutional amendment. Consequently, Community law is recognized as valid by the national legal systems, and is applied by the courts of the Member States, only because the national legal systems *say* that it is to have that effect. In this respect, Community law is different from the national law of most States. British law, for example, is not valid in Britain because international law or some foreign legal system says so: its validity is not dependent on any other legal system.

However, even if a legal system was created by another legal system, it does not follow that its *continuing* existence and validity depend on that other legal system. The Canadian legal system is an example. At one time, Canada was a British dependency; as a result, the British Parliament had the power to legislate for Canada. In 1867,

judgment). The fact that the Treaties have a constitutional character does not, however, mean that they cannot also be treaties under international law. In a later decision, the first *EEA* case, Opinion 1/91, [1991] ECR I-6079, the European Court again referred to the EC Treaty as the constitutional charter of the Community, but added the phrase "albeit concluded in the form of an international agreement" (para. 21 of the judgment). For further discussion of this theory and of the ambiguity of the word "constitution", see below, Chapter 9, pp. 180–181. In any event, the national courts and governments still regard the treaties as international agreements: whenever they are amended, a process that occurs frequently, the amendments take the form of new treaties—for example, the Treaty of Amsterdam.

it passed a statute, the British North America Act (subsequently amended on various occasions), which gave Canada a constitution. Thus the Canadian legislature, executive and judiciary owed their existence to a British statute. The Canadian legal system was separate from the British legal system—Canadian laws did not have to be the same as British laws—but it was not *independent* in the sense explained above. Not only was it brought into being by the British legal system, but its continuing existence was dependent on that legal system. At any time, the British Parliament could have stepped in and altered it, or even abolished it.[55]

This state of affairs continued for many years, during which time Canada gained *de facto* independence.[56] Its constitution, however, continued to be that contained in the British North America Acts. It could be amended by the British Parliament, though there was an understanding that this would be done only at the request of Canada.[57] Canada finally decided that it wanted to "patriate" its constitution.[58] So the British Parliament passed a new statute, the Canada Act 1982, which contained the Canadian Constitution in a schedule. The preamble to the Act recited that Canada had requested and consented to the enactment of the Act; section 1 said that the Constitution had the force of law in Canada; and section 2 said that no future British statute would apply in Canada.

It might be thought that the Canada Act, after giving legal validity to the new Constitution, had then severed the umbilical cord, so that the continuing validity of the Canadian legal system no longer depended on the British legal system. That was no doubt the intention. However, it will be remembered that the doctrine of the sovereignty of Parliament states that Parliament can never limit its own powers; consequently, it could be argued that the British Parliament can still legislate for Canada and that it could amend, or even repeal, the Canadian Constitution. If correct, this would mean that the Canadian legal system remained dependent on the British legal system. *Is* this correct? As far as the British legal system is concerned, it

---

[55] This is still the position, for example, with regard to the Northern Ireland legal system.

[56] This is conventionally regarded as having taken place when the Statute of Westminster 1931 came into force.

[57] The Statute of Westminster stated that thenceforth the United Kingdom Parliament would legislate for the Dominions (as they were then called) only at their request; however, under the doctrine of the sovereignty of Parliament, this limitation on the powers of the British Parliament was not binding.

[58] Not "repatriate", because it had always been foreign.

may be; but as far as the Canadian legal system is concerned, it almost certainly is not. If Britain tried to legislate for Canada in future, the Canadian courts would almost certainly rule that such legislation was invalid.[59] They would rule that the Canadian legal system had become independent of the British legal system. Since there would then be no way of enforcing the British legislation in Canada, it would remain a dead letter.

Is the same true of the Community legal system? Though it was created by international law and the legal systems of the Member States, has it subsequently gained independence? This question is best examined by considering situations in which the issue could arise.

Amending the Treaties: Procedure

The Community Treaties themselves contain rules for their amendment. Today, these are contained in Article N {48} of the Treaty on European Union. Under this provision, the Council must deliver an opinion (after consulting the European Parliament and, where appropriate, the Commission) in favour of calling a conference of the representatives of the governments of the Member States. The conference is then convened and must determine unanimously what amendments are to be made. Though not specified by Article N {48}, the amendments take the form of a new Treaty amending the existing Treaties. This new Treaty must then be ratified by all the Member States "in accordance with their respective constitutional requirements"—in other words, it must be constitutionally valid in the legal systems of each of the Member States.[60] This constitutes express recognition by the Community legal system itself that it is dependent on the legal systems of the Member States: if an amendment is not valid law under the legal system of even one Member State, it will not be valid in the Community legal system.[61]

---

[59] Since there is no longer an appeal from the highest court in Canada to the Privy Council in London, the decision of the Canadian courts would be final as far as Canada was concerned.

[60] Art. N {48}, third para., TEU.

[61] De Witte, "Rules of Change in International Law: How Special is the European Community?" (1994) 25 Neth.Yb.Int.L 299 at pp. 331–332, points out that the procedure in Art. N {48} is "more respectful of national sovereignty than the amendment procedures of many other multilateral treaties". Thus, under Art. 108 of the United Nations Charter, amendments to the Charter enter into force (for all members) if adopted by a two-thirds

Would it be *sufficient* if the amendment was valid under international law and under the legal systems of the Member States?[62] Let us assume that all the Member States agree to the amending treaty and that it is ratified by all of them according to their respective constitutional requirements. If this were done, would the amendment be valid even if the additional requirements of Community law—consulting the European Parliament, for example—were omitted?[63] The European Court has indicated its view in a *dictum* in *Defrenne* v. *Sabena*,[64] in which it said:[65]

> In fact, apart from any specific provisions, the Treaty can only be modified by means of the amendment procedure carried out in accordance with Article 236 [now Article N {48} TEU].

It is not clear from this statement whether the amendment would be invalid if the correct procedure was not followed. Even if this is what the Court meant,[66] however, the fact of the matter is that on two occasions in the past the ECSC Treaty *has* been amended without going through the procedure laid down in it.[67] The first was the Treaty of 27 October 1956, which brought about certain amendments consequent on the return of the Saar to Germany, and the second was the Convention on Certain Institutions Common to

majority in the General Assembly and ratified by two-thirds of the members, including the permanent members of the Security Council (*ibid.*, p. 308).

[62] For the view that it would, see Deliège-Sequaris, "Révision des traités européens en dehors des procédures prévues" [1980] CDE 539, a closely reasoned analysis which takes the views of a wide range of writers into account. For a study which contrasts the position under the various legal systems involved, see Diarmuid Rossa Phelan, *Revolt or Revolution: The Constitutional Boundaries of the European Community* (Dublin, 1997), pp. 148–154.

[63] It seems generally accepted that, under international law, the additional requirements in Art. N {48} do not have to be followed: even if an international treaty lays down special procedures for its amendment, the treaty may be validly amended without going through those procedures—provided all the States concerned agree: see Deliège-Sequaris, n. 62 above; Weiler and Haltern, "Response: The Autonomy of the Community Legal Order—Through the Looking Glass" (1996) 37 Harv.Int.LJ 411, at p. 418, n. 26 (and authorities cited therein); Weiler and Haltern, "Constitutional or International? The Foundations of the Community Legal Order and the Question of Judicial *Kompetenz-Kompetenz*" in Anne-Marie Slaughter, Alec Stone Sweet and Joseph H H Weiler, *The European Courts and National Courts—Doctrine and Jurisprudence* (1998) 331, at p. 337, n. 27 (a revised version of the previous article); Cruz Vilaça and Piçarra, "Y a-t-il des limites matérielles à la révision des traités instituant les Communautés européennes?" [1993] CDE 3, at p. 14.

[64] Case 43/75, [1976] ECR 455.

[65] Para. 58 of the judgment.

[66] See Cruz Vilaça and Piçarra, n. 63 above, at p. 16.

[67] At the time, this procedure was contained in Art. 96 ECSC. It was slightly different from that now contained in Article N {48} TEU.

the European Communities, which was signed at the same time as the EEC and Euratom Treaties.[68] No one has ever questioned the validity of these amendments.

Of course, the statement in *Defrenne* v. *Sabena* was made almost twenty years later and it could be argued that the position had changed. However, if the treaty making the amendments was valid under international law and under the law of each of the Member States, it is hard to see how the European Court could deny its validity. If it was valid under the constitutional law of the Member States, it would be accepted as valid by the courts of the Member States. There is little that the European Court could do to persuade them otherwise: to do so, it would have to induce them to treat their own national constitutions as subordinate to Community law. As we shall see in the next chapter, few, if any, of them would do this. Consequently, if the European Court refused to treat the amendment as valid, it would open up a gap between Community law as applied by the Community institutions and Community law as applied in the Member States. This would undermine the whole system. If the Member States were unanimous in wanting the amendment, there would be little chance of persuading them to reverse it: this could be done only by a new treaty, to which all of them would have to agree.

A second obstacle of a more technical nature is that, although the European Court has power to rule on the validity of Community legislation and can annul it on various grounds, including an infringement of an essential procedural requirement,[69] it has no such power with regard to a Treaty provision.[70] Thus, though the European

---

[68] See Pierre Pescatore, *L'ordre juridique des Communautés européennes* (1975), pp. 62–63.

[69] Art. 173 {230} EC. See also sub-para. (b) of the first paragraph of Art. 177 {234} EC.

[70] It has no such power under Art. 173 {230} EC: *Roujansky* v. *Council*, Case T-584/93, [1994] ECR II-585 (para. 15 of the judgment) (Court of First Instance); *LAISA* v. *Council*, Cases 31 and 35/86, [1988] ECR 2285 (para. 18 of the judgment). It might have an implied power to determine whether a Treaty provision exists and, if it does not, to declare it "non-existent", but it would be hard to justify holding an amendment non-existent merely because the European Parliament had not been consulted: although failure to consult the European Parliament can make legislation invalid (see, for example, *Roquette* v. *Council*, Case 138/79, [1980] ECR 3333), it has never been suggested that it renders it non-existent; even serious defects of procedure have been held not to have this effect: see, for example, *Commission* v. *BASF*, Case C-137/92P, [1994] ECR I-2555 (appeal from Cases T-79/81 (etc.), [1992] ECR II-315). For a fuller discussion, see T C Hartley, *The Foundations of European Community Law* (4th ed. 1998), pp. 341–344. The suggestion that the Court could declare a Treaty amendment "inapplicable" in proceedings under Arts 169–171 {226–228} EC (Cruz Vilaça and Piçarra, "Y a-t-il des limites matérielles à la révision des traités instituant les Communautés européennes?" [1993] CDE 3, at p. 15) has no basis in the Treaties. It

Court might try to stop the Member States from going ahead with the amendment, there is little that it could do once it was in force: it would have to accept it.[71] It would probably say that, though the procedure under which it was adopted was defective, it was nevertheless valid.

Amending the Treaties: Substance

Apart from the question of form (procedure), the Treaties contain no limits on their amendment: no provision in them is unamendable nor is there any restriction on the new provisions that may be included. Not only is there no express limit or restriction, but there is no provision that could even remotely be regarded as imposing an implied restriction; nor is there any reason to suppose that the Member States *intended* that there should be any restrictions. In spite of this, the European Court has nevertheless hinted that it may impose restrictions of its own.

This occurred in the first *EEA* case,[72] a case under Article 228(1) EEC as it existed at the time (see now Article 228(6) {300(6)} EC). This provision states that where an agreement is envisaged between the Community and one or more non-member States (or an international organization), the European Court may be asked to give an

is of course true that, despite the lack of any legal power to do so, the Court might nevertheless declare an amendment invalid or "inapplicable". Such a ruling would not, however, be accepted in at least some of the Member States: see below at pp. 154–162.

[71] If the Parliament brought proceedings against the Council before the amendment was adopted, it might be able to obtain a ruling from the Court under Art. 175 {232} EC that the failure of the Council to consult it was contrary to the Treaty. Such a ruling would not, however, prevent the Member States from agreeing to the amendment. The Commission might be able to obtain a ruling against the Member States under Arts 169–171 {226–228} EC that, by going ahead with the revision of the Treaty without consulting the Parliament, they had failed to fulfil an obligation under Article N {48} TEU. The proceedings would have to be brought against all the Member States, a bizarre prospect. If the ruling was given before ratification of the amendment had taken place, it might induce some of the national parliaments to reject the amendment. If it did not, or if the amendment was already ratified, the judgment would have the effect of imposing an obligation on the Member States to repeal it—repeal could constitute a "necessary measure" in terms of Art. 171 {228}—and, if they failed to do so, further proceedings could be brought to impose fines on them. If all the Member States were fined, however, there would be no way of collecting the fines: the Commission would be politically unable to oppose the combined will of the Member States. If the Court gave such a judgment, therefore, it would remain a dead letter; consequently, the Court would probably not give it.

[72] Opinion 1/91, [1991] ECR I-6079.

opinion on whether the agreement is compatible with the EC Treaty. Article 228 then says that if the Court's opinion is adverse, the agreement may enter into force only if there is an amendment to the EC Treaty. The Commission had asked the Court to give an opinion on whether the proposed EEA Agreement was compatible with the EC Treaty, and the Court held that it was not, partly because the European Court regarded the new court to be set up under the Agreement as a threat to its own position. The Commission also asked whether an amendment to the relevant provision of the EC Treaty (Article 238 {310}) would solve the problem, to which the Court replied that such an amendment "could not cure the incompatibility with Community law of the system of courts to be set up by the agreement".[73] This could be read simply as a statement that the European Court's objections to the new court would still exist; on the other hand, however, it could be read as an indication that an amendment to the EC Treaty expressly permitting the Community to enter into the EEA Agreement would be regarded as invalid by the Court, despite the express words of Article 228 to the contrary. The Member States never put this to the test: they amended the proposed Agreement to meet the European Court's objections.[74]

It need hardly be said that any ruling by the European Court that certain provisions of the Treaties cannot be amended would itself be a gross violation of the Treaties. However, we saw in Chapter 2 that the Court is capable of giving judgments contrary to both the clear words of the Treaties and the evident intention of their authors. Nevertheless, some authors read the judgment in the first *EEA* case as implicitly suggesting that some Treaty provisions cannot be amended.[75] It is doubtful whether the Court would be foolhardy

---

[73] Para. 72 of the opinion.

[74] For the background to the case, see Hartley, "The European Court and the EEA" (1992) 41 ICLQ 841.

[75] Cruz Vilaça and Piçarra, "Y a-t-il des limites matérielles à la révision des traités instituant les Communautés européennes?" [1993] CDE 3, at pp. 25–26. For other authors supporting this view, see *ibid.*, n. 66; for authors rejecting it, see nn. 65, 76, 77 and 78. Another supporter of the idea that there are substantive limits to the amendment of the Treaties is Bieber, "Les limites matérielles et formelles à la révision des traités établissant la Communauté européenne" [1993] RMC 343. To some extent, these authors base their contentions on the constitutions of the Member States; to this extent, of course, their arguments are not relevant to the question we are discussing since an amendment that was contrary to the constitution of a Member State could not be validly ratified under the law of that State. See, further, Diarmuid Rossa Phelan, *Revolt or Revolution: The Constitutional Boundaries of the European Community* (Dublin, 1997), pp. 154–158.

enough to try to prevent the Member States from adopting an amendment to which they were all agreed. If it was, the comments made in the previous section would apply: if the Member States were sufficiently determined, there is no way in which the Court could stop them doing what they wanted. It would have to accept it.

One can conclude, therefore, that the Community legal system is not independent of international law and Member-State law in so far as amendments to the Treaties are concerned.

Winding Up the Community

Can the Member States abolish the Community? It seems clear that they can, if they are unanimous. A new treaty would be needed, which would have to be ratified in the form required by the constitutional law of each Member State. That is all that would be necessary. The Community could then be wound up: the Member States would cease to pay money to the Community; the officials and judges would cease to receive their salaries; ownership of the buildings housing the Community institutions would revert to the Member States. The Community judges would not like what was happening, but they would be powerless to prevent it: they would have been ousted from their buildings in Luxembourg; their officials would have left; their library would have been dispersed. They would have lost their powers and be private citizens again. The fact that Community law makes no provision for winding up the Community[76] is irrelevant: it would not matter if the winding up were contrary to Community law and invalid under it, since the Community legal system would, for all practical purposes, have ceased to exist. This position may be contrasted with that in Canada if the British Parliament tried to abolish Canada's statehood. In such a situation, the British legislation would simply be ignored in Canada. The reason is that Canada has its own territory, its own armed forces and its own means of collecting revenue. The Community has none of these things.

---

[76] The ECSC Treaty was concluded for a period of fifty years from its entry into force on 23 July 1952; the EC and Euratom Treaties were concluded for an indefinite period.

Conclusions

It will be seen from what has been said that, as long as they act together, the Member States can do what they like with regard to the Community legal system. They created it and they can change it, or abolish it: in the words of the *Bundesverfassungsgericht* (German Constitutional Court), the Member States are the "masters of the Treaties" ("*Herren der Verträge*").[77] It follows from this that the *continuing* validity of the Community legal system depends on other legal systems, those of the Member States and international law. Community law is not an independent legal system in the sense that Canadian law is an independent legal system. It may be separate from international law and the law of the Member States, but it is not *independent* from them.

---

[77] German *Maastricht* case, *Brunner* v. *European Union Treaty*, *Bundesverfassungsgericht* (German Constitutional Court), decision of 12 October 1993, [1994] 1 CMLR 57 (para. [55] of the judgment).

8

The Question of Sovereignty—II

[N]o power to extend its powers [*Kompetenz-Kompetenz*] is conferred on the European Union . . .

The *Bundesverfassungsgericht* (German Constitutional Court) in
the German *Maastricht* case.[1]

We saw in the last chapter that the Community legal system is separate from the legal systems of the Member States and (we assumed)
from international law; however, it is not independent: it owes its
creation and continuing validity to other systems of law. In continuing our examination of sovereignty, we must now shift the focus of
our discussion from the Community legal system to the European
Court, its main interpreter and staunchest defender.

THE EUROPEAN COURT

As might be expected, the European Court sees it as its mission to
protect Community law from encroachment by other legal systems[2]
and, where possible, to extend its dominion over them.[3] As shown
in Chapter 2, it uses its existing jurisdiction to grant itself further
jurisdiction and, in so far as it can, to cut down the jurisdiction of the

---

[1] *Brunner* v. *European Union Treaty*, *Bundesverfassungsgericht*, decision of 12 October 1993,
[1994] 1 CMLR 57 at para. [33] of the judgment.
[2] Its declaration that Community law is separate from international law (*Costa* v. *ENEL*,
Case 6/64, [1964] ECR 585) was presumably made with this objective in mind, as was its
ruling that Community legislation cannot be challenged on the basis of international treaties
which are not directly effective (*Germany* v. *Council* (*"Banana"* case), Case C-280/93, [1994]
ECR 4973).
[3] See, for example, the Court's rulings on the direct effect of Treaty provisions and of
directives, as well as its doctrine of supremacy (all discussed in Chapter 2).

national courts.[4] The question we must now ask ourselves is whether the European Court could use its powers to advance the position of Community law to such an extent that the sovereignty of the Member States was undermined or even extinguished.

In this respect, the European Court's most valuable power is that of giving rulings on a reference from a national court. In so far as the EC Treaty is concerned, this is based on Article 177 {234}, which states that the European Court has jurisdiction to give rulings on:

(a) the interpretation of this Treaty;
(b) the validity and interpretation of acts of the institutions of the Community and of the ECB . . .[5]

As mentioned previously, any court of a Member State may request such a ruling, but a court from which there is no appeal (or other judicial remedy) *must* request a ruling if it considers that a decision on the question is necessary to enable it to give judgment.

We said in the previous chapter that this power enables the European Court to penetrate directly into the judicial process of the Member States and, to the extent that it is permitted to do so, to take control of that process. Could this be carried to the point where the sovereignty of the Member States was undermined? Let us take the example of a Treaty amendment that was valid under international law and under the legal systems of the Member States. Let us assume that the European Court objects to the amendment: this might be on procedural grounds—for example, if the additional requirements of Community law have not been complied with—or on grounds of substance—for example, if the amendment provides for the establishment of a new court which threatens its position. In such a situation, could the European Court use its power under Article 177 {234} to declare the amendment invalid?

It was said previously that the European Court has no jurisdiction to declare Treaty provisions invalid. It will be seen from the extract from Article 177 {234} EC set out above that paragraph (a) only gives it jurisdiction to *interpret* the Treaty (amendments to the EC

---

[4] See, for example, the ruling that it, rather than the courts of the Member States, has power to determine the effect of Community law in the national legal systems (*Van Gend en Loos*, Case 26/62, [1963] ECR 1), and the ruling that only it, and not the courts of the Member States, has power to declare Community legislation invalid (*Foto-Frost*, Case 314/85, [1987] ECR 4199).

[5] "ECB" stands for "European Central Bank". There is also a third sub-paragraph, but this is of no importance.

Treaty would of course form part of that Treaty), while paragraph (b) only gives it jurisdiction to rule on the validity of *Community* acts. As we saw in Chapter 2, however, the European Court does not scruple to create new rules of law where this would serve its purposes. What would happen, therefore, if it proclaimed that a power to annul Treaty provisions was "inherent in the Treaty": could it then force national courts to reject a Treaty amendment even if that amendment was valid by the Member States' own law? It could be argued that, since Article 177 {234} undoubtedly gives jurisdiction to the European Court to interpret the Treaty, a ruling that jurisdiction to annul the Treaty was "inherent in the Treaty" would itself constitute an "interpretation" of the Treaty, and would therefore be binding on the courts of the Member States. Once this was accepted, there would seem to be no way in which the national courts could lawfully prevent the European Court from forcing them to accept its view: the European Court could declare that the amendment was invalid and the national courts would have to follow the ruling. Then, the Member States would no longer be masters of the Treaties: the European Court would be master of the Member States.

The national courts might respond to such a possibility by refusing to refer the question to the European Court. Such a refusal could be justified on the ground that an obligation to refer arises only if the national court is faced with a question of *interpreting* the Treaty; a question of interpretation, however, arises only if the Treaty is not clear, and since it is clear beyond doubt that the Treaty does not give the European Court jurisdiction to annul a Treaty provision, no question of interpretation arises; therefore, there is no obligation to refer the matter to the European Court.[6] This argument, which is usually called the *"acte clair"* doctrine,[7] has been accepted by the European Court[8]—though its acceptance was so hedged about with

---

[6] The third paragraph of Art. 177 {234} requires a national court against the decisions of which there is no judicial remedy to make a reference only if "such a question" is raised before it. The phrase "such a question" refers back to the first paragraph, which is the one (quoted above) giving the European Court jurisdiction to rule on "the interpretation of this Treaty". If no question of interpretation arises, therefore, there is no obligation to refer the matter to the European Court.

[7] The French term, *"acte clair"* means "clear provision" and indicates that a provision that is clear requires no interpretation.

[8] *CILFIT*, Case 283/81, [1982] ECR 3415.

qualifications that it has been doubted whether it really wanted to accept it at all.[9]

The European Court might try to defeat this strategy by tacking a ruling on the Treaty-amendment issue onto its answer to some other question referred to it by a national court. In such a case, however, the national court could argue that it was not bound by the ruling because the European Court has jurisdiction to give rulings only on questions referred to it: if the national court did not *refer* the question of Treaty amendments, any ruling on that question would be outside the jurisdiction of the European Court. This argument has already been used by the French *Conseil d'Etat*.[10]

Expedients of this kind, however, avoid the real issue, which is whether the European Court should be allowed to abuse its powers in this way. For an answer to this question, we must turn to Germany and Denmark.

THE THEORY OF *KOMPETENZ-KOMPETENZ*

The higher German courts, in particular the *Bundesverfassungsgericht* (German Constitutional Court), have a particularly strong tradition of basing their judgments on a thorough analysis of the legal principles at stake. It is hardly surprising, therefore, that they have been the first to deal squarely with the question we are considering. The way they have approached it is by asking whether the European Court has "*Kompetenz-Kompetenz*". In German, "*Kompetenz*" means "jurisdiction"[11]: in legal terminology, "jurisdiction" is the power to give a binding ruling on a question. If a judicial authority has jurisdiction to decide a given question, its ruling on that question has to be accepted by everyone else: no one can question it (unless an appeal lies to some higher authority). "*Kompetenz-Kompetenz*", therefore, means jurisdiction to give a binding ruling on the extent of one's own jurisdiction.

Most decision-makers have limited jurisdiction: they can give a binding ruling only on particular questions. A ruling outside their

---

[9] Rasmussen, "The European Court's *Acte Clair* Strategy in *CILFIT*" (1984) 9 ELRev. 242.

[10] *Maïseries de Beauce, Conseil d'Etat*, 26 July 1985, [1985] Recueil des Décisions du Conseil d'Etat 233; [1985] L'Actualité Juridique: Droit Administratif 615; [1986] Revue Trimestrielle de Droit Européen 158.

[11] From the French, "*compétence*" (jurisdiction).

jurisdiction is not, therefore, binding: individuals or courts do not have to accept it. An English lawyer would say that it was *ultra vires*. To give an illustration from the world of sport, a referee in a football match has jurisdiction to give rulings on whether a player has broken a rule of the game in the course of the match: his ruling must be accepted by all the players even if it is wrong. However, if the referee were to rule on whether a player owed another player a sum of money as a result of a business transaction, the ruling would be outside his jurisdiction, and would not be binding on the persons concerned.

The next question is who decides whether a decision on a particular question is within the jurisdiction of the decision-maker. Is this a matter which can be decided by the person to whom the decision was addressed? Or should it be decided by some other body, perhaps a court? Or should it be decided by the decision-maker himself? This depends (in the terminology we are using) on whether the decision-maker has *Kompetenz-Kompetenz*. If he has, he can first decide whether the question before him is within his jurisdiction; if he decides that it is, he can then proceed to decide it. Then, both the jurisdictional decision and the substantive decision will be binding on all concerned: no one can challenge the substantive decision on the ground that it is outside his jurisdiction (*ultra vires*), since his decision that it is within his jurisdiction is itself binding.[12] If, on the other hand, he not does have *Kompetenz-Kompetenz*, it will be open to an appropriate court—or perhaps even to the person to whom the decision is addressed—to decide whether the substantive ruling was within the jurisdiction of the decision-maker: if it was not, it will not be binding.

We can now reformulate the problem we are considering by asking whether the European Court has *Kompetenz-Kompetenz*. If it has, it will indeed be master of the national courts and, through them, master of the Member States themselves.

---

[12] A higher-level problem is who decides whether a decision-maker has *Kompetenz-Kompetenz*: if the decision-maker can decide *this* question too, he may be said to have *Kompetenz-Kompetenz-Kompetenz*. This is more easily understood if we adopt quasi-mathematical notation: if *Kompetenz* is called "K" and *Kompetenz-Kompetenz* is referred to as "K^2", *Kompetenz-Kompetenz-Kompetenz* would be "K^3". If the decision-maker has jurisdiction to decide whether he has "K^3", he could be said to have "K^4". It does not take much imagination to see that this is the beginning of an infinite series of concepts.

THE GERMAN *MAASTRICHT* DECISION

The German *Maastricht* case[13] was a decision of the *Bundesverfassungsgericht* (German Constitutional Court) in proceedings brought by a group of German citizens who claimed that it would be unconstitutional for Germany to ratify the Maastricht Agreement (Treaty on European Union). One of the arguments put forward was that the transfer of wide powers to the Community would be contrary to the principle of democracy, a principle enshrined in the German Constitution:[14] matters which previously would have been decided by the German Parliament, a body elected by the German voters, would pass outside the control of the German electorate.[15]

The *Bundesverfassungsgericht* rejected this argument (partly) on the ground that the powers given to the Community were limited to those specified in the Treaty, which had been approved by the German Parliament. The Community legal system was applicable in Germany, it said, only because the German laws ratifying the Community Treaties said that it was.[16] Any increase in the powers of the Community would require an amendment to the Treaties, which

---

[13] *Brunner* v. *European Union Treaty, Bundesverfassungsgericht*, decision of 12 October 1993, [1994] 1 CMLR 57; (1994) 33 ILM 388; 89 BVerfGE 155; 20 EuGRZ 429; [1993] NJW 3047. For a full discussion and analysis, see Everling, "The *Maastricht* Judgment of the German Federal Constitutional Court and its Significance for the Development of the European Union" (1994) 14 YEL 1; Foster, "The German Constitution and EC Membership" [1994] PL 392; Herdegen, "Maastricht and the German Constitutional Court: Constitutional Restraints for an 'Ever Closer Union'" (1994) 31 CMLRev. 233; Kokott, "Report on Germany" in Anne-Marie Slaughter, Alec Stone Sweet and Joseph H H Weiler, *The European Courts and National Courts—Doctrine and Jurisprudence* (1998), 77; MacCormick, "The *Maastricht-Urteil*: Sovereignty Now" (1995) 1 ELJ 259.

[14] The basic provision is Art. 20 of the *Grundgesetz* (German Constitution), which says that all State authority emanates from the people. The right to participate in elections to the German Federal Parliament is guaranteed by Art. 38. It should be noted that Art. 79(3) provides that certain basic principles of the Constitution, including the principle of democracy, are unalterable. It follows from this that if the *Bundesverfassungsgericht* had declared that the principle of democracy would be infringed by ratification of the Maastricht Agreement, it would not have been possible to circumvent the judgment by means of a constitutional amendment.

[15] The existence of the European Parliament is not generally regarded as sufficient to solve the problem. The theory prevalent in Germany is that democracy on a European level is not possible because there is no European nation: there is a French nation, a German nation, an Italian nation, etc., each with its own values, attitudes and culture, but no European nation. Democracy, according to this theory, requires that each nation should have its own representation.

[16] [1994] 1 CMLR 57, at para. [55].

would be subject to approval by the German Parliament.[17] The Community, it said, had no power to grant itself further powers: it had no *Kompetenz-Kompetenz*.[18] If it tried to assume further powers, anything done under those additional powers would be invalid in Germany: German public authorities would be constitutionally prohibited from giving effect to it. The *Bundesverfassungsgericht* said that it would itself determine whether any legal acts adopted by an institution of the Community went beyond the powers given to the Community.[19] This, in the view of the *Bundesverfassungsgericht*, provided sufficient guarantees that the Community would not take further powers for itself without the consent of the Member States and their parliaments; consequently, the democratic rights of German voters would not be infringed by ratification of the Maastricht Agreement. The Court thus rejected the claim that ratification was unconstitutional, but it did so on grounds that dismayed European federalists.

Three features of this judgment should be emphasized. First, the *Bundesverfassungsgericht* implicitly rejects the ruling of the European Court in the *Foto-Frost* case[20] that national courts have no power to declare Community legislation invalid.[21] This ruling might seem to be more concerned with restricting the jurisdiction of the national courts than increasing that of the European Court; nevertheless, it could be regarded as being outside the jurisdiction of the European

---

[17] *Ibid.*, para. [33].

[18] According to German ideas, a federation has *Kompetenz-Kompetenz*: it can determine the extent of its own powers without the consent of its component parts (in Germany, the *Länder*). According to the *Bundesverfassungsgericht*, however, the Community is not a federation (*Bundesstaat*), but a *Staatenverbund*, a word that cannot easily be translated into English, but which means something like "association of States", "confederation of States" or "union of States". The Community is not a State. Consequently, it has no power to determine the extent of its powers and to increase them without the consent of its component parts, the Member States. See Everling, n. 13 above, pp. 6–7.

[19] [1994] 1 CMLR 57, at para. [49].

[20] Case 314/85, [1987] ECR 4199 (discussed in Chapter 2).

[21] The *Bundesverfassungsgericht* might argue that it does not claim the right to declare Community acts invalid, but merely to hold them *inapplicable* in Germany. The difference between these two concepts is that the former purports to deal with the status of the act in the Community legal system, while the latter merely holds that it has no effect in the German legal system. However, since all directly effective Community acts are supposed to be applicable in the national legal systems, and since the ground on which the act would be declared inapplicable in Germany would be that it was beyond the powers of the Community, the practical effect of the two concepts would seem to be virtually identical; in any event, the European Court would almost certainly consider that the *Foto-Frost* case covers both.

Court, since the Treaty does not give it jurisdiction to determine the jurisdiction of national courts. It is probably for this reason that the *Bundesverfassungsgericht* considers that it is not bound by it.

Secondly, the *Bundesverfassungsgericht* said that neither the Community as a whole, nor any of its institutions, has *Kompetenz-Kompetenz*. Its ruling is not limited to the European Court, but applies to all the Community institutions. *Kompetenz-Kompetenz* can in fact apply to any governmental body. A legislative body, for example, might pass legislation giving itself power to pass further legislation: if it has *Kompetenz-Kompetenz*, it can do this; if it does not, it cannot. This is sometimes called legislative *Kompetenz-Kompetenz*, as distinct from judicial *Kompetenz-Kompetenz* (the concept we have been considering up to now). Legislative *Kompetenz-Kompetenz*, of course, poses just as great a threat to national sovereignty as judicial *Kompetenz-Kompetenz*; so the *Bundesverfassungsgericht* had to deal with it as well.

The logic of the *Bundesverfassungsgericht's* position demands that any ruling by the European Court increasing the power of another Community institution, or affirming an act of an institution which is beyond the powers of that institution, must also be invalid in Germany. It too could be reviewed by the *Bundesverfassungsgericht*. Such a ruling by the European Court would not necessarily be outside the jurisdiction of the European Court, since it would normally involve the interpretation of one of the Treaties; nevertheless, its effect would be to increase the powers of the Community as a whole. If the Community as a whole has no *Kompetenz-Kompetenz*, a ruling by one of its institutions that increases the powers of another institution must also be subject to review by the national courts.

Thirdly, there is a passage in the judgment of the *Bundesverfassungsgericht*[22] which seems to reproach the European Court for extending Community power too far in the past, especially by giving a wide interpretation to Article 235 {308} EC[23] and by relying on the doctrines of implied powers and *effet utile*. (The doctrine of implied powers is the theory that if the Treaty gives a Community institution a particular *task* or *activity*, it must be regarded as impliedly

---

[22] [1994] 1 CMLR 57, para. [99]. On the meaning of this passage, see Everling, n. 13 above, at p. 13.

[23] This is the provision, discussed in Chapter 5, which states that if, in the course of the operation of the common market, action by the Community is necessary to attain its objectives and the Treaty has *not* provided the necessary powers, the Council can take the appropriate measures anyway.

conferring the powers necessary to carry it out;[24] the doctrine of *effet utile* is the theory that the Treaties must be interpreted so as to enhance their practical effectiveness.) The *Bundesverfassungsgericht* said that it would have to be understood in future that there is a distinction between the exercise of powers conferred for limited purposes and the amendment of the Treaty: if the European Court fails to appreciate this, its rulings may be without effect in Germany.[25]

Interestingly, in the next case to come before it on Article 235 {308},[26] the European Court said:[27]

> That provision [Article 235 {308}], being an integral part of an institutional system based on the principle of conferred powers,[28] cannot serve as a basis for widening the scope of Community powers beyond the general framework created by the provisions of the Treaty as a whole and, in particular, by those that define the tasks and the activities of the Community. On any view, Article 235 cannot be used as a basis for the adoption of provisions whose effect would, in substance, be to amend the Treaty without following the procedure which it provides for that purpose.

Could this be regarded as the European Court's response to the *Bundesverfassungsgericht?* If so, it is interesting that, while it conceded the point regarding Treaty amendments, the European Court was not willing to give up the doctrine of implied powers.

THE DANISH *MAASTRICHT* DECISION

The Danish *Maastricht* decision[29] in many ways covers the same ground as the German one; however, the relative brevity of the

---

[24] See *Germany v. Commission*, Cases 281, 283–5, 287/85, [1987] ECR 3203. For a comment on this case, see Hartley, "The Commission as Legislator under the EC Treaty" (1988) 13 ELRev. 122.

[25] The European Court is not mentioned by name in this passage—the *Bundesverfassungsgericht* refers to "Community institutions and agencies"—but it is nevertheless clear what is meant.

[26] The *ECHR* case, Opinion 2/94, [1996] ECR I-1759. This judgment was given on 28 March 1996, some two and a half years after the judgment of the *Bundesverfassungsgericht* in the *Maastricht* case.

[27] Para. 30 of the Opinion.

[28] The principle of conferred powers is the principle that the Community has only those powers conferred on it. It is expressly laid down in the first paragraph of Art. 3b {5} EC, as amended by the Maastricht Agreement (Treaty on European Union).

[29] Danish Supreme Court, judgment of 6 April 1998, Case I 361/1997, *Carlsen v. Rasmussen* (not yet reported: English text available from the Danish Foreign Ministry).

Court's reasoning and the less abstract language in which it is expressed mean that the judgment is easier for foreign lawyers to understand. The case also began with a legal action by a group of citizens to challenge ratification of the Maastricht Agreement. The provision of the Danish Constitution permitting Denmark's membership of the Community is section 20, which states that powers may be delegated to an international authority "to an extent specified by statute", a requirement that precludes the delegation of unlimited or undefined powers. The appellants argued that the powers delegated to the Community under the Maastricht Agreement were too ill-defined to satisfy the requirements of section 20. In particular, they referred to the open-ended nature of the Council's legislative power under Article 235 {308} EC[30] and the law-making activities of the European Court.

The Danish Supreme Court rejected these arguments and held that Denmark could ratify the Maastricht Agreement. It began its reasoning by stating that section 20 does not permit an international organization (such as the Community) to be given power to adopt legal acts or to make decisions that are contrary to the provisions of the Danish Constitution.[31] Secondly, it made clear that an international organization cannot be permitted to determine for itself what its powers are: in German terminology, it cannot have *Kompetenz-Kompetenz.*[32]

Having specified the requirements of the Constitution, the Supreme Court next considered whether they had been met. It first noted that the EC Treaty is based on the principle of conferred powers, the principle that the Community possesses only those powers given to it by the Treaties.[33] It then turned its attention to Article 235 {308}. This provision was discussed in Chapter 5: it will be remembered that it states that if, in the course of the operation of the common market, action by the Community is necessary to attain its objectives and the Treaty has *not* provided the necessary powers, the Council can take the appropriate measures anyway. The Supreme Court gave a fairly restrictive interpretation to the provi-

---

[30] This will be explained shortly.

[31] Section 9.2 of the judgment.

[32] *Ibid.* It is not, however, necessary that the powers should be specified so precisely that there is no room left for discretion or interpretation.

[33] See Arts 3b {5} (first paragraph) and 4(1) {7(1)} EC.

sion,[34] partly on the basis of the passage from the European Court's judgment in the *ECHR* case quoted above.[35] It concluded that if Article 235 {308} was applied no more widely than this, the requirements of section 20 of the Danish Constitution would be satisfied. If an attempt were made to apply it on a wider basis, the Danish Government would be obliged to veto it.[36]

The Supreme Court next dealt with the argument that the European Court's methods of "interpreting" Community law are contrary to section 20 of the Constitution. It indicated that it was prepared to allow the European Court a great deal of latitude: it was in fact prepared to accept the European Court's law-making activities, provided these remained within the scope of the EC Treaty.[37] The Supreme Court recognized that the European Court had been given jurisdiction to rule on the validity of Community acts; as a consequence, it said, Danish courts cannot declare Community acts inapplicable in Denmark without first referring the question of their validity to the European Court. The European Court's ruling on such questions should, in general, be accepted by Danish courts. However, the Supreme Court held that the requirement of specificity in section 20 of the Danish Constitution meant that Danish courts cannot be deprived of their right to judge for themselves whether EC acts go beyond the powers conferred on the Community. Consequently, if the European Court held the act valid, the Danish courts could in exceptional situations nevertheless hold it inapplicable in Denmark. The same applies, said the Supreme Court, to legal principles derived from the case law of the European Court.[38]

On these grounds, the Supreme Court ruled that neither the open-ended nature of Article 234 {308} nor the law-making activities of the European Court rendered Danish ratification of the Maastricht Agreement unconstitutional.[39]

---

[34] It noted that Art. 235 {308} applies only "in the course of the operation of the common market". The precise meaning of this restriction has been subject to much speculation, but the Supreme Court seems to consider that it precludes the application of Art. 235 {308} with regard to economic and monetary union or the implementation of common policies and actions.

[35] Opinion 2/94, [1996] ECR I-1759 (para. 30 of the Opinion).

[36] Measures may be adopted under Art. 235 {308} only if the members of the Council are unanimous.

[37] See the last paragraph of section 9.5 of the judgment.

[38] Section 9.6 of the judgment.

[39] Section 9.7 of the judgment.

CONCLUSIONS

We began this chapter by considering whether the European Court could use its powers to advance the position of Community law to such an extent that the sovereignty of the Member States would be undermined. It is clear from the two cases we have been considering that, at least in Germany and Denmark, this is not possible. If the European Court tried to give itself, or another institution, powers that are not conferred by the Treaties, the resultant judgments and legal acts would be inapplicable in Germany and Denmark. For example, if the European Court sought to strike down a Treaty amendment that complied with the requirements of international law and the legal systems of the Member States, its judgment would almost certainly not be followed in Germany and Denmark. It is likely that the same would be true in most, if not all, of the other Member States.[40]

Would this be justified? It is suggested that it would, provided that such action was taken only in extreme cases. When they signed the Treaties, the national governments could hardly have intended to do anything that was contrary to the constitutions of their countries. They could not have intended to confer on the Community powers that the national constitutions would not allow the Community to exercise. Moreover, it was always clear that the powers conferred were intended to be limited: right from the beginning, Article 4 {7} EC stated that each institution of the Community had to act within the limits of the powers conferred on it by the Treaty.[41] Moreover, since the Maastricht Agreement has come into force, the first paragraph of Article 3b {5} EC has stated:

> The Community shall act within the limits of the powers conferred upon it by this Treaty and the objectives assigned to it therein.

[40] For the view that the French *Conseil Constitutionnel* considers that *Kompetenz-Kompetenz* lies with the Member States, see Plötner, "Report on France" in Anne-Marie Slaughter, Alec Stone Sweet and Joseph H H Weiler, *The European Courts and National Courts—Doctrine and Jurisprudence* (1998), 41 at 53 (for a similar statement by the French Minister for Justice, see Diarmuid Rossa Phelan, *Revolt or Revolution: The Constitutional Boundaries of the European Community* (Dublin, 1997), p. 217). For a similar view regarding the *Corte Costituzionale* (Italian Constitutional Court), see Cartabia, "The Italian Constitutional Court and the Relationship between the Italian Legal System and the European Union", in Slaughter, Sweet and Weiler, above, 133 at pp. 142–144 and Laderchi, "Report on Italy", *ibid.*, 147 at pp. 169–170.

[41] See also Art. 6, last paragraph, ECSC.

This eliminates the possibility of the Community's having legislative *Kompetenz-Kompetenz*.

Judicial *Kompetenz-Kompetenz* is more difficult because the European Court would maintain that it never gives itself new powers, but merely discovers that—contrary to what was previously thought—certain powers were inherent in the Treaty all along. In doing so, it would argue, it is simply carrying out its task of interpreting the Treaty. However, while the Member States clearly intended that the European Court would resolve doubts as to the meaning of the Treaty, they can hardly have intended that it should have the power to give itself, and the other institutions, powers that were never there in the first place. They cannot have intended that the European Court should have *Kompetenz-Kompetenz*, except in cases of genuine doubt.[42] Since it is clear that the German and Danish courts would refuse to follow judgments of the European Court only in cases of blatant abuse,[43] one can conclude that their approach is in line with what the authors of the Treaties must have intended.[44]

[42] There are many examples in other areas of law in which a decision-maker is given a margin of error within which his ruling is conclusive; if he goes beyond that margin of error, however, his decision will be struck down. One example is the way the European Court treats other institutions of the Community, especially the Commission. It often happens that the Treaty gives the Commission power to take action if, and only if, certain conditions are fulfilled. In such a case, the Commission must first decide whether the conditions are fulfilled; if they are, it must then decide whether it should exercise the power. The first decision is one of fact, or (more usually) mixed fact and assessment—for example, whether there is a threat to market stability; the second decision is discretionary. If the action is taken and the European Court is asked to review it, the first decision could be regarded as concerning the Commission's jurisdiction and this could be analysed in terms of *Kompetenz-Kompetenz*. At least in some cases, the approach of the European Court is to hold that it has power to review the first decision, but that it will set it aside only if the Commission is guilty of a manifest error or a misuse of power, or if it has clearly exceeded the limits of its power of evaluation. See, for example, *Racke*, Case 136/77, [1978] ECR 1245 (para. 4 of the judgment). This analogy is not entirely apposite because the judgments of the European Court involve decisions of law; nevertheless, an appropriate test might be whether the European Court has clearly exceeded the limits of its interpretative power, those limits being set by the national courts.

[43] This was clearly stated by the Danish Supreme Court in the last paragraph of section 9.6 of its judgment. It is implicit in the judgment of the *Bundesverfassungsgericht* in the *Maastricht* case and is explicit in earlier cases: see, for example, *Kloppenburg*, *Bundesverfassungsgericht*, decision of 8 April 1987, [1988] 3 CMLR 1; (1987) 75 BVerfGE 223.

[44] See Schilling, "The Autonomy of the Community Legal System: An Analysis of Possible Foundations" (1996) 37 Harv. Int. LJ 389; for the opposite view, see Weiler and Haltern, "Response: The Autonomy of the Community Legal Order—Through the Looking Glass", *ibid.* 411, especially at pp. 423 *et seq.* The earlier pages of Weiler and Haltern's article are marred by an unattractive form of sarcasm directed against Schilling, something the authors perhaps regard as a substitute for legal analysis. A version of the article purged of

There is of course the danger that if national courts decide these questions for themselves, they might reach conflicting conclusions. For this reason, it would be desirable if there was some way in which they could reach a joint decision; in the absence of any mechanism to achieve this, they should co-ordinate their approaches by taking into account the case law of courts in other Member States.[45]

this element appears in Anne-Marie Slaughter, Alec Stone Sweet and Joseph H H Weiler, *The European Courts and National Courts—Doctrine and Jurisprudence* (1998), 331.

[45] Weiler has put forward an interesting proposal to solve this problem. He suggests that a new court, modelled on the French *Conseil Constitutionnel*, should be established. It should consist of the presidents of each of the national constitutional courts (or their equivalents), presided over by the President of the European Court. It would have jurisdiction to determine, prior to enactment, whether Community acts are within Community jurisdiction. See Weiler and Haltern, n. 44 above, at pp. 346 (Harv. LJ) and 364 (book). For a more elaborate description of the proposal, see Weiler, Haltern and Mayer, "European Democracy and its Critique" [1995] *West European Politics* 4. Though valuable, Weiler's proposal is, however, too limited. Until the Community act has come into operation and it is apparent how it is to be applied, and in particular until it has been interpreted by the European Court, it will be impossible to tell whether it goes beyond the powers of the Community. Moreover, it would also be necessary to determine whether legal principles created by the European Court go too far. For these reasons, the proposed court should, like most constitutional courts, be able to determine the constitutionality of Community law *after* it has been adopted: it should hear appeals from the European Court and should not, therefore, contain a member of the European Court. In order to limit its work-load, it should only hear appeals involving constitutional issues of major importance, a question to be determined by the court as a preliminary issue of admissibility. Only Member States should be entitled to lodge an appeal.

9

The Question of Sovereignty—III

If the time should come when our Parliament deliberately passes an Act with the intention of repudiating the Treaty or any provision in it or of intentionally acting inconsistently with it and says so in express terms then I should have thought that it would be the duty of our courts to follow the statute of our Parliament.

Lord Denning MR in *Macarthys Ltd* v. *Smith* [1979] 3 All ER 325 at 329 (CA).

We saw in Chapter 7 that, if they act together, the Member States can do whatever they want. They are the masters of the Treaties: they can amend the Treaties in any way they want and could even wind up the Community. We saw in Chapter 8 that if the European Court tried to stop them—for example, by striking down Treaty amendments—its judgment would not be followed in at least some Member States. Now, we must consider the position where one or more Member States take action independently of the others.

UNILATERAL ACTION BY MEMBER STATES

In considering this question, we must remember that there are three levels of law involved: the highest level is international law; next comes Community law; then there are the legal systems of the Member States. Where the Member States take joint action, what they do will (we assume) be valid under international law and under their own legal systems. The question we considered previously was whether it would matter if their action was contrary to Community law. Where a Member State takes unilateral action, on the other hand, its action will almost certainly constitute a breach of the

Treaties and will, therefore, be contrary to international law. However, it will continue (we assume) to be valid under its own legal system.

The two most important cases in which this situation is likely to arise are withdrawal by a Member State from the Community, and the expulsion of a Member State. We will consider each of these in turn.

Leaving the Community

There is no provision in the Treaties for a Member State to leave. However, if a Member State wanted to leave, it would be legally able to do so.[1] It would just have to take the steps necessary under its legal system to deprive Community law of any validity within its territory. In the case of Britain, all that would be constitutionally required would be to repeal the European Communities Act 1972. Community law would then cease to have effect in Britain: as far as British law was concerned, Britain would no longer be a Member.[2] Under Community law, on the other hand, Britain would still be a Member State, but the obligations resulting from this could not be enforced. The European Court could do nothing: its judgments would no longer have validity in Britain. The other Member States could, if they wished, take sanctions against Britain, but this would be a two-edged weapon which could harm them as well. At the very worst, Britain would be back to the position in which she found herself in 1940 when trade with the Continent was cut off.

Unilateral departure from the Community would also constitute a violation of international law, and the other Member States would be entitled to such remedies as international law might afford. These would, however, be limited by virtue of the fact that Article 219 {292} EC precludes the Member States from submitting any dispute concerning the interpretation or application of the Treaty to any method of settlement other than those provided in it. This would seem to exclude all avenues of redress other than adjudication by the

---

[1] The *Bundesverfassungsgericht* (German Constitutional Court) said in the German *Maastricht* case that Germany could leave the Community if it wanted to: *Brunner v. European Union Treaty*, *Bundesverfassungsgericht*, decision of 12 October 1993, [1994] 1 CMLR 57, para. [55] of the judgment.

[2] This is discussed further below.

European Court, though some Member States might argue that, since the departing Member State no longer accepted the judgments of the European Court, that provision could no longer apply.

In practice, if a country wanted to leave, the others would permit it to do so. This has already happened in the case of Greenland, a territory which is small in population but large in area. Greenland is part of the Kingdom of Denmark, but has home rule. It was originally part of the Community, but in a referendum held in 1982 there was a narrow majority in favour of withdrawal. Denmark then negotiated with the other Member States on Greenland's behalf and Greenland left the Community in 1985. This was done by the normal procedure for the amendment of the Community Treaties.[3] The withdrawal of Greenland, therefore, was valid under Community law; however, it can hardly be doubted that the other Member States would accept the withdrawal of a Member even if it left without going through the procedures required by Community law for an amendment to the Treaties.[4]

Expulsion

There is no provision in the Treaties for the expulsion of a Member State. What would happen if one State was so obstreperous that the others could no longer accept it as a Member of the Community? If it refused to leave of its own accord, there might seem to be little that could be done. No doubt the others could apply pressure. If this did not work, the only possibility would be to wind up the Community and reconstitute it without the objectionable Member State. If the latter refused to agree, however, there would be two problems. First, the existing Community Treaties would still be valid under international law as between it and the other Member States: it could insist that the other Member States uphold the rights given to it by the Treaties. Secondly, the existing Treaties would still be valid under Community law, since under Article N {48} TEU any amendment to the Community Treaties must be agreed unanimously. On both

[3] For further details, see Weiss, "Greenland's Withdrawal from the European Communities" (1985) 10 ELRev. 173.

[4] For further discussion, see Weiler, "Alternatives to Withdrawal from an International Organization: The Case of the European Economic Community" (1985) 20 Israel LRev. 282.

these issues, however, the comments made above would also be applicable.

In practice, the objectionable Member State—particularly if it were a small country—would probably have to accept the position. In view of this, it would no doubt prefer to negotiate its withdrawal and agree to the necessary amendments to the Treaties.

Conclusions

In the two cases discussed above, unilateral action would be legally possible. It might be impractical for political and economic reasons, though this would depend on the circumstances: if a large country decided to leave the Community, it might have sufficient bargaining power to force the others to accept an arrangement that was in the interests of both sides.

Unilateral action short of withdrawal is more problematic. If a Member State wanted to remain in the Community, but refused to apply Community legislation in a particular area, the Commission and the other Member States could take the proceedings in the European Court described in Chapter 6. Penalties could be imposed on the recalcitrant Member State, though their effectiveness might depend on the circumstances.

In addition, proceedings could be brought in the national courts of the Member State concerned and a reference might be made to the European Court for a ruling under Article 177 {234} EC. Whether the national courts would do this, and whether, if they did, they would accept the European Court's ruling would depend on considerations specific to each Member State. In Britain the issue would be one of sovereignty of Parliament, assuming—as would almost certainly be the case—that the British action took the form of an Act of Parliament. This question will be considered below.

In any event, if the other Member States were sufficiently determined, they could probably make life so unpleasant for the delinquent Member State that it would be forced to withdraw from the Community. On the other hand, if they felt their interests were not seriously threatened, they might reach an accommodation with the Member State in which it was given an opt-out, possibly in return for concessions in another area. This would legitimate its action. Alternatively, the rebellious Member State might agree to terminate its unilateral action in return for concessions to solve the problem that led it to take the action in the first place. This, it will be remembered, is what happened when France unilaterally decided to ban imports of lamb and mutton from Britain: once the other Member States agreed to institute a scheme to support French sheep farmers, France ended the ban.[5]

SUPREMACY

Nowhere in the Treaty is it said that directly effective Community law prevails over Member-State law; nevertheless, this principle has been laid down by the European Court in numerous cases.[6] According to the Court, it does not matter whether the Community provision or the national provision was enacted first, nor does it matter what form the national provision takes: even a provision in the constitution of a Member State is overridden by directly effective Community law.[7] The principle of Community supremacy is largely accepted by the courts of the Member States; however, most, if not all, national courts would not accept it with regard to at least some of the provisions of their national constitutions. In the Danish *Maastricht* case,[8] the Danish Supreme Court expressly said that the Community cannot be given the power to adopt legislation that would be contrary to the Danish Constitution;[9] the *Bundesverfassungsgericht* has made clear that a transfer of powers to the Community cannot affect the basic framework of the constitutional order in Germany,[10] and the *Corte Costituzionale* (Italian Constitutional Court) considers that Community law cannot prevail over the fundamental principles of

---

[5] See Chapter 6.
[6] The first of these were *Van Gend en Loos*, Case 26/62, [1963] ECR 1 (discussed in Chapter 2) and *Costa* v. *ENEL*, Case 6/64, [1964] ECR 585.
[7] See, for example, *Internationale Handelsgesellschaft*, Case 11/70, [1970] ECR 1125 (para. 3 of the judgment).
[8] Danish Supreme Court, decision of 6 April 1998, Case I 361/1997, discussed in Chapter 8.
[9] See the fourth paragraph of section 9.2 of the judgment.
[10] *Bundesverfassungsgericht, Internationale Handelsgesellschaft* v. *EVGF*, decision of 29 May 1974, [1974] 2 CMLR 540 (para. [22]); 37 BVerfGE 271 at 279–280; *Wünsche Handelsgesellschaft*, decision of 22 October 1986, [1987] 3 CMLR 225 (para. [32]); 73 BVerfGE 339 at 374.

the Italian Constitution.[11] A similar view is implicit in decisions of the French *Conseil Constitutionnel*[12] and would almost certainly be taken by courts in other Member States.[13]

This means that if there was a provision of Community law that conflicted with a fundamental principle of the constitution of a Member State, that provision would prevail in the Community legal system, but would be overridden in the legal system of the Member State in question. There is thus a discrepancy between the "super-rule" in the Community legal system and that in the legal systems of the Member States. The existence of such a discrepancy was one of the reasons why it was said in Chapter 7 that Community law and the law of the various Member States must be regarded as separate legal systems.

THE BRITISH PARLIAMENT

In Chapter 7, we defined sovereignty (in the sense in which we are discussing it) as ultimate constitutional authority. We also said that, according to the traditional doctrine, Parliament was sovereign in Britain. The question we posed was whether this state of affairs has been changed by Britain's membership of the European Union. The time has now come to answer this question. To do so, we must consider the constitutional position of Community law in the United Kingdom.

[11] See, for example, *Frontini, Corte Costituzionale*, decision No. 183 of 27 December 1973, [1974] 2 CMLR 372 (para. [21] of the judgment); [1974] RDI 154; *Fragd, Corte Costituzionale*, decision No. 168 of 21 April 1989, English translation in A Oppenheimer (ed.), *The Relationship between European Community Law and National Law—The Cases* (1994), p. 653; [1990] I Foro Italiano 1855. See, further, Cartabia, "The Italian Constitutional Court and the Relationship between the Italian Legal System and the European Union" in Anne-Marie Slaughter, Alec Stone Sweet and Joseph H H Weiler, *The European Courts and National Courts—Doctrine and Jurisprudence* (1998), 133 at pp. 138–139; De Witte, "Sovereignty and European Integration: The Weight of European Legal Tradition", *ibid.*, 277 at pp. 288–289.

[12] For example, in its decision of 9 April 1992, [1993] 3 CMLR 345, it held that French ratification of the Maastricht Agreement would be unconstitutional, a ruling which necessitated an amendment to the French Constitution: this judgment would make no sense if the French Constitution did not prevail over Community law in France.

[13] The position in the United Kingdom is considered below.

The European Communities Act

When the United Kingdom joined the Community, it did not amend its Constitution; indeed, given the fact that it is largely unwritten, it is hard to see how it *could* have amended it. Instead, it passed a simple statute, the European Communities Act 1972. Since the United Kingdom is a strictly dualist country in its attitude to international treaties,[14] the Community Treaties could have no effect in the British legal system without an Act of Parliament. This was made clear by Lord Denning MR in *McWhirter* v. *Attorney-General*,[15] a case decided after the EC Treaty had been signed but before the European Communities Act had been passed:

> Even though the Treaty of Rome has been signed, it has no effect, so far as these Courts are concerned, until it is made an Act of Parliament. Once it is implemented by an Act of Parliament, these Courts must go by the Act of Parliament.

As will be seen from this, not only is an Act of Parliament needed, but, once passed, it is pivotal: it is to the Act of Parliament that the courts look in order to ascertain the effect of the Treaties in the British legal system.

Provision for the direct effect of Community law in the United Kingdom is made by section 2(1) of the European Communities Act. It reads:

> All such rights, powers, liabilities, obligations and restrictions from time to time created or arising by or under the Treaties, and all such remedies and procedures from time to time provided for by or under the Treaties, as in accordance with the Treaties are without further enactment to be given legal effect or used in the United Kingdom shall be recognized and available in law, and be enforced, allowed and followed accordingly . . .

It should be noted that the words "from time to time" in this provision were intended to indicate that it applied to provisions of Community law that would be adopted in the future as well as to those in existence when the European Communities Act was passed.

---

[14] On the meaning of "dualist", see p. 31, n. 33, above.
[15] [1972] CMLR 882 at 886 (CA).

Section 2(1) says that Community law will be given legal effect in the United Kingdom; it does not say what happens when it conflicts with British law. This is dealt with in section 2(4) of the European Communities Act, which provides:

> . . . any enactment passed or to be passed, other than one contained in this Part of this Act, shall be construed and have effect subject to the foregoing provisions of this section . . .

What does this mean? The word "enactment" refers to legislation, and covers Acts of Parliament as well as lesser measures. The phrase "passed or to be passed" covers Acts of Parliament passed both before and after the European Communities Act. It, therefore, covers both past and future Acts of Parliament and lays down a rule of construction:[16] Acts of Parliament are, it says, "to be construed and have effect" subject to the foregoing provisions of section 2. One such provision is section 2(1), an extract from which was quoted above; consequently, section 2(4) means that all past and future Acts of Parliament must be interpreted and applied subject to the rule in section 2(1) that directly effective Community law is to be applied in the United Kingdom. In other words, Parliament is expressing the intention in section 2(4) that all future Acts passed are to have effect subject to any conflicting rule of directly effective Community law.

The Sovereignty of Parliament

The traditional doctrine of parliamentary sovereignty may be expressed in three simple propositions. The first is that there are no legal limits to the laws that Parliament may pass.[17] The second, which is an exception to the first, is that Parliament cannot validly limit its own future powers.[18] The third is that, in the event of a conflict between two Acts of Parliament, the later prevails over the earlier. (The rule that Parliament cannot validly limit its own future powers could almost be regarded as an application of this last proposition.)

---

[16] Whether it contains anything else *in addition* to the rule of construction is considered below.

[17] See Stanley de Smith and Rodney Brazier, *Constitutional and Administrative Law* (7th ed. 1994 by Rodney Brazier), pp. 75–80, where examples are given.

[18] *Vauxhall Estates Ltd* v. *Liverpool Corporation* [1932] 1 KB 733; *Ellen Street Estates Ltd* v. *Minister of Health* [1934] 1 KB 590.

Questions may exist about what exactly constitutes Parliament (the traditional answer is that it consists of the House of Commons, the House of Lords and the Queen, each consenting separately), whether Parliament can abolish itself, and what exactly constitutes "passing" an Act of Parliament;[19] subject to one minor exception,[20] however, none of this is relevant to our enquiry.[21]

Parliamentary Sovereignty and Community Law

How have the British courts reacted when faced with a conflict between an Act of Parliament and a directly effective provision of Community law? The answer is that they have looked to the European Communities Act as providing the key. This was made clear in the passage from the judgment of Lord Denning in the *McWhirter* case quoted above, and is equally clear in the most recent pronouncement on the subject by the House of Lords, the judgment of Lord Bridge in *R* v. *Secretary of State for Transport, ex parte Factortame* (*No 2*).[22] In this, Lord Bridge said:

> Under the terms of the [European Communities Act 1972] it has always been clear that it was the duty of a United Kingdom court, when delivering final judgment, to override any rule of national law found to be in conflict with any directly enforceable rule of Community law.

For this purpose, the most important provision in the European Communities Act is section 2(4), which was set out above. It was said above that this lays down a rule of construction (interpretation) to the effect that future Acts of Parliament are not intended to prevail over directly effective Community law. No one can dispute that section 2(4) does this; however, it might be argued that it does something else in addition: the words "and shall have effect" in section 2(4) could be regarded as laying down more than a rule of construction.[23]

---

[19] For a summary of the arguments, see de Smith and Brazier, n. 17 above, pp. 81–99.

[20] The exception is whether Parliament can bind itself as to the form in which it expresses its intention.

[21] Parliament did not redefine or abolish itself when it passed the European Communities Act, nor did it redefine what constitutes an Act of Parliament or change the procedures required to enact one.

[22] [1991] 1 AC 603 at 659.

[23] See de Smith and Brazier, n. 17 above, p. 85.

If it is more than a rule of construction, what is it? If, by enacting it, Parliament sought to deprive itself of the power of legislating contrary to Community law, that would constitute an attempt by Parliament in 1972 to limit its own future powers. This, as we have seen, is something which cannot be done. It is of course true that the traditional theory of Parliamentary sovereignty could change, but since it constitutes the bedrock of the British constitution, its change would be a serious matter. It is not something that could be done casually or without good reason. In any event, it is not something that Parliament itself could do; indeed, it is the only thing that *cannot* be done by Act of Parliament. For this reason, one cannot believe that Parliament's intention in inserting the words "and shall have effect" in section 2(4) was to limit its own future powers.[24]

If Parliament was not trying to deprive itself of the power to legislate contrary to Community law, what was it trying to do? Surely, by saying that future Acts of Parliament are to have effect subject to the rule of Community-law supremacy, it was explaining to the courts, and to the citizens of Britain, that it does not intend to legislate contrary to Community law in the future: it was asking the courts to take this into account when applying Acts of Parliament in future. In other words, it was saying that when applying Acts of Parliament in future, each Act should be read as if it contained the words, "Nothing in this Act is to be applied in a way which conflicts with Community law". This, according to Lord Bridge in *R v. Secretary of State for Transport, ex parte Factortame (No 1)*,[25] is precisely the effect of section 2(4). If this view is correct, the section does not purport to deprive future Parliaments of the power to legislate contrary to Community law, but merely tries to ensure that the courts understand what Parliament means in future legislation. One could

---

[24] It should be said that as regards Acts of Parliament passed *prior* to the European Communities Act 1972, Parliament *can* limit their effect in any way it wants: this follows from the third proposition on Parliamentary sovereignty set out above. As regards such Acts, therefore, s. 2(4) can be, and no doubt is, more than a rule of interpretation. The words "and shall have effect" impliedly amend such legislation to the extent that it would otherwise conflict with Community law, including Community law that might be adopted in the future. The same applies to delegated legislation if the parent Act was passed prior to the European Communities Act 1972, even if the delegated legislation was itself passed subsequently. This is because the validity and effect of delegated legislation can never be greater that it would be if it had been contained in the parent Act, a rule which itself follows from the principles of Parliament sovereignty.

[25] [1990] 2 AC 85 at 140. This judgment was given in earlier proceedings in the same legal action as the judgment quoted from previously.

say that it provides the key to the code Parliament will use in expressing its intention: "If we say X, we mean we want X, provided it does
not conflict with Community law".[26]

If this is all Parliament was doing in section 2(4), it was not restricting its own future powers, except perhaps as to the manner in which
it would have to express itself. Whenever Parliament passes an
Interpretation Act, something which most parliaments (at least in the
English-speaking world) have done,[27] it is doing something similar.
An Interpretation Act, for example, might say: "whenever any (past
or future) Act of Parliament uses the word 'man', it means 'man or
woman'".[28] The only difference between section 2(4) and an
Interpretation Act is that the rules laid down in an Interpretation Act
apply only to the extent that the context does not reveal a contrary
intention.[29] In the case of section 2(4), on the other hand, it is doubtful whether the rule of construction that all British legislation is subject to Community law can be negated simply by implication. If it
can, if would certainly have to be a strong and clear implication.[30]

However this may be, it is unlikely to make much difference in
practice. Even if we assume that no such limitation is imposed on
Parliament, the courts still have the task of determining what the true
intention of Parliament was. In view of section 2(4) and of Britain's
commitments under the Community Treaties, it is hardly likely, if
Parliament intended to legislate contrary to Community law, that it
would not say so expressly. Consequently, it would be entirely reasonable for the courts to assume that, in the absence of an express
statement, an Act of Parliament is not intended to prevail against
Community law. An exception could exist only in the most unusual
circumstances.

This, however, is taking us away from our inquiry. The question
we are considering is whether Parliament is still sovereign in the sense

---

[26] For a similar view, see Laws, "Law and Democracy" [1995] PL 72 at p. 89.

[27] For the United Kingdom, see the Interpretation Act 1978.

[28] Or, in more elegant and draftsmanlike language, "Words importing the masculine gender include the feminine": see the Interpretation Act 1978, s. 6(a).

[29] In the words of the Interpretation Act 1978, ss. 5 and 6, "unless the contrary intention
appears".

[30] It seems likely that express words must be used: this was the view of Lord Denning in
Macarthys Ltd v. *Smith* [1979] 3 All ER 325 at 329 (CA) (quoted below); see also Laws, "Law
and Democracy" [1995] PL 72 at p. 89, where it is suggested that there are other areas of
law where a particular statutory construction is likely to be accepted by the courts only if it
is stated in express words.

traditionally understood. Do the three propositions set out above still apply? We are not concerned with limitations as to form. The question to be considered is one of substance: assuming that Parliament uses the correct words, is its legal power to legislate limited as a result of Britain's membership of the Community? The two situations in which this question is most likely to arise are, first, if Britain sought to leave the Community without the permission of the other Member States; and, secondly, if it sought, while still remaining a Member, to legislate contrary to Community law. We will consider each of these in turn.

Leaving the Community

Does Britain have the legal power to leave the Community, even if the other Member States do not grant their permission? Previously, we discussed this question from the point of view of Community law and international law. We saw that there was little that the other Member States or the European Court could do to stop a Member State from leaving. We said that all Britain had to do was to pass a short Act of Parliament repealing the European Communities Act 1972. Community law would then cease to have legal effect in the United Kingdom and the same would be true of the judgments of the European Court. This follows from the fact that it is due to the European Communities Act, and to nothing else, that Community law and the judgments of the European Court have legal effect in the United Kingdom. Since Britain is a dualist country, the Treaties in themselves have no legal effect. As Lord Denning said, the Treaty of Rome has no effect, as far as the English courts are concerned, "until it is made an Act of Parliament":[31] if the Act of Parliament is repealed, it can no longer have any effect. Consequently, as far as British law is concerned, Parliament still has the legal power to end Britain's membership of the Community.

Legislating Contrary to Community Law

While it is generally recognized that Britain could leave the Community even if this was contrary to Community law, some

---

[31] *McWhirter* v. *Attorney-General* [1972] CMLR 882 at 886 (CA).

writers have cast doubt on the legal ability of Parliament to legislate contrary to Community law while Britain remains a Member.[32] Let us therefore put the matter to the test by imagining a situation in which, without terminating Britain's membership, Parliament knowingly, deliberately, unmistakeably and in the correct form, passes a statute that conflicts with Community law. It will be remembered from Chapter 6, that in the late 1970s France banned imports of British lamb, knowing full well that such action was contrary to Community law. It will be remembered also that France was successful in its defiance of Community law: despite a judgment from the European Court, it stuck to its guns until the other Member States agreed to a scheme to support French sheep farmers. Let us assume, therefore, that Britain decides to do the same thing. We will not concern ourselves with what might happen at the Community level and whether Britain might win concessions by such a tactic. We will concern ourselves solely with the question whether it would be legally possible, as far as the legal system of the United Kingdom was concerned, for Parliament to pass the necessary legislation. Let us assume, therefore, that a statute of the normal kind is passed by the normal procedure in the House of Commons and the House of Lords. The Queen assents to it. The statute is called the "European Communities (Amendment) Act". It amends section 2(1) of the European Communities Act by inserting the italicised words into the following passage:

> All such rights, powers, liabilities, obligations and restrictions *other than those specified in the proviso to this sub-section* from time to time created or arising by or under the Treaties, and all such remedies and procedures *other than those specified in the proviso to this sub-section* from time to time provided for by or under the Treaties, as in accordance with the Treaties are without further enactment to be given legal effect or

[32] See, for example, Craig, "Report on the United Kingdom" in Slaughter, Sweet and Weiler, n. 11 above, 195 at p. 204. The author there expresses the "conjecture" that, no matter how clearly Parliament expressed its intention, the British courts would not give effect to an Act of Parliament if it conflicted with a provision of Community law. This view is, however, based on the assumption that the Community provision falls within the Community's area of competence. (Where the Community has clearly acted beyond its powers, British courts might, he suggests, refuse to accept the validity of the measure: see pp. 207–209.) It should be noted that the "Report on the United Kingdom" is largely based on an earlier work, Craig, "Parliamentary Sovereignty in the United Kingdom after *Factortame*" (1991) 11 YEL 221, in which he carefully leaves open the possibility that Parliament may still have the power to legislate contrary to Community law: see (1991) 11 YEL at pp. 251 and 253.

used in the United Kingdom shall be recognized and available in law, and be enforced, allowed and followed accordingly . . . *provided that, notwithstanding anything contained in any provision of this Act, no provision of Community law and no remedy or procedure provided by Community law shall have legal effect or be available in law in the United Kingdom in so far as it—*

(a)   *gives any person the right to import lamb or any product containing lamb into the United Kingdom; or*

(b)   *impugns the validity of this Act or any part thereof; or*

(c)   *imposes any penalty, or makes any provision, consequential on the passing of this Act; or*

(d)   *permits or requires the making of a reference to the European Court from a court or tribunal in the United Kingdom concerning the validity or effect of this proviso or of anything done under it; or*

(e)   *permits or requires legal effect to be given to any judgment of the European Court concerning any of the above matters.*[33]

In addition, a new section is inserted into the European Communities Act which prohibits all imports of lamb, and empowers customs officials to turn back any such imports. This section is stated to have effect notwithstanding anything contained in the Act.

After the new Act comes into force, a Frenchman arrives at Dover with a consignment of lamb destined for the British market. Customs officials turn the consignment back. The importer brings proceedings in the English courts claiming that, notwithstanding the Act, he has a right to import the lamb. Can it be seriously asserted that the courts would find in his favour? They could not do so on the basis of Community law, because the relevant rules of Community law would have no legal effect in the United Kingdom: the only basis on which they could have effect—the European Communities Act 1972—would expressly exclude them. The courts could not lawfully refer the matter to the European Court, since the provisions allowing or requiring such references would no longer have any effect in the United Kingdom. If they did, or if the European Court somehow took it upon itself to give a ruling anyway, its ruling would have no legal validity in the United Kingdom. In short, there would be no legal ground for granting the importer a remedy. No one could quibble regarding the manner or form in which the new Act was passed. No one could argue that it was not an Act of Parliament.

---

[33] This attempt at legislative drafting would horrify a professional draftsman; let us assume, therefore, that it has been put into the appropriate form.

It might be said that, because Britain has joined the Community, Parliament is bound by the Community Treaties and cannot legislate against them:[34] "[W]hile the United Kingdom remains in the EEC, it cannot pick and choose what norms of EEC law to comply with".[35] It is, however, well established that Parliament *can* legislate contrary to a Treaty that is binding on the United Kingdom.[36] No one disputes this with regard to other treaties, even those establishing international organizations of which the United Kingdom is a member: no one has ever suggested that Parliament cannot legislate contrary to, for example, the United Nations Charter.

There is no legal reason why the Community Treaties should be different. In 1979 Lord Denning thought that Parliament could, if it expressed itself clearly enough, legislate contrary to the Community Treaties. In the passage from his judgment in *Macarthys Ltd* v. *Smith*[37] quoted at the beginning of this chapter, he said:

> If the time should come when our Parliament deliberately passes an Act with the intention of repudiating the Treaty or any provision in it or of intentionally acting inconsistently with it and says so in express terms then I should have thought that it would be the duty of our courts to follow the statute of our Parliament.

In the twenty years since he made this statement, there has not been a single statement by a British court suggesting that Parliament could not legislate contrary to Community law if it expressed itself clearly enough.[38]

---

[34] This appears to be what Craig means when he says that Lord Bridge's judgment in *R* v. *Secretary of State for Transport, ex parte Factortame (No 2)* [1991] 1 AC 603 at 659 is founded on reasoning which is "essentially contractarian": Craig, "Parliamentary Sovereignty in the United Kingdom after *Factortame*" (1991) 11 YEL 221 at p. 249.

[35] Craig, n. 34 above, p. 253.

[36] *Mortensen* v. *Peters* (1906) 14 SLT 227; *Cheney* v. *Conn* [1968] 1 WLR 242.

[37] [1979] 3 All ER 325 at 329 (CA).

[38] For an analysis of the cases, see Lawrence Collins, *European Community Law in the United Kingdom* (4th ed. 1990) pp. 30–39. Lord Bridge's *dictum* in *R* v. *Secretary of State for Transport, ex parte Factortame (No 2)* [1991] 1 AC 603 at 658–659 is no exception. It reads: "[W]hatever limitation of its sovereignty Parliament accepted when it enacted the European Communities Act 1972 was entirely voluntary. Under the terms of the 1972 Act it has always been clear that it was the duty of a United Kingdom court, when delivering final judgment, to override any rule of national law found to be in conflict with any directly enforceable rule of Community law". The phrase "limitation of sovereignty" in the first sentence refers to sovereignty in the sense explained at the beginning of Chapter 7 (pp. 123–124). In this sense, sovereignty means practical power. Parliament's practical power certainly has been limited by Britain's joining the Community. That Lord Bridge was not referring to sovereignty in the sense in which we are using the term is made clear by the fact that

It might of course be argued that, in some mysterious and inexplicable way, the traditional doctrine of Parliamentary sovereignty has been altered. Since Britain joined the Community, it might be claimed, the basic rule of the British constitution is that Community law—not Parliament—is supreme. This would mean that the will of the British nation, as expressed through Parliament, would no longer count: while Britain remained in the Community, Brussels and Luxembourg would rule Britain; Parliament would no longer be sovereign. If the British courts accepted this, it would mean they had transferred their allegiance from Parliament to Europe. At least as things stand today, it is hard to believe that this is the case.

For this reason, Community protagonists have begun to suggest that the national courts of the Member States should no longer be regarded simply as national courts, but also (perhaps first and foremost) as *Community* courts.[39] The hope clearly is that, if this idea takes root, the national courts will one day be weaned away from their national loyalties and will give their allegiance to Europe. Clearly, this has not worked in the case of the *Bundesverfassungsgericht* or the Danish Supreme Court. Can it be imagined that the House of Lords would be any different? Until the British courts transfer their allegiance to the Community, Parliament will retain the right to legislate contrary to Community law. At least if it expresses itself clearly enough, its sovereign powers have not been affected by Britain's membership: in the memorable words of Sir John Laws,[40] the limits which for the time being Community law sets to the power of Parliament are "at the grace of Parliament itself". This is the answer to the question posed in Chapter 7.[41]

---

he bases his statement four-square on the European Communities Act 1972: it is under the terms of this Act that national law is to be overridden. If the Act were to be repealed or amended, that consequence would no longer follow.

[39] See, for example, Lang, "The Duties of National Courts under Community Constitutional Law" (1997) 22 ELRev. 3.

[40] Laws, "Law and Democracy" [1995] PL 72 at p. 89.

[41] See Clarke and Sufrin, "Constitutional Conundrums: The Impact of the United Kingdom's Membership of the Communities on Constitutional Theory" in M P Furmston, R Kerridge and B E Sufrin (eds.), *The Effect on English Domestic Law of Membership of the European Communities and of Ratification of the European Convention on Human Rights* (1983), 32; Lawrence Collins, *European Community Law in the United Kingdom* (4th ed. 1990), pp. 26-43. For further references, see Collins, p. 28, n. 11.

CONCLUSIONS

In the final analysis, Community law is an essentially dependent system of law. It is not valid in its own right, but owes its validity to international law and the legal systems of the Member States. Ultimately, it is controlled by the Member States: if they act together, they can change it in any way they want, and can even abolish it. If the European Court tried to take away the powers of the Member States, its judgment would not be followed in at least some of them. In Britain, Parliament retains the legal power to legislate contrary to Community law. In view of these facts, one cannot say that sovereignty (in the sense of ultimate legal power) has passed to the Community. The Member States remain sovereign.

European federalists have sought to remedy this state of affairs by proposing that the Community should have a constitution.[42] At this point, it must be said that the word "constitution" is ambiguous: it can simply mean the instrument that creates an entity and lays down its powers (for example, the constitution of a club, society, trade union or political party); on the other hand, it can mean an instrument that creates a new legal system without deriving its own validity from any other legal system (the constitutions of countries such as France and Germany are examples).[43] It is in the former (wide) sense that the word is used in the title of this book; it is in the latter (narrow) sense, however, that we shall use it in the following pages: should the Community have a constitution in the narrower sense? If it had such a constitution, its legal system would then become truly independent, and the Member States would lose their authority over it.

The problem with this idea is that it is not clear how a Community constitution could be brought into existence. It could not take the form of a treaty, since it would then derive its validity from international law; nor could it be created by legislation on the part of the Member States, since it would then derive its validity from national

[42] See, for example, the *Draft Constitution for the European Union* of 9 September 1993, presented by the European Parliament's Institutional Committee, revised on 10 February 1994, OJ 1994 C61/155.

[43] See Schilling, "The Autonomy of the Community Legal System: An Analysis of Possible Foundations" (1996) 37 Harv. Int. LJ 389 at pp. 390–393; see, further, Grimm, "Does Europe Need a Constitution?" (1995) 1 ELJ 282.

law. It could be proclaimed by the Commission or the European Parliament,[44] but if this was its only claim to legitimacy, it would not be accepted by the Member States. At the very least, it would have to be approved in a referendum by the peoples of Europe. However, even if there was an overall majority in its favour, what if it was rejected in one or more of the individual Member States? Those States would not accept it. As things stand at present, one cannot imagine a European constitution being accepted in Germany, France or Britain—to name just three countries—and one can hardly imagine that the Community could exist without at least France and Germany. Though things may change, the adoption of a European constitution is not at present a realistic proposition.

In view of this, some bold commentators have said that there is no need for the Community to adopt a constitution: they claim that it already has one.[45] They argue that the basic Treaties have lost their character as treaties and, by a process described by two of its exponents as "circular or, rather, spiral",[46] have been transformed into a constitution (in the narrow sense). This is known as the "constitutionalization" of the Treaties,[47] a theory that comes in both a weak and a strong form. In its weak form, it means no more than that the Treaties display some of the characteristics of a constitution in the *wide* sense: no one can object to this, since it is clearly correct.[48] In its strong form, it means that the Treaties have become a constitution in the *narrow* sense: it is this form of the theory that is relevant for our present purposes. Constitutionalization in this sense has come about, it is said, as a result of the judgments of the European Court criticized in Chapter 2 as going beyond the Treaties. The argument is that these judgments would not be appropriate, both as regards their method of "interpretation" and as regards the results they reach, if the Treaties were treaties; consequently, they must be regarded as a constitution

[44] It seems that the European Parliament intended that its "Draft Constitution of the European Union" (see above) would be adopted by the Member States and the European Parliament: see the second-last paragraph of the Preamble.

[45] See Grimm, "Does Europe Need a Constitution?" (1995) 1 ELJ 282 at pp. 282 *et seq.*

[46] Cruz Vilaça and Piçarra, "Y a-t-il des limites matérielles à la révision des traités instituant les Communautés européennes?" [1993] CDE 3 at p. 10.

[47] See Stein, "Lawyers, Judges and the Making of a Transnational Constitution" (1981) 74 AJIL 1; Mancini, "The Making of a Constitution for Europe" (1989) 26 CMLRev. 595; Weiler, "The Transformation of Europe" (1991) 100 Yale LJ 2403; Weiler, "The Reformation of European Constitutionalism" (1997) 35 JCMS 97.

[48] See Hartley, "Federalism, Courts and Legal Systems: The Emerging Constitution of the European Community" (1986) 34 Am. Jo. Comp. L 229.

in the narrow sense. (It is at this point in the argument that one begins to hear the sound of bootstraps being tightened.[49]) Since they now have this new character, the Treaties are no longer dependent for their validity on international law or on the legal systems of the Member States,[50] and all the consequences of this dependence disappear with a wave of the jurist's magic wand.

The problem with this theory is that, even if it is accepted by the European Court, there is no evidence that it is accepted by any of the governments of the Member States or by any of their courts.[51] The *Bundesverfassungsgericht* and the Danish Supreme Court—to name but two—clearly reject it.[52] And without acceptance by the Member States, the theory will not work. At present, therefore, it suffers from a "reality deficit": at the crucial moment, the rabbit stubbornly refuses to come out of the hat, no matter how frantically the magician waves his wand.

---

[49] It might be argued that the birth of a new constitution (in the narrow sense) always involves the use of bootstraps. However, if the element of *general acceptance* is missing, bootstraps will be of no avail.

[50] They are "self-validating": see Cruz Vilaça and Piçarra, n. 46 above, at p. 9.

[51] See Schilling, "The Autonomy of the Community Legal System: An Analysis of Possible Foundations" (1996) 37 Harv. Int. L J 389 at pp. 396 *et seq.*

[52] In the German *Maastricht* case, the *Bundesverfassungsgericht* said that the Treaties are valid law in Germany *because German law says so*: decision of 12 October 1993, [1994] 1 CMLR 57, para. [55] of the judgment. See also the Danish *Maastricht* case, Danish Supreme Court, judgment of 6 April 1998, section 9.2 of the judgment. The same view is implicit in the statement by Lord Bridge in *R* v. *Secretary of State for Transport, ex parte Factortame (No 2)* [1991] 1 AC 603 at 659 (set out at p.171, above).

Select Bibliography

1. BACKGROUND

Books

ANDERSEN, S, and ELIASSEN, K, *The European Union: How Democratic is it?* (1996).
CORBETT, R, JACOBS, F, and SHACKLETON, M, *The European Parliament* (3rd ed. 1995).
DIEBOLD, WILLIAM, *The Schuman Plan* (1959).
HARTLEY, T C, *The Foundations of European Community Law* (4th ed. 1998).
HAYES-RENSHAW, F, and WALLACE, H, *The Council of Ministers* (1997).
HIX, S, and LORD, C, *Political Parties in the European Union* (1997).

Articles

DASHWOOD, "States in the European Union" (1998) 23 ELRev. 201.
HARTLEY, "Federalism, Courts and Legal Systems: The Emerging Constitution of the European Community" (1986) 34 Am.Jo.Comp.L 229.
NICOLL, "The Luxembourg Compromise" (1984) 23 JCMS 35.
TEASDALE, "The Life and Death of the Luxembourg Compromise" (1993) 31 JCMS 567.
WEILER, "The Community Legal System: The Dual Character of Supranationalism" (1981) 1 YEL 267.
WEILER, "European Democracy and Its Critique" (1995) 18 West European Politics 4.

2 AND 3. THE EUROPEAN COURT

Books

BRITISH INSTITUTE OF INTERNATIONAL AND COMPARATIVE LAW, *The Role and Future of the European Court of Justice* (1996).

BROWN, L N, and JACOBS, F G, *The Court of Justice of the European Communities* (4th ed. 1994 by L Neville Brown and Tom Kennedy).

HOWE, MARTIN, *Europe and the Constitution after Maastricht* (Nelson & Pollard, Oxford, 1993).

HUNNINGS, NEVILLE MARCH, *The European Courts* (1996).

NEILL, SIR PATRICK, *The European Court of Justice: A Case Study in Judicial Activism* (published by European Policy Forum, 20 Queen Anne's Gate, London SW1H 9AA, August 1995; also published in House of Lords Select Committee on the European Communities, Minutes of Evidence, 18th Report, p. 218 (HL Paper 88, 1994–95)).

RASMUSSEN, HJALTE, *On Law and Policy in the European Court of Justice* (Martinus Nijhoff, Dordrecht, 1986).

—— *The European Court of Justice* (Gad Jura, Copenhagen, 1998).

Articles

ALTER, "Explaining National Court Acceptance of European Court Jurisprudence: A Critical Examination of Theories of Legal Integration" in Anne-Marie Slaughter, Alec Stone Sweet and Joseph H H Weiler, *The European Courts and National Courts—Doctrine and Jurisprudence* (1998), p. 227.

ARNULL, "The Community Judicature and the 1996 IGC" (1995) 20 ELRev. 599.

—— "Does the Court of Justice Have Inherent Jurisdiction?" (1990) 27 CMLRev. 683.

BURLEY and MATTLI, "Europe before the Court: A Political Theory of Legal Integration" (1993) 47 International Organization 41.

BZDERA, "The Court of Justice of the European Community and the Politics of Institutional Reform" (1992) 15 West European Politics 122.

CAPPELLETTI, "Is the European Court of Justice 'Running Wild'?" (1987) 12 ELRev. 3.

JACOBS, "Is the Court of Justice of the European Communities a Constitutional Court?" in Deirdre Curtin and David O'Keeffe, *Constitutional Adjudication in European Community Law* (Butterworths, Dublin, 1992).

LANG, "Community Constitutional Law: Article 5 EEC Treaty" (1990) 27 CMLRev. 645.

—— "The Division of Powers between the Community and the Member States" (1988) 39 Northern Ireland Legal Quarterly 209.

MANCINI and KEELING, "Language, Culture and Politics in the Life of the European Court of Justice" (1995) 1 Columbia Jo. Euro. Law 397.

RASMUSSEN, "Between Self-Restraint and Activism: A Judicial Policy for the European Court" (1988) 13 ELRev. 28.

TRIDIMAS, "The Court of Justice and Judicial Activism" (1996) 21 ELRev. 199.

USHER, "How Limited is the Jurisdiction of the European Court of Justice?" in Janet Dine, Sionaidh Douglas-Scott and Ingrid Persaud, *Procedure and the European Court* (1991), p. 72.

VOLCANSEK, "The European Court of Justice: Supranational Policy-Making" (1992) 15 West European Politics 109.

WEILER, "Journey to an Unknown Destination: A Retrospective and Prospective on the European Court of Justice in the Arena of Political Integration" (1993) 31 JCMS 417.

—— "The Court of Justice on Trial" (1987) 24 CMLRev. 555.

4. THE UNCERTAINTY PROBLEM IN COMMUNITY LAW

HARTLEY, "Five Forms of Uncertainty in European Community Law" [1996] CLJ 265.

RAWLINGS, "The Eurolaw Game: Some Deductions from a Saga" (1993) 20 Jo. of Law and Society 309.

5. THE DIVISION OF POWER: THE MEMBER STATES AND THE COMMUNITY

Books

NIELSEN, R, and SZYSZCZAK, E, *The Social Dimension of the European Union* (3rd ed. Handelshøjskolens Forlag, Copenhagen, 1997), Chapter 4.

WEATHERILL, STEPHEN, *EC Consumer Law and Policy* (1997).

Articles

BERMANN, "Taking Subsidiarity Seriously: Federalism in the European Community and the United States" (1994) 94 Columbia Law Rev. 331.

CASS, "The Word that Saves Maastricht? The Principle of Subsidiarity and the Division of Powers within the European Community" (1992) 29 CMLRev. 1107.

COMMISSION (EC), *The Principle of Subsidiarity*, Com. Doc. SEC(92) 1990, 27 October 1992, p. 5.

CONSTANTINESCO, "Who's Afraid of Subsidiarity?" (1991) 11 YEL 33.

EMILIOU, "Subsidiarity: Panacea or Fig Leaf?" in David O'Keeffe and Patrick M Twomey, *Legal Issues of the Maastricht Treaty* (1994), p. 65.

—— "Subsidiarity: An Effective Barrier against 'the Enterprises of Ambition'?" (1992) 17 ELRev. 383.

GIBSON, "Subsidiarity: The Implications for Consumer Policy" (1992) 16 Journal of Consumer Policy 323.

SCHILLING, "A New Dimension of Subsidiarity: Subsidiarity as a Rule and a Principle" (1994) 14 YEL 203.

STEINER, "Subsidiarity under the Maastricht Treaty" in David O'Keeffe and Patrick M Twomey, *Legal Issues of the Maastricht Treaty* (1994), p. 49.

TOTH, "A Legal Analysis of Subsidiarity" in David O'Keeffe and Patrick M Twomey, *Legal Issues of the Maastricht Treaty* (1994), p. 37.

—— "Is Subsidiarity Justiciable?" (1994) 14 ELRev. 268.

—— "The Principle of Subsidiarity in the Maastricht Treaty" (1992) 29 CMLRev. 669.

VAN KERSBERGEN and VERBEEK, "The Politics of Subsidiarity in the European Union" (1994) 32 JCMS 215.

6. ENFORCING COMMUNITY LAW

AUDRETSCH, H A H, *Supervision in European Community Law* (2nd ed. North-Holland, Amsterdam, 1986).

COMMISSION (EC), *Annual Reports to the European Parliament on the Monitoring of the application of Community Law:*
    First Annual Report (1983), COM(84) 181;
    Second Annual Report (1984), COM(85) 149;
    Third Annual Report (1985), COM(86) 204;
    Fourth Annual Report (1986), COM(87) 250;
    Fifth Annual Report (1987), COM(88) 425;
    Sixth Annual Report (1988), COM(89) 411;
    Seventh Annual Report (1989), COM(90) 228;
    Eighth Annual Report (1990), COM(91) 321;
    Ninth Annual Report (1991), COM(92) 136;
    Tenth Annual Report (1992), COM(93) 320;
    Eleventh Annual Report (1993), COM(94) 500;
    Twelfth Annual Report (1994), COM(95) 500;
    Thirteenth Annual Report (1995) COM(96) 600;
    Fourteenth Annual Report (1996) COM(97) 299.

7–9. SOVEREIGNTY

General Aspects, the Community Legal System and Constitutionalism

Book

PHELAN, DIARMUID ROSSA, *Revolt or Revolution: The Constitutional Boundaries of the European Community* (Round Hall Sweet and Maxwell, Dublin, 1997).

Articles

BIEBER, "Les limites matérielles et formelles à la révision des traités établissant la Communauté européenne" [1993] RMC 343.

CRUZ VILAÇA and PIÇARRA, "Y a-t-il des limites matérielles à la révision des traités instituant les Communautés européennes?" [1993] CDE 3.

DOWRICK, "A Model of the European Communities' Legal System" (1983) 3 YEL 169.

ELEFTHERIADIS, "Aspects of European Constitutionalism" (1996) 21 ELRev. 30.

GRIMM, "Does Europe Need a Constitution?" (1995) 1 ELJ 282.

HARDEN, "The Constitution of the European Union" [1994] PL 609.

LENAERTS, "Constitutionalism and the Many Faces of Federalism" (1990) 38 Am.Jo.Comp.L 205.

MANCINI, "The Making of a Constitution for Europe" (1989) 26 CMLRev. 595.

OBRADOVIC, "Repatriation of Powers in the European Community" (1997) 34 CMLRev. 59.

SCHILLING, "The Autonomy of the Community Legal System: An Analysis of Possible Foundations" (1996) 37 Harv.Int.LJ 389.

SØRENSEN, "Autonomous Legal Orders: Some Considerations Relating to a Systems Analysis of International Organizations in the World Legal Order" (1983) 32 ICLQ 559.

STEIN, "Lawyers, Judges and the Making of a Transnational Constitution" (1981) 74 AJIL 1.

WEILER, "Alternatives to Withdrawal from an International Organization: The Case of the European Economic Community" (1985) 20 Israel LRev. 282.

—— "The Transformation of Europe" (1991) 100 Yale LJ 2403.

—— "The Reformation of European Constitutionalism" (1997) 35 JCMS 97.

WEILER and HALTERN, "Response: The Autonomy of the Community Legal Order—Through the Looking Glass" (1996) 37 Harv.Int.LJ 411.

—— and —— "Constitutional or International? The Foundations of the Community Legal Order and the Question of Judicial *Kompetenz-Kompetenz*" in Anne-Marie Slaughter, Alec Stone Sweet and Joseph H H Weiler, *The European Courts and National Courts—Doctrine and Jurisprudence* (1998) p. 331 (a revised version of the previous article).

ZULEEG, "The European Constitution under Constitutional Constraints: The German Scenario" (1997) 22 ELRev. 19.

Community Law and International Law

Books

BOWETT, D W, *The Law of International Institutions* (4th ed. 1982).

COLLINS, LAWRENCE, *European Community Law in the United Kingdom* (4th ed. 1990), pp. 2–43.

JACOBS, FRANCIS G, *European Community Law and Public International Law—Two Different Legal Orders?*, Institut für Internationales Recht an der Universität Kiel (Schücking Lecture, 1983).

—— and ROBERTS, SHELLY (eds.), *The Effect of Treaties in Domestic Law* (1987).

JACOT-GUILLARMOD, OLIVIER, *Droit communautaire et droit international public* (1979).

ROBERTSON, A H, *European Institutions* (3rd ed. 1973).

SCHERMERS, H G, and WAELBROECK, M, *Judicial Protection in the European Communities* (4th ed. 1987), pp. 89–95.

Articles

DELIÈGE-SEQUARIS, "Révision des traités européens en dehors des procédures prévues" [1980] CDE 539.

LOUIS, "Quelques considérations sur la révision des traités instituant les Communautés" [1980] CDE 552.

LYSÉN, "The EC as a Self-Contained Regime, as an International Law 'Bubble'" (paper given at a conference in Uppsala in 1997, to be published in 1998 in the first issue of *Europarättslig Tidskrift*, a journal of the Faculty of Law of the University of Stockholm).

PESCATORE, "International Law and Community Law—A Comparative Analysis" (1970) 7 CMLRev. 167. Further references may be found on p. 168, n. 5, of this article.

PLENDER, "The European Court as an International Tribunal" [1983] CLJ 279.

SCHILLING, "The Autonomy of the Community Legal System: An Analysis of Possible Foundations" (1996) 37 Harv.Int.LJ 389.

SPIERMANN, "The Making of the Community Legal Order" (paper given at a conference in Uppsala in 1997, not yet published, revised under the title "The Other Side of the Story: An Unpopular Essay on the Making of the European Community Legal Order").

WEILER and HALTERN, "Response: The Autonomy of the Community Legal Order—Through the Looking Glass" (1996) 37 Harv.Int.LJ 411.

DE WITTE, "Rules of Change in International Law: How Special is the European Community?" (1994) 25 Neth.Yb.Int.L 299.

WYATT, "New Legal Order, or Old?" (1982) 7 ELRev. 147.

Community Law and Member-State Law

Books

OPPENHEIMER, A (ed.), *The Relationship between European Community Law and National Law—The Cases* (1994).

PHELAN, DIARMUID ROSSA, *Revolt or Revolution—The Constitutional Boundaries of the European Community* (Round Hall Sweet and Maxwell, Dublin, 1997).

SLAUGHTER, A-M, SWEET, A S, and WEILER, J H H, *The European Courts and National Courts—Doctrine and Jurisprudence* (1998).

Articles

CARTABIA, "The Italian Constitutional Court and the Relationship between the Italian Legal System and the European Union" in Anne-Marie Slaughter, Alec Stone Sweet and Joseph H H Weiler, *The European Courts and National Courts—Doctrine and Jurisprudence* (1998), p. 133.

EVERLING, "The *Maastricht* Judgment of the German Federal Constitutional Court and its Significance for the Development of the European Union" (1994) 14 YEL 1.

FOSTER, "The German Constitution and EC Membership" [1994] PL 392.

GENEVOIS, "Le Traité sur l'Union européenne et la Constitution" (1992) 8(3) *Revue Française de Droit Administratif* 374.

HERDEGEN, "Maastricht and the German Constitutional Court: Constitutional Restraints for an 'Ever Closer Union'" (1994) 31 CMLRev. 233.

KOKOTT, "Report on Germany" in Anne-Marie Slaughter, Alec Stone Sweet and Joseph H H Weiler, *The European Courts and National Courts—Doctrine and Jurisprudence* (1998), p. 77.

LADERCHI, "Report on Italy", in Anne-Marie Slaughter, Alec Stone Sweet and Joseph H H Weiler, *The European Courts and National Courts—Doctrine and Jurisprudence* (1998), p. 147.

MACCORMICK, "The *Maastricht-Urteil*: Sovereignty Now" (1995) 1 ELJ 259.

OLIVER, "The French Constitution and the Treaty of Maastricht" (1994) 43 ICLQ 1.

LA PERGOLA and DEL DUCA, "Community Law and the Italian Constitution" (1985) 79 AJIL 598.

WEISS, "Greenland's Withdrawal from the European Communities" (1985) 10 ELRev. 173.

DE WITTE, "Sovereignty and European Integration: The Weight of European Legal Tradition" in Anne-Marie Slaughter, Alec Stone Sweet and Joseph H H Weiler, *The European Courts and National Courts—Doctrine and Jurisprudence* (1998), p. 277.

The British Parliament

Books

DE SMITH, S A, *Constitutional and Administrative Law* (2nd ed. 1973) (the last edition for which de Smith was responsible), Chapter 3.

DE SMITH, S, and BRAZIER, R, *Constitutional and Administrative Law* (7th ed. 1994 by Rodney Brazier), Chapters 4 and 5.

Articles

ALLAN, "The Limits of Parliamentary Sovereignty" [1985] *PL* 614.

CLARKE and SUFRIN, "Constitutional Conundrums: The Impact of the United Kingdom's Membership of the Communities on Constitutional Theory" in M P Furmston, R Kerridge and B E Sufrin (eds.), *The Effect on English Domestic Law of Membership of the European Communities and of Ratification of the European Convention on Human Rights* (1983), p. 32.

CRAIG, "Parliamentary Sovereignty in the United Kingdom after *Factortame*" (1991) 11 YEL 221.

—— "Report on the United Kingdom" in Anne-Marie Slaughter, Alec Stone Sweet and Joseph H H Weiler, *The European Courts and National Courts—Doctrine and Jurisprudence* (1998), p. 195.

LAWS, "Law and Democracy" [1995] PL 72 (at pp. 84–89).

TRINDADE, "Parliamentary Sovereignty and the Primacy of European Community Law" (1972) 35 MLR 375.

WADE, "The Basis of Legal Sovereignty" [1955] CLJ 172.

—— "Sovereignty—Revolution or Evolution?" (1996) 112 LQR 568.

Index

Index